Heiss übern Afrikboden die Sonne glüht,
Unsere Panzermotoren singen ihr Lied.
Panzer ziehen in Wüstensand
Stehen im Kampf gegen Engeland.
Es rasseln die Ketten,
Es dröhnt der Motor,
Panzer rollen in Afrika vor.

Hot above African soil the sun glows
As our Panzer motors sing their song.
Panzers are grinding through the desert's sand
Standing in the fight against England.
The chains rattle
The motors threaten
Panzers roll forward in Africa.

AFRIKA KORPS

LT. COL. A.J. BARKER

DOMUS

A Bison Book

USA/Quality Books

Library of Congress Catalog Card Number:

ISBN 78-70063

Printed in Hong Kong
Produced by Bison Books Limited
4 Cromwell Place, London, England
Published by Quality Books Inc.

I am indebted to all those who fought with or against the Deutsche Affika Korps, who have helped to make this book possible; to my old friend Generalmajor aD J H Löser and to General der Panzertruppe aD Gerhard Graf von Schwerin. To my wife Alexandra who has translated, interpreted, and typed with infinite patience and who has selected most of the photographs which have been used to illustrate the text, I am especially grateful.

Finally I must acknowledge the courtesy and help afforded by Dr Haupt and his staff of the Bundesarchiv Koblenz, and thank Messrs George G Harrap & Co for permission to quote a passage from Alexander Clifford's *Three Against Rommel*, the Oxford University Press for permission to quote from Brigadier Howard Kippenberger's *Infantry Brigadier*, and Purnell & Sons (SA) Ltd. to quote from Brigadier Eric 'Scrubbs' Hartshorn's *Avenge Tobruk*.

Cape Town,
March 1978.

Introduction

by

General Count von Schwerin

The Afrika Korps! Service with this exclusive force and with it the privilege of wearing the distinctive palm tree cuff-title and sand-coloured uniform was something coveted by every German soldier. In 1941 its deeds and achievements in what to most Germans was a novel, mysterious and romantic setting captured the imagination of the whole German people. The very name 'Africa' suggested something out of the ordinary – waving palms, exotic plants and strange animals, camels, caravans, desert, dark-skinned tribesmen in flowing white burnous, dusky maidens with hot glowing eyes peering from behind their veils. It was also soon apparent that the conflict there was different from that of other theatres of war. The so-called 'desert' war was one where tanks and motorised columns were not constrained by the terrain; under a scorching sun they could cruise around like battleships on the high seas.

The Afrika Korps, although quite a small force, was certainly a *corps d'élite*, but contrary to popular belief outside Germany its members were not hand-picked volunteers. Without exception they were just ordinary run-of-the-mill Wehrmacht soldiers of exactly the same calibre as those who fought in France or in Russia. Furthermore their equipment – with minor variations in dress and personal kit necessitated by the climate – was also the same as that issued to troops in the other theatres of war. As newcomers to the desert they adapted the experience gained in Poland and France and developed new methods and techniques suited to the war in North Africa. Unlike our Italian allies or our British adversaries, the Afrika Korps was prepared to waive the rules and methods devised for the conduct of war during the colonial era. Moving by night its columns would suddenly appear at sunrise on the enemy's flank or surprise him in his rear areas, and its 8.8cm AA guns were used with devastating effect. Movement, manoeuvre and concentration of effort were everything, and Erwin Rommel, the Afrika Korps' commander, was a master of all three. It was Rommel that made the Afrika Korps what it was, and its sensational successes were due to his grasp of what was essential in an unorthodox war. His leadership, plus his masterly employment of manoeuvre, tactical surprise and imaginative bluff, blitzkrieg techniques developed in Poland and France, and all-arms co-operation in battle, combined with the daring inculcated in his subordinates turned the Afrika Korps into a first-class fighting machine. The Korps was in fact tailored to Erwin Rommel's character. He asked a lot of his troops, but he was just as unsparing of himself – something which earned him the affection and respect of his own 'Afrika' men and the admiration of the German public at large. Rommel was an eminently successful commander-in-chief and the only German general of World War II who was as popular with our adversaries as with us. This popularity stemmed as much from the chivalrous code of conduct he upheld as on his successes in battle. And those of us who served with the Afrika Korps under Rommel were proud to belong to an army which enjoyed the enemy's respect.

Gerhard Graf von Schwerin.

Has Rommel's popularity and charisma been overrated? In the writer's opinion the answer is 'No'. The Afrika Korps' achievements were both unique and exemplary, and when its advance on Alexandria and the Suez Canal was halted by Field Marshal Montgomery before Alamein, Rommel was not to blame. When the Americans landed in Tunisia, Rommel flew to the Führer's headquarters, the 'Wolf's Lair', in East Prussia to explain the seriousness of the situation and to ask for the prompt transfer of the Afrika Korps to Italy. Hitler treated him with disdain, refused to countenance any withdrawal, and – figuratively speaking – had Rommel thrown out of the headquarters. The fate of the Afrika Korps was sealed just as that of the Sixth Army at Stalingrad was sealed at about the same time – with far worse consequences. Rommel's distrust and hostility towards the German High Command in general and Hitler in particular dates from the humiliation he suffered at this time. As is well known his hostility towards Hitler steadily increased as the war progressed, and this led eventually to the order that he should commit suicide.

Frederick the Great would have called Rommel a 'lucky' general. And he would have been right in so far as Lady Luck seemed to favour Rommel and the Afrika Korps as far as Alamein. Much of his good fortune can be attributed to audacity combined with unscrupulousness. Time and again the British armour were in a position to cut off the Afrika Korps columns during the latter's long outflanking marches in Cyrenaica and 'Afrika' men would have died of thirst even if the British had not been able to administer the *coup de grâce*. Audacity did not always pay off. For example half the Afrika Korps was sacrificed in a fruitless attempt to capture Tobruk because Rommel underestimated the strength of the defences and the determination of the Australians and New Zealanders who were garrisoning it at the time. And but for the protests of some of his subordinates he would have sacrificed the other half of the Korps.

On the other hand daring sometimes

produced extraordinary dividends. In April 1941 the writer was commanding the vanguard of the force which moved through the desert towards Mechili. By the time we reached our objective our vehicles had very little petrol left, we had no water, and the supply column which was supposed to rendezvous with us had missed us because we had changed our course during the night and nobody had thought to tell the supply column commander. Moreover as we had been spotted by British aircraft it was clear our situation was somewhat precarious. However I decided to try a bluff and sent our medical officer – because he spoke and understood English – across to the British lines under a white flag. 'You're surrounded,' he announced, 'And my commander is prepared to accept your surrender.' The British response was a courteous rejection of my offer. 'We have no intention of surrendering' was their laconic message. In the end they did surrender however and the negotiations were conducted all according to form, and with due ceremony – with the two British generals concerned presenting me with a captured Italian regimental standard. (This in due course I handed over to the Italian liaison officer attached to Rommel's headquarters, who burst into tears when he took it.)

Finally, it is perhaps fitting to conclude this foreword to Colonel Barker's book with two more anecdotes to illuminate the spirit of camaraderie that developed between friend and foe in the desert. The first is also related to the battle for Mechili, when a British officer who had been seriously wounded asked if I could get a message to his wife in Alexandria. I said that I would try, and my signallers transmitted a call in clear on the British radio frequency. Somewhat to our surprise the message was promptly acknowledged, and even more to my surprise an hour later a further call was received to say that our message had been passed to the officer's wife.

The second story reflects the British attitude towards 'good form' and correctness even in war – a characteristic that we Germans sometimes find difficult to understand. During Operation Battleaxe and the battle for Halfaya Pass in May 1942 we knocked out a large number of new heavily-armoured British tanks and one of the tank commanders asked me if he could see one of the weapons responsible for the wholesale destruction of the British armour. So I took him across to the 8.8cm AA Battery. The Englishman looked astounded, as he turned to me and said indignantly but seriously: 'But it's not cricket to use anti-aircraft guns against tanks!'

Such was the war in North Africa: those of us who served with the Deutsche Afrika Korps are proud to have fought there under command of the 'Desert Fox'.

Prologue

Italy's entry into World War II was late. Mussolini waited until Germany had mortally wounded France before delivering a stab in the back. Then, while Germany was fighting the Battle of Britain to bring the English to their knees the Duce embarked on what he termed a parallel operation – a glorious adventure in Africa which would restore the old Roman Empire. From the Italian colony of Libya an Italian Army was ordered to march to the Nile to conquer Egypt, and on 13 August 1940 this army of over 300,000 men began a ponderous and cautious advance from its Libyan base and main supply port of Tripoli.

Prospects of an Italian success were high, for Marshal Rudolfo ('Butcher') Graziani, the army's commander, had as high a reputation as any general in the Italian Army. But Graziani's campaigns had all been waged against primitive peoples and his plan for the invasion of Egypt was both ill-conceived and mismanaged. Nor were his troops equipped for a desert war against a sophisticated enemy – even if that sophisticated enemy was thin on the ground. The Italians' weapons were obsolete and they were short of mechanical transport. Their tanks were light and underpowered, their huge ten-ton Diesel lorries were too heavy to operate in the desert off the road, and their light vehicles were for the most part ordinary Fiats built for the Italian *autostrada*; artillery pieces were of 1918 vintage, anti-tank weapons were few and far between and infantry weapons were as outdated as the artillery. Nevertheless the sheer size of the invasion force was such that the handful of British troops in the Middle East at that time had no hope of stopping the Italian invasion, and they fell back nimbly without attempting to give battle. Thus, within three days the Italians had crossed the Egyptian border and occupied Sidi Barrani. There they stopped and dug in to await supplies of food, water, petrol and ammunition, and to build a tarmac road to link Sidi Barrani with the Libyan base above Sollum.

They waited in vain. Graziani had shot his bolt, for not only was the Duce ill-prepared to furnish the supplies which his armies in Africa sorely needed, but his ambitions were now dictating to his good sense. Resources which should have been sent to Graziani's army were allocated to another Italian adventure in Greece. Meanwhile the British had hurriedly assembled a modern mechanised army in Egypt, and with dramatic suddenness it went onto the offensive. An attack was launched on 9 December, and the Italians – who had spent much of their time trying to convert the stretch of desert around Sidi Barrani into a home-from-home – were caught completely by surprise. Sidi Barrani was captured on 11 December, Bardia on the Egyptian border fell on 5 January, Tobruk surrendered 18 days later and the Italian garrison at Derna, 600 miles further west, withdrew before the advancing British columns were even in sight. The British had not only swept the Italians out of Egypt in the space of a fortnight, they had also conquered half of Libya. The Duce's men were now facing an overwhelming defeat; Tripolitania was threatened, and if Tripoli fell it was possible that a British force might advance on Tunisia. If this happened the French administration there, shakily loyal to the Vichy government, might well decide to join the Free French on the British side. This was something which Hitler could not tolerate. Furthermore the Italian defeat had removed the threat to Egypt and to Britain's entire position in the Eastern Mediterranean. They could now send forces from Egypt to Greece – something they had in fact already started to do. When the Italians had suffered their first defeats in Greece and the Western Desert towards the end of 1940 Hitler had declared that he was not prepared to send a single man nor spend one *pfennig* on pulling Italy's chestnuts out of the North Africa fire. But the fantastic British advance which the Italians were clearly incapable of stopping was a development which the Führer regarded with grave misgivings.

On 11 January 1941 the OKW (*Oberkommando der Wehrmacht*) headquarters in Berlin issued a 'Führer Directive' stating that 'for strategic, political and other reasons Germany must assist Italy in Africa', and authorising the formation of a *Sperrverband* – a blocking force – to defend Tripolitania. Following a meeting between Hitler and Mussolini at the Obersalzberg a week later, the status of the *Sperrverband* was upgraded. The two dictators had agreed that the policy in North Africa was to be offensive rather than passively defensive, and for this a highly mobile mechanised formation commanded by a man who knew how to handle such a formation was needed. Meantime the Luftwaffe's *Fliegerkorps X* was ordered to move to Sicily from where its 500 Stukas and fighters could disrupt the supply line of the advancing British and generally support Graziani's retreating army.

The plan implementing these decisions constituted the birth certificate of the Deutsche Afrika Korps. The code name given to the venture was *Sonnenblume* (Sunflower) and the man, the 'incredibly hard' man, selected to command the new force was the recently promoted Generalleutnant Erwin Johannes Eugen Rommel.

It would have been difficult to find a better man for the job or a more captivating German officer. Handsome, buoyant and talented, he was a devoted husband and father who wrote a few lines to his wife every day. A professional soldier, he was never a Nazi; indeed he had little interest in politics until much later in the war when he was an uncomfortable conspirator in the

German field artillery in action.

plot to assassinate Hitler. Yet it was Hitler who recognised Rommel's proficiency and fostered his career. Because he was a Württemberger, Rommel's accomplishments had been denigrated by the Prussian hierarchy which dominated the officer corps of the Reichswehr until Hitler came to power. Then he made rapid progress. Under the Führer's patronage he was a colonel in 1939, a major-general a year later, and a field marshal in 1942 who had been decorated with Germany's highest military award.

Originally an infantryman, but a leading exponent of the blitzkrieg theory, Rommel had shown in France that he could execute it with remarkable results. In February 1940 during the so-called Sitzkrieg 'phoney war', he had taken command of a Panzer division which a few months later was in the forefront of the breakthrough that brought Germany a heady victory and France a dismal defeat. This, then, was the man who flew in to Berlin on 6 February 1941 to report to the Wehrmacht's Commander-in-Chief, Feldmarschall Walther von Brauchitsch, to be told of his assignment, and to be given his orders for the deployment of what the Führer himself was now calling the Deutsche Afrika Korps.

The Afrika Korps did not actually come into being until Rommel's appointment on 6 February. But two motorised divisions had already been earmarked for it. One, the 15th Panzer Division under command of Generalmajor von Prittwitz, was equipping and training for its new role; the second, a light division – known first as the 'Ceremonial' Division and subsequently as the 5th Light Division until it was converted to become the 21st Panzer Division – was still being formed from elements of the 3rd Panzer Division; this formation was particularly strong in anti-tank units. Together, at full strength, the two divisions would muster about 24,000 men.

At his interview with von Brauchitsch, Rommel was told that the first units of the light division were already on their way to Italy, and were expected to embark for Tripoli on, or about, 15 February. The 15th Panzer Division would follow a month later and the whole of the Afrika Korps ought to be in Africa by the middle of May. This schedule, said von Brauchitsch, would enable Rommel to familiarise himself with the terrain and get to know his Italian allies. In saying this it was clear that the German Commander-in-Chief reckoned that the Italians might be as difficult as the desert terrain. The Führer believed that he not only had to prevent Italy from suffering a humiliating defeat, but he also had to demonstrate Axis solidarity. However having decided that Africa did not count, so far as his ideas of the role of the Third Reich in the greater scheme of things was concerned, he had also decided that Rommel would be subordinated to the Italian Commander-in-Chief, who was responsible to the *Comando Supremo*, Graziani and took his orders from Rome. On the other hand the German expeditionary force – the Afrika Korps – was to be employed as a formation only and not split up over the front. If Rommel was given an order that would in his opinion lead to failure he had the right of appeal to Berlin.

Turning to a map of the North African coast von Brauchitsch ran his finger along the coast line from Tripoli along the Gulf of Sirte, past Mersa Brega to Benghazi, and then on to Derna, Tobruk, Sollum, and finally to Alexandria and inland to Cairo – indicating a stretch of over a thousand miles of sandy wilderness. This, he said, would be Rommel's theatre of operation, and there was only one road through it – the Via Balbia (called after Marshal Balbo). North of the road there was the sea, south of it the limitless desert – shimmering ranges of sand dunes, vast plains of broken stone, steep cliffs and waterless lakes. The very nature of this terrain, von Brauchitsch continued, presented special problems – great distances, lack of water and absence of cover. To Rommel however it already seemed that its very size and featurelessness offered many advantages to an army which had superior mobility.

Writing to his wife that night to tell her of his new appointment, Rommel bypassed security about where he was going. 'I shall be able to do something for my rheumatism at long last,' he wrote. When Frau Rommel remembered that a doctor who had treated her husband for rheumatism in France had said, 'You need sunshine, General; you ought to be in Africa,' the inference was not too difficult to draw.

Rommel flew to Rome the next day, 7 February, accompanied by a smooth and personable young officer, Oberst Rudolf Schmundt. In so far as Schmundt was supposed to iron out any differences that might arise between Rommel and the Italians, it seems that Hitler had anticipated that there would be problems with Rommel's subordination to the Italian High Command. Once he overcame his initial suspicions of the man he must have seen as a Nazi watchdog, Rommel and Schmundt became good friends.

On arrival at Rome the two Germans were met by the news that Benghazi had fallen, and that Graziani had been replaced by General Italo Gariboldi. At the *Comando Supremo* headquarters, senior Italian officers greeted Rommel with polite condescension. To them he was an unknown and relatively unimportant German, who would take his orders from Gariboldi. Questioned by Rommel as to what the Italians were doing to stop the British reaching Tripoli now that they had overrun Benghazi General Alfred Guzzoni, the Deputy Chief of Staff, shrugged his shoulders. 'We shall try to hold Buerat until your troops arrive,' he replied. Buerat is on the edge of a marshy plain, about 180 miles from the capital of Tripolitania. Rommel realised that the Italians were on the run. To Schmundt he said, 'There's only one way to stop the rot! – To go on the offensive. It should be possible to do so even with a small force – provided we have the right

A Messerschmitt Bf 109 fighter.

General Ugo Cavallero (centre) was the pro-German Italian Chief of Staff from 1940 until January 1943.

kind of equipment. And the sooner we get on with it the better. The desert is wide enough to outflank the enemy in order to strike him where he is not expecting to be struck.'

From Rome, Rommel and Schmundt flew on to Catania, where the headquarters of General Geissler's *Fliegerkorps X* were located. 'The Italians have been routed,' Rommel told Geissler, 'and unless we can stop the British from advancing at the rate they are now moving, my troops will never get to Tripoli in time to be of any use. The only way to slow the British is to bomb Benghazi and attack their convoys in the Gulf of Sirte.' 'Impossible,' Geissler replied, 'the Italians will never agree.' 'Why?' 'Because many of the officers in their Libyan army have nice houses in Benghazi.'

A telephone call by Rommel to the *Comando Supremo* confirmed Geissler's view that bombing Benghazi was taboo. But another telephone call – this time by Schmundt direct to Hitler – quickly brought a change in attitude, and next morning, as Rommel waited to emplane for Tripoli, he watched the Luftwaffe bombers taking off and heading south-east towards Benghazi. For the first time since the start of their victorious campaign the British were going to have to reckon with the Germans. The Luftwaffe struck the first blow; the Deutsche Afrika Korps would soon take over.

Heia Safari

Rommel flew from Catania in one of the aircraft ferrying the advance parties of the 5th Light Division to Tripolitania. General Streich, the divisional commander, travelled with him and like his men he was wearing one of the tropical uniforms which had been issued before emplaning. Not having had any experience of equipping German troops for service in the tropics since the Cameroon expedition in 1914, the Wehrmacht's *Intendantur* had taken its cue from the Italians. Trousers, shorts and field tunic were of light weight canvas drill dyed 'sage-green' – a dull sand colour, which in time would fade under the combined effects of sun, heat, desert air and washing. A colonial-style pith helmet had also been issued, and this together with the British style shorts and knee stockings caused a certain amount of hilarity among the troops. 'We look like a lot of bloody Tyroleans,' said one. (In the event these Italian-German equivalents of the British 'Bombay-bowler' had a short life. Being neither attractive nor practical they were soon replaced by the tropical *Einheitsfeldmütze* – the sloppy peaked 'fore-and-aft' which became a symbol of the Afrika Korps. The pattern of dress, like that of the British Eighth Army, later became less and less formal.)

None of these men who 'looked like Tyroleans' had had any special training before embarkation. Medical officers had merely given them a cursory medical examination, pronounced them 'fit for service in the tropics' and – apart from a lecture at which they were cautioned about their relations with the Arabs 'who have a sense of honour and are fiercely jealous,' and warned of the dangers of the women, the vice, the dirt, the disease, the vermin, the water, the heat and the peculiarities of the climate – that was all. Arrangements for the units and reinforcements which followed were more elaborate. At Hamburg's Tropical Institute scientists and technicians were put to work producing antidotes and palliatives; and foot-powders, ointments, vitamin pills, 'pep' pills, eye-lotions, water-purifiers and insecticides were shipped across to North Africa. The advice and the warnings were also incorporated in a little book which was handed to every German soldier posted to the Afrika Korps. But all this was in the future; Streich's men first had to blaze the trail.

Oberstleutnant Heggenreimer was waiting when Rommel's plane landed at Castel Benito, some $12\frac{1}{2}$ miles south of Tripoli. Heggenreimer was the liaison officer with the *Comando Supremo* in Africa and he had been sent to ensure Rommel reported straight to General Gariboldi. He also had a few things to say to Rommel before the latter's interview with the Italian Commander-in-Chief. The Italian retreat would be better described as a rout, Heggenreimer said. Many of the Italians had simply thrown away their weapons and scrambled on to the already overloaded vehicles, in a desperate attempt to get away to the West, and there had been some ugly scenes. It was Heggenreimer's opinion that the whole Italian army in North Africa was completely demoralised. To Rommel it seemed that this might well be so. As their car sped northwards towards Tripoli, they passed Italian soldiers moving in both directions. Disciplined detachments were few and far between; most of the men were unshaven; many were not wearing headgear; quite a number had no weapons; and all of them looked haggard and disgruntled. Defeat was written on their faces.

At Gariboldi's headquarters there was more evidence of despair and even signs of panic. Some staff officers appeared to be more concerned with what would happen to their houses and personal possessions when the British arrived, than in arrangements to stop them. Gariboldi himself – a big, burly man six inches taller than Rommel – was clearly at the end of his tether. He looked tired and he spoke in a tone of disillusionment. 'I am pulling all the *bouches inutiles* out of Tripoli and shipping them back to Italy,' he told Rommel. 'We shall stand and fight at Buerat.' 'It would be better to dig in 40 miles further east – at Sirte – and counter-attack from there,' Rommel responded. 'The British will continue to advance just so long as there is no organised resistance. Their supply line is the weak link. If we attack with everything we've got – including the German units now on their way here – and the Luftwaffe concentrates on stopping supplies getting forward to the British, General O'Connor will be in trouble.' Gariboldi argued that Rommel

German troops on parade, February 1941, in Tripoli.

Rommel (right) next to Gariboldi.

did not know what he was up against. Desert warfare, he said, was something Rommel knew nothing about. 'There is no such thing as "desert" warfare,' Rommel snapped back; 'war is war, wherever you are. The only difference is that the desert allows more scope for manoeuvre and a war of movement. But only the offensive pays. We must strike where the enemy is least expecting us by outflanking him.' Somewhat reluctantly the Italian Commander-in-Chief conceded that there might be something in Rommel's theory. In any case he had nothing to lose by permitting the Germans to make an air reconnaissance of the Sirte region.

Thus it was that on the morning of 13 February Rommel was in the air with Oberst Schmundt examining what Rommel called 'the soil of Africa'. In a Heinkel III they flew over the desert east of Tripoli – 'a belt of sand which had the appearance of being difficult country for either wheeled or tracked vehicles and thus forming a good natural obstacle in front of Tripoli.' The flight continued over the hilly country around Tarhuna, Homs and Buerat and finally circled over Sirte. 'The flight confirmed me in my plan to fortify Sirte and the country on either side of the coast road and to reserve the motorised forces for the mobile defence,' Rommel confided to his diary.

Their aircraft had been spotted by British troops on the ground. But the British had more pressing problems than concern about a lone Heinkel circling over their front line. In ten weeks General Sir Richard O'Connor's victorious army had advanced 500 miles, cut the Italian army to shreds and taken 130,000 prisoners. But on the very same day as Rommel flew to Tripoli, O'Connor was ordered to halt the advance. His experienced units were needed elsewhere, and he himself was to be pulled back to become General Officer Commanding British troops in Egypt. Within a week O'Connor's spearhead divisions were on their way to Greece, and O'Connor's successor Lieutenant General Philip Neame was left with a much reduced and ill-equipped force of inexperienced replacements.

Just as O'Connor and Neame knew nothing of Rommel and his plans, Rommel was not aware of what was happening behind the enemy front. He was not told that the Germans would march into Greece if the British responded to Greece's appeal for an army to help them drive out the Italians who had invaded their country. But Rommel had quickly grasped the tactical and strategic situation in North Africa and his decision 'in view of the tenseness of the situation and the sluggishness of the Italian command, to depart from my instructions to confine myself to a reconnaissance and to take command at the front as soon as possible . . .' was soon to be proved right.

During the flight back to Castel Benito Rommel chatted with Schmundt. 'What do you propose to do?' the latter asked. 'To attack, of course – just as soon as we can get the teeth units of

General Sir Archibald Wavell.

An Italian Fiat G-50, a useful single-seater fighter plane.

Streich's division up to Buerat,' Rommel replied. 'O'Connor has over-stretched himself. He should have stopped at Mersa Brega; with the sea on his right and marshland on his left he would have been in an ideal defensive position. As it is, at El Agheila he is in the plain and we can outflank him by the south.'

Back in Tripoli Rommel went straight to the docks to see how the disembarkation of the 5th Light Division was progressing. To the Italians it was progressing very well indeed; accustomed as they were to a more leisurely pace and to a long break at midday it seemed to them that men, tanks and lorries were coming ashore at a phenomenal rate. But they were not moving fast enough for Rommel. The unloading must continue throughout the night, he ordered. To do so meant the use of floodlights. 'What about the British bombers?' the Italians asked. Rommel shrugged his shoulders. 'We have every confidence in the Luftwaffe,' he said.

Streich's men were glad to get off the ship. Their voyage across the translucent sea – which their allies persisted in calling '*Mare Nostrum*' and subsequent contingents of the Afrika Korps dubbed the 'German swimming pool', had been without incident, and Rommel's confidence in Luftwaffe air superiority at this stage of the war was completely vindicated. The convoys bound for Tripoli sailed from ports in southern Italy under an umbrella of fighters which effectively prevented British bombers, submarines and warships getting to them. Of 220,000 tons of cargo for Rommel's men in North Africa loaded in February and March 1941 only 20,000 failed to arrive.

On 14 February the officers of those units which had disembarked were assembled to meet their new commander. 'Gentlemen,' Rommel said, in what passed for his welcoming address, 'We are here to defend Tripoli. But I have no intention of sitting and waiting for the enemy to come to us; we are going to go on the offensive as soon as possible. You will not have very much time to get acclimatised and to get to

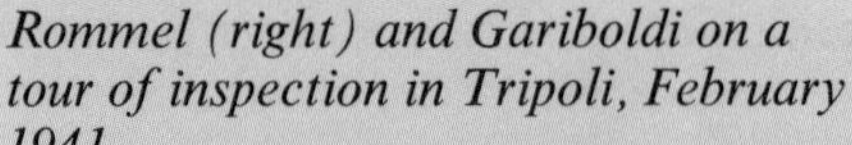

Rommel (right) and Gariboldi on a tour of inspection in Tripoli, February 1941.

know the desert. But time is of the essence; we must seize the initiative and keep it. Our campaign begins tomorrow . . . the desert is waiting for us. We are about to embark on a great safari!' *'Heia Safari,'* shouted one enthusiastic young subaltern straight from the Hitler Youth. *'Heia Safari,'* echoed others in the audience, and the words were to become the Afrika Korps' battle-cry – comparable with the war-cry of the Gurkhas: *'Ayo Gurkhali'*.

Next morning the Afrika Korps and detachments of the Italian Brescia and Ariete ('Battering Ram') armoured divisions paraded through Tripoli. Rommel was inclined to regard ceremonial affairs like this as a waste of time – time which could be better spent in training. But he had decided that the sight and sound of German mechanised might would impress the local populace. Furthermore a report on the quantity and quality of weapons and equipment on show would be certain to get back to the enemy, for Tripoli was known to be swarming with agents in British pay. Properly staged, therefore, a display of force could be used to deceive the enemy and induce the British to believe that the newly arrived German contingent was more powerful in terms of men and machines than it actually was.

Rommel, accompanied by Italian officers, inspects German troops newly arrived in Tripoli, 1941.

It was a glorious day when the parade formed up on the Via Balbia west of the town, to follow a circular route past the civic centre before ending up back on the coast road where the sunburned desert began again at the town's western limits. To demonstrate Axis solidarity buildings along the route had been bedecked with German and Italian flags. As the Panzers rumbled down the avenues, however, there could be little doubt about the feelings of the locals. Axis solidarity meant little to the Italian population in Tripoli, and literally nothing to the Arabs who lived there. They watched impassively as the Tedesco column rattled and clanked its way through the streets; the Italians' cheers were reserved for the vehicles of the Brescia and Ariete Divisions. These were thinly armoured two-man light tanks, and the better-looking, but mechanically inferior M-13s. Neither type was in the same class as the 50 German Mk III and Mk IV Panzers on the parade – 22- and 24-ton leviathans armed with 50mm guns which, it was soon to be seen, could outrange and outshoot the British tanks in the Western Desert. But the two-man 'coffins' and the 14-ton, four-man M-13s were Italian: and although the Italians needed the Germans, the Germans were still foreigners.

Thirty armoured cars of Oberstleutnant Freiherr Irmfeld von Wechmar's 3rd Reconnaissance Abteilung headed the German column. Behind them came the Mk III and Mk IV Panzers, all bearing the newly painted sign of the Afrika Korps – a palm tree surmounted by a swastika. Infantry riding in trucks and half-track personnel carriers came next, then the men of the motorcycle battalion on their motorcycles and sidecars; and two batteries of the famous 8.8cm anti-aircraft guns brought up the rear – although to spectators watching the parade it appeared that there were another 50 Mk III and Mk IV tanks. This was an illusion, for there was only

one group of Panzers which – when they had trundled past the saluting base behind von Wechmar's armoured cars – turned off the route to rumble down roads which brought the group back to the parade to rejoin the tail of the column.

By noon with the parade behind them, the motorised column was clattering along the Via Balbia heading for a concentration area near Sirte, where the Afrika Korps was to train and prepare itself for desert warfare. Acclimatisation would come with the training and the men would grow tough and lean and seasoned, their skins burnt by the sun to the colour of old shoe-leather. The units which had not taken part in the ceremonial send-off were waiting to join the column outside Tripoli and there was a pause while this assortment of the 5th Light Division's base unit and headquarter vehicles – ambulances, workshop and recovery trucks, signals vans and the like – were slotted into position and the convoy shook out into a tactical formation. Finally there came a shout which rippled down the road – *'Heia Safari!'* and the Afrika Korps was on its way.

On the move the column stretched back almost two miles, each vehicle keeping ten yards behind the one in front and tanks advancing as flank guards on the south side of the road where the desert terminated in a narrow fringe of green palms. It took 26 hours to cover the 300 miles from Tripoli, and when the convoy dispersed in a patch of desert near Sirte the troops were tired and both they and the vehicles had lost the Wehrmacht gloss; faces were chapped and sore, uniforms and vehicles were dusty. Those who might have been expecting to find a North African version of the summer holiday resorts of Heringsdorf or Bansin at Sirte were quickly disillusioned. Nothing remains of the ancient Phoenician city which gave its name to the largest bay on the North African coast; Sirte itself turned out to be a shabby little Arab village of mud huts, clustered on the banks of a foul-smelling stream. A few poverty-stricken Bedouins – none of whom turned out to have 'a sense of honour or to be fiercely jealous' – with a few half-starved sheep and goats lived there, but the principal residents in the region were flies and fleas. The flies roamed around in swarms by day, descending on eyelids, mouths and nostrils in nauseous clinging clouds – their place being taken by night by the fleas which emerged from the sand, probing their way through clothes to exposed flesh which they bit till the blood ran.

South of the village there was a primitive airfield, with its limits marked by empty white-painted oil drums, which the Italians had staked out in the desert. Near this airfield there were the few battered and deserted buildings which the Italian garrison had once occupied; that was all. Here, in a region almost unimaginably devoid of luxuries, the men of the Afrika Korps were to spend the next six weeks. Strip life of everything that makes it worthwhile and that was their existence at Sirte. Water was scanty and brackish; even the coffee they brewed tasted salty however strong it was made; the rations were just a means of keeping alive in the most economical way. (In these early days the rations were mainly Italian and often consisted of unappetising tins of meat. With the passage of time the quality of rations improved and by the end of 1941 the food supplied to the Afrika Korps was undeniably good – full corn 'Kommiss' bread wrapped in cellophane and silver paper; succulent German sausage, tinned fruits, chocolate, dehydrated soups, dried vegetables, wine, beer and orange concentrate.) But the mens' bodies gradually grew accustomed to stark simplicity, hard living, and monotonous eating, only the flies and fleas never ceased to bother them.

Under Rommel's direction conventional battle procedures designed for Europe were discarded and units dispersed into detachments which were then amalgamated to form all-arms battle groups. The mechanised battle groups were then sent off into the desert to learn to navigate by compass, sextant, the stars and dead reckoning – like ships at sea. It was tough going and in the early days the men loathed the desert, and were filled with an almost morbid homesickness for the green hills of Northern Europe. One young lieutenant tells the story of how his group of tanks attempted to charge across a flat sandy plain. But the plain turned out to be a dry salt lake, the surface of which had been obscured by drifting sand, and the tanks sank up to their bellies. When recovery vehicles eventually came to their rescue it took the best part of a day to pull the tanks out; then – as they cautiously manoeuvred round the side of the salt-pan – they ran into an unmarked and unrecorded minefield, and the Afrika Korps suffered its first casualties. Writing home the lieutenant told of his frustrations, the horrors of Africa and how on this occasion some of his men had actually been reduced to tears.

Gradually, however, the men conquered their fears, learned to find their way without landmarks, and acclimatised to the furnace-like heat of the sun by day and biting cold at night. They also developed new battle drills, and to 'laager' in all-round defensive positions when halted – very much as the pioneers in North America or the voortrekking Boers in South Africa had done in the days of the covered wagons and marauding natives.

Meantime Rommel was brooding on strategy and tactics. He had already decided on an early offensive, though he was not prepared to reveal what he had in mind or von Brauchitsch in Berlin and Gariboldi in Tripoli would have promptly vetoed it. But Streich, a man who was apt to see difficulties and disaster round every corner, suspected his commander was up to something and expressed concern about his division being flung into an offensive prematurely – before it was joined by the 15th Panzer Division. Rommel placated him by telling him that what he had in mind was merely a 'reconnaissance in force'. Whether or not this was what he did have in mind originally, on 5 March he was writing to his wife, 'Speed is the thing that matters here.' However if speed was the main issue, strength was its concomitant, and as the 15th Panzer Division would not be available until the middle of May the Afrika Korps could only hope to convey the *impression* of strength in any attack before that date. Some deceptive measure was necessary therefore. Thus it was that the Cardboard Division came into being.

'Put yourself in the enemy's shoes,' Rommel said at a conference of unit commanders. 'The British do not know precisely how many tanks we have, and what types they are. Nor in an attack can they know where we have concentrated them. When we advance what do they see?' The answer, of course, was dust, and the outlines of vehicles – not tanks necessarily, but the outlines of tanks. The solution therefore was to create a lot of dust and to deploy vehicles which looked like tanks. So the Afrika Korps' workshops were ordered to manufacture a 100 dummy tanks by mounting wooden and canvas frames

Top left: Afrika Korps men sing and march on parade, February 1941.
Above: Rommel and his staff inspect a front-line position on a Libyan beach.
Right: Tanks are unloaded in Tripoli.

on motorcars commandeered in Tripoli. These were then moved forward to Sirte and handed over to the Reconnaissance Group commander, von Wechmar.

On 19 March when Rommel flew to Berlin to report on the situation in North Africa, von Brauchitsch accepted the arguments Rommel had used to persuade Gariboldi to move the front forward from Buerat. But he stressed that German troops and equipment were not going to be frittered away in Africa: there was no intention of striking a decisive blow in Africa. The Führer and the High Command might agree to a limited offensive – to recapture Benghazi perhaps – but not until the whole of the German Expeditionary Force reached Africa. 'The British,' said von Brauchitsch, 'are far too strong for a single light division. . . . You will have to wait until the 15th Panzer Division arrives in May.' Rommel agreed, and made no mention of the fact that he had already issued orders for the 'reconnaissance in force' which he had every intention of making the first phase of an offensive.

While Rommel was in Berlin General Archibald Wavell went up to see O'Connor's successor, General Philip Neame, at his desert headquarters near Benghazi, and he was profoundly disturbed by what he saw and heard. Holding the British front lines east of Benghazi was a single armoured brigade, equipped with old and ailing medium and light tanks, an infantry brigade, and the 9th Australian Division. Being thin on the ground was bad enough – considering the terrain on which the forward troops were deployed was clearly vulnerable to attack by a mechanised force. Worse was the fact that morale was not high and relationships between at least two of the commanders was strained. General Leslie Morshead GOC of the Australian division who was worshipped by his troops (who called him 'Ming – the merciless') had two major worries: the shortage of anti-tank weapons in his division – which he blamed partly on the British, and Neame's attitude towards his unruly 'diggers'. Neame, for his part, considered the Australians to be an undisciplined, drunken lot and said so. Even on 31 March, while the Australians were fighting desperately at Mersa Brega, Neame was writing to Wavell complaining bitterly of their lack of discipline. On the credit side however – as Wavell saw it – there was time to put things right, for it was certain that the enemy could not mount an offensive until after 15 May. Wavell was quite positive about this, for he had received secret information from the highest source. Allied code-cracking experts in London had been monitoring signals passing between the German High Command and Africa and Churchill had passed on the news concerning the arrival of the 15th Panzer Division in Africa, and the German High Command's views on another Axis offensive.

But Rommel was a law unto himself and events were soon to show that neither the men in Berlin nor Wavell in Cairo could count on his behaving in an orthodox fashion. Back in Africa he proceeded to completely disregard the instructions he had received from von Brauchitsch.

By this time the men of the Afrika Korps had already clashed with their British opponents. Three British armoured cars patrolling beyond Agedabia had met and passed three German armoured cars on the Via Balbia. All six had slithered to a standstill and deployed in the desert according to text-book tactics. A brisk action followed, at the conclusion of which the Germans had suffered no casualties, while the British had lost two armoured cars and three men who had been taken prisoner.

Rommel's 'reconnaissance in force' got under way at dawn on 22 March, when von Wechmar's armoured cars drove down the Via Balbia and deployed on the edge of the El Agheila plain. 'Rather far for a reconnaissance in force,' Streich commented drily when he was told that his Reconnaissance Abteilung had reached the British front line. Von Wechmar's men had in fact covered 190 miles in the two days since they left Sirte. From the turret of his vehicle von Wechmar could see an old fort, a square brick building overlooking the road and below the fort the trenches and wire of defensive positions astride the road. Behind these positions there were tents and further back above the road, where the ground was hilly a

Wavell (right) and O'Connor discuss the situation in Bardia, January 1941.

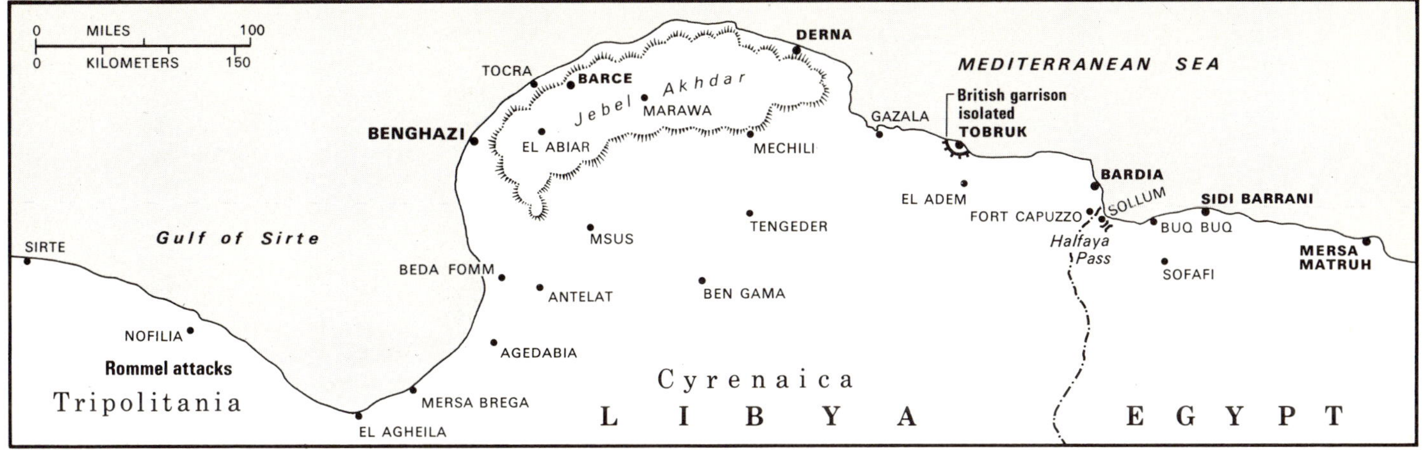

The DAK advance through Libya.

number of tanks, hull down, could be discerned in the half light. Even allowing for a surprise attack and successful deception by the Cardboard Division, it was clear to von Wechmar that the opposition was formidable.

However there was no stopping now. As the sun rose von Wechmar signalled his men to advance, and his cars – in two groups – raced forward to envelop the British positions on the road. The initial attack was completely successful and within 15 minutes the trenches had been overrun and the men who had been defending them were being hustled back down the Via Balbia. But the British armour still had to be reckoned with. Leaving their positions the tanks moved down towards the Via Balbia with the obvious intention of forming up for a counter-attack.

But now the German anti-tank guns, under command of Hauptmann Wilhelm Bach, opened up. The Reverend Captain Bach, who was destined to become a legendary figure in the Afrika Korps, had been ordained as a priest before the war. Mobilised as a private soldier in 1939 his true calling appeared during the campaign in France when his expertise as an anti-tank gunner led to his being commissioned in the field. He was now 50 years of age, ('Rather long in the tooth for this sort of game' Rommel said when he met him) walked with a limp because of an old wound, and his fondness for beer was reflected in the overhang of his stomach. Rommel had taken an instinctive dislike to him, but his opinion was soon to change.

In the first salvo from Bach's guns one tank was set on fire and two others were hit; others turned tail and roared off, wheeling south into the desert to get out of range. As they did so a crescent-shaped cloud of dust appeared on the horizon: the Cardboard Division, deployed on a very wide frontage, was charging down, seemingly bent on enveloping the British armour. The latter wheeled again and headed back towards Mersa Brega, 30 miles east across the desert. The Afrika Korps had won its first battle, and Rommel was still in Berlin.

The Afrika Korps did not attempt to advance beyond El Agheila for a week, although von Wechmar's armoured cars patrolled to points about 6 miles from Mersa Brega without seeing any enemy. Meantime Rommel had returned from Berlin determined to press forward, despite the advice of his tubby little chief of staff, Oberstleutnant Klaus von dem Borne. Mersa Brega, the latter pointed out, was at the head of a defile, and the terrain favoured the defence; with the sea on one side and marshland on the other the British position could not be outflanked. So, unless an amphibious operation was envisaged, it would have to be attacked frontally. Reports by Luftwaffe pilots suggested that the British were hard at work digging and wiring. Therefore it would be better to delay the attack until the Afrika Korps was at full strength.

Rommel was in no mood to wait until 15 May however. 'We've got the enemy on the run,' he said. 'And we must capture Mersa Brega before it becomes more of an obstacle than it is already. We attack on 31 March.' From this date on the war in Africa steadily escalated.

For the Mersa Brega operation Rommel divided his force into three battle groups. The first, the 104th Infantry Regiment, under command of Oberst von Holtzendorff, was ordered to seize the height overlooking the village at the head of the defile. This meant a flank attack, and to get to their objective Holtzendorff's Panzergrenadiers were to move through marshland, which armoured fighting vehicles could not negotiate. The second battle group was composed of von Wechmar's armoured cars, and Bach's guns. Its task was to drive straight down the road and assault the British defences frontally. The remaining group, Oberst Herbert Olbrich's 5th Panzer Regiment, was the mailed fist which Rommel expected to deliver the decisive blow.

The frontal attack was scheduled for noon, but Olbrich's Panzers were in action an hour before von Wechmar's cars charged up the road. Moving along the strip of desert between the Via Balbia and the sea, the leading tanks paused a few hundred yards away from the strong points and trenches blocking the road while the remainder clanked into position. Then, turning in towards the road the Panzers resumed their advance in an inverted 'V' formation. As they began to move Bach's guns opened fire on the British defences.

The enemy positions were manned by men of the 9th Australian Division. Few of them had ever been in battle before, and besides being inexperienced they were also ill-equipped to fight tanks. Rifles and bayonets were of little use against 22-ton Panzers, and Australian resistance at the entrance to the defile was quickly crushed.

Von Wechmar came up at midday, according to plan, but neither his armoured cars nor Olbrich's tanks were able to get very far beyond the entrance to the defile. Olbrich's Panzers had dealt effectively with the road block, but the main British positions in the centre of the village were showing plenty of fight, and any of the Afrika Korps vehicles which tried to get up the road were greeted with shells from 25-pounder field guns firing over open sights and two-pounder anti-tank guns. Up in the hills above the village the Panzergrenadiers were also having a tough time. The Australians, supported by fire from the 25-pounders in the village, stubbornly refused to give ground and the battle looked like going on for ever. By the middle of the afternoon Rommel decided to bring in the Luftwaffe and he had a message radioed to the Luftwaffe command in Tripoli. In response shortly before 1700 hours, about 50 Stukas screamed down to bomb targets indicated by smoke shells fired from Bach's guns. The effect was immediate and devastating. The fire of the 25 pounders slackened; Olbrich's tanks found that at long last they could move up the defile, and Holtzendorff's men up in the hills were no longer pinned down either, so both Panzers and Panzergrenadiers moved in for the kill. By 1800 hours the battle was over and the Afrika Korps could begin to count the spoils.

These spoils, which included enough petrol to take the Afrika Korps' vehicles deep into Cyrenaica and a bonus of 50 fairly new Bren carriers, far exceeded the optimistic hopes that Rommel had nurtured. But captured material was less important than the tactical advantage which this successful action brought. The British had lost the only position along the Libyan coast where outflanking tactics could be blocked. The Afrika Korps had established a foothold in Cyrenaica, the door of which was now open, and the tables had been turned on the British – for it was they that were now on the run. There was nearly 500 miles of desert between Mersa Brega and the Egyptian border and Rommel was determined to go after the British and annihilate them somewhere in this stretch of wasteland.

Next morning (1 April) a reformed battle group consisting of Olbrich's tanks and a motorised battalion of Panzergrenadiers set off up the road to Agedabia, about 30 miles from Mersa Brega. After a brief action with the tiny garrison that had been left to delay the Afrika Korps' advance, Agedabia was occupied and next morning (2 April) the Panzers were on the move once more, scouring the desert around the village. Olbrich knew that a clash with British armour could not be long delayed, and at 1100 hours with the temperature about 60°C, it came; Stuart tanks of the 3rd Armoured Brigade had been sent to halt the Afrika Korps' advance. There were three Stuarts to every Mk III and Mk IV Panzer, but the technical superiority of the German tanks more than made up for their numbers. Shot from the 37mm cannon mounted on the Stuarts merely bounced off the armour of the Panzers while rounds fired by the

Nazi propaganda pictures from Signal: Far right: Relaxing in the scorching sun. Above: A first taste of action.

latter were devastatingly effective. Within minutes five tanks of the 5th Royal Tank Regiment had been knocked out and in a scramble to get away two others broke down and had to be abandoned. As Agedabia was now in German hands Major-General Gambier-Parry, the Commander of the 2nd British Armoured Division ordered the brigade to fall back on Antelat.

Meantime Rommel was planning the next phase of his offensive. 'We must press on,' he told von Wechmar. 'There are three routes open to us – the first along the Via Balbia towards Benghazi, Derna and Tobruk; the second, running north-eastwards via an oasis called Msus to another called Mechili; and a third, running further to the east and bypassing the "Green Mountains", which joins the second above Mechili.'

Rommel's decision was to use all three and to organise his force into three battle groups once more to do so. The first of the groups, under the ubiquitous von Wechmar, would move along the Via Balbia; the second – and most powerful, since it included the 5th Panzer Regiment – would be commanded by General Streich and take the middle route; Rommel himself would command the third battle group, which would move by the long detour through the desert, to join hands with Streich's column at Mechili. The *Ariete* Division following Rommel's column would also converge on Mechili.

All seemed set but, before the operation could get under way, Rommel was suddenly presented with two new problems. The first was precipitated by Streich, who announced that his vehicles were running short of petrol and needed time off the road for maintenance. 'How much time?' asked Rommel. 'Four days,' replied Streich. 'Ridiculous!' Rommel exploded. 'We are not going to let success slip away just because you reckon you're short of petrol and want time off to grease the vehicles. Take petrol from the non-essential trucks; they can catch up later. As for the maintenance: it will have to wait.' Streich's 'Jawohl' settled that particular problem so far as Rommel was concerned. But Rommel was not to forget it; he had never liked the commander of the 5th Light Division and this incident was another nail in the coffin of Streich's career.

The second problem was one which von Brauchitsch had envisaged when Rommel's appointment was made. Gariboldi, on learning of the capture of Agedabia, had taken umbrage. No doubt he felt entitled to some share of the glory. 'In continuing your advance you are contravening the *Comando Supremo*'s orders,' he announced pompously, when he presented himself at Rommel's headquarters on 13 April. The supply situation was 'very risky', he averred; Rommel should have halted at the Tripolitanian border. Anyway Rommel must now call a halt and await orders from Rome. But the commander of the Afrika Korps was not going to be stopped by Gariboldi at this critical juncture and when he flatly refused to comply a long and bitter argument developed, which ended with the Italian giving way. 'In that case,' he said, 'I shall myself command the operation for the recapture of Benghazi.'

In actual fact while this conversation was taking place von Wechmar's troops were already in Benghazi. The British had pulled out without a fight and when Italian troops arrived two days later von Wechmar was already well on his way to Derna.

Fiat G-50 accompanies a Bf 110.

Led by two companies of infantry and another of sappers in carriers and half-tracks the column taking the long desert route to Mechili left Agedabia at first light on 5 April. It was a composite force consisting mainly of motorised infantry, Panzergrenadiers from von Holtzendorff's regiment, a detachment of machine-gunners from Major Ponath's battalion, the reconnaissance company of light tanks from Olbrich's Panzers, and the 5th Light Division's machine gun battalion commanded by Major Knabe – a man who looked like an ageing middle-weight boxer, which is what he was. Total strength amounted to about 1500 men, and although Rommel had said that he would command it personally, he did not actually travel with the group. His Fieseler Storch bearing the registration 'YK' was already a familiar sight to the Afrika Korps, and it was from this plane that Rommel exercised his command, flying above and forward of all three columns – four if one considers the Ariete Division to have been a separate column – dropping messages and, on occasions, landing to discuss the situation and urge on the commander. Command of the Mechili desert column thus devolved on the dashing young Oberst Graf von Schwerin, who had relinquished command of the Wehrmacht's élite formation the Grossdeutschland Regiment, in order to serve with the Afrika Korps.

Von Schwerin's group unquestionably had to negotiate the most difficult terrain. From Agedabia the stony track to Ben Gama and the Green Mountains ran across a flat and empty plain, winding between ridges and for the most part only faintly discernible. The region was completely devoid of vegetation – there was no grass, no trees, no life. As the column moved it raised a cloud of fine dust which fell back and settled on vehicles and men alike. The fact that it was blistering hot – hotter than anything the Afrika Korps had known so far because their activities had been confined mostly to the coastal plain where a cool wind swept in from the sea – added to the discomfort. There was no wind; the sun glared down and the only movement of the dust-laden air was created by the vehicles. As the column rolled on most of the troops dozed and gradually lost all sense of time. Drivers had to be changed every hour or so because of the strain, the monotony, and the mirages which to tired men seemed like distant vistas of shimmering water expanses. The sappers in the advance guard had a particularly onerous time, for they were responsible for maintaining direction, and this meant frequent halts and compass checks at places where the track was no longer visible or diverged.

DAK men examine a captured Matilda.

The centre column, commanded by General Streich, was experiencing the same sort of conditions. Towards noon Olbrich's Panzers passed the deserted collection of mud huts which was the village of Antelat and one *Unterfeldwebel* commented 'There's more gaiety in a graveyard!' During the afternoon the *khamsin* – the hot dust-laden wind that in Egypt and Cyrenaica gets up every day for six months starting in March – added to the problems of the safari. On the coast it did not obliterate landmarks and stop traffic, but in the desert movement was impossible while the *khamsin* raged. When the columns halted the troops sheltered under their vehicles, cradling their heads in their arms to stop the sand blowing into eyes, nostrils, and ears. Throats were parched, water was scarce, and for the men of the Afrika Korps thirst was at this moment a more important factor than the enemy.

Had they but known it the enemy was actually in a more sorry state than the Afrika Korps. Wavell, astounded at the success of Rommel's unexpected onslaught and Neame's inability to cope with it, had ordered O'Connor to return to the desert and take over again from Neame. O'Connor, a good friend of Philip Neame, did not believe that 'changing horses in mid-stream' was a good idea, and Wavell wavered and compromised. Neame would not be sacked, but O'Connor would help him to sort out the current situation. Meanwhile Gambier-Parry would withdraw the 3rd Armoured Brigade – the brigade which had already taken a hammering from Olbrich's tanks. However as Gambier-Parry's headquarters (2nd Armoured Division) had only a tenuous radio contact with the brigade, the order to pull back compounded a first-class muddle, with units not knowing when or where to go and what to do. When the man in charge of the British supply dump at Msus set fire to the petrol stocks on being told that German tanks were heading in his direction, the muddle degenerated into chaos. Not being able to fill up their tanks at Msus many of the 3rd Armoured Brigade's vehicles were stranded.

Rommel on the airstrip at Agedabia knew nothing of this. But a Luftwaffe reconnaissance report was handed to him while von Schwerin's men lay panting under their trucks waiting for the *khamsin* to blow out. The Mechili

area appeared to be clear of enemy, so a message was sent to von Schwerin telling him to push on as fast as possible, and another to Streich ordering him to drive flat out to Mechili.

As soon as the wind had dropped the columns were on the move again and by nightfall that of von Schwerin had reached the foothills of the so-called Green Mountains. There was no question of halting and waiting here for daybreak, before continuing the advance, for Rommel had made it clear that he expected the column to press on despite the hazards involved. But the track, normally used by sure-footed camels, followed knife-edge ridges and crossed near vertical ravines. Moreover to get vehicles across the mountains was a veritable nightmare for the sappers and infantrymen who spent a long hard night widening the track, filling crevasses, building makeshift bridges across the dry wadis and then heaving and hauling the trucks out of places where they had bogged down. Fortunately there was a full moon. But night brought no respite from the heat, for the furnace-like heat of the sun absorbed by the rocks during the day was now being re-radiated. To make matters worse water bottles and the reserve tins of water were nearly all empty. Men worked stripped to the waist, bathed in perspiration, and cursing in hoarse whispers.

With the dawn (6 April) conditions improved a little; the temperature had dropped a few degrees by the time the column topped the last ridge as the sun started to rise. The open plain lay at the bottom of the slope and it was easy going from there on. Not that the sappers and Panzergrenadiers cared much; they were too weary now to worry about what happened, and as von Schwerin mustered his strike force of armoured vehicles they flopped down, exhausted by their efforts.

Within an hour von Schwerin was racing towards Mechili and a squadron of Stuarts which saw him coming promptly turned round and made off. But a motorised brigade of Indian troops – Neame's only reserve force – dug in around Mechili still had to be dealt with, and when Rommel realised what von Schwerin was up against he decided it was too tough a nut for von Schwerin to crack on his own. Flying over in 'YK', he dropped a message advising von Schwerin to await Olbrich's Panzers. The latter were in fact driving to Mechili as fast as their tracks would carry them, urged on by Rommel's promise that: 'If you don't move, I'll come down and move you myself.'

Further north von Wechmar had run into trouble on the coast road north of Benghazi. His route was blocked by tanks deployed to stem the German advance while the British and Australian garrisons holding Barce and Derna were withdrawn. 'Get round them,' Rommel directed. 'They're just playing for time while their troops get away from the coastal towns. I'm going to cut them off at Derna.' Von Wechmar, who had been trying to outflank the British position for the past 18 hours, ordered another attempt, which this time was successful. By 2200 hours he was driving through parties of forlorn Australian and Indian infantrymen trudging towards Derna through the desert east of the Via Balbia. When they saw the Afrika Korps vehicles many of them threw down their rifles and raised their hands in the traditional gesture of surrender. But von Wechmar took no notice. 'We can round them up later,' he told his section commanders when one of them asked what he was supposed to do about the men who already considered themselves to be prisoners of war.

Von Schwerin was not noted for his patience, nor was he one who liked sharing success with others. So although Rommel had advised him to wait for Olbrich, von Schwerin decided to attack the British positions with what he had. By his reckoning it would be at least five hours before the 5th Panzers arrived, and Rommel had repeatedly said that time was of the essence. The Indians defending Mechili outnum-

DAK men advance in Cyrenaica. The machine gun is a Mauser MG-34, one of the best German light arms.

bered von Schwerin's force by about four to one, and they were dug in in a box formation the centre of which was the Mechili oasis. In many ways their deployment resembled the old 'square' formation which a European force would take up when threatened by hordes of natives during the colonial wars of the Victorian age. To deal with it von Schwerin planned to use the same sort of tactics that Red Indians had used when attacking a white encampment, or Zulus assaulting a Boer laager. The German vehicles were formed up out of small arms range, facing one side of the British box, and when the order to advance was given they swept forward in open order firing as they moved. As they neared the defences the advancing front divided and swung round the box to encompass it and then converge once more on the rear of the defences. With the light tanks and armoured cars spitting fire and racing round on the inside, and the trucks carrying the Panzergrenadiers and motorcycles tearing round in a second circle, the manoeuvre may well have seemed more like a Wild West rodeo than an operation of war. But it worked; von Schwerin's armour was probing for a weak spot in the British defensive perimeter, and when it had found the chink the Afrika Korps plunged in to spray death and wreak destruction in the camp which the Indians' defences encircled. The battle started at midday, and it was over by the late afternoon. More than 4000 men were taken prisoner – among them Major-General Gambier-Parry, the commander of the 2nd Armoured Division, Brigadier R G W Rimington, the commander of the 3rd Armoured Brigade and the staffs of their respective headquarters.

Olbrich and his Panzers arrived while von Schwerin was marshalling the prisoners and sorting out the booty – not the least important of which were the Indian Brigade's vehicles. Rommel flew in soon after that, having narrowly escaped capture or death while looking for units which had straggled from Streich's column. Spotting an armoured column moving towards Mechili the pilot of 'YK' was about to land on a flat stretch of desert in the path of the column when Rommel saw that the trucks were British and their occupants were aiming Brens in his general direction. Gunning the engine the pilot climbed away. But it was a near thing. (Coincidentally Wavell had a similar adventure next day. Flying back to Cairo from a conference with O'Connor and Neame, some mechanical defect in one of the engines of his Lockheed Lodestar compelled the pilot to make a forced landing in the desert. Luckily for the British Commander-in-Chief there were no German patrols in the area. Nevertheless Wavell was taking no chances and went off into the desert away from the plane in order to burn papers he was carrying.)

After congratulating von Schwerin on the success of his action Rommel briskly announced that the operations were not finished yet. A new battle group from Mechili was to drive to Derna, 37 miles to the north of Mechili, leaving as soon as possible and driving flat out in an effort to get there before nightfall. As the 5th Light Division's machine gun battalion would be the backbone of the group Major Ponath, its commanding officer was appointed its commander.

The Ponath Group left Mechili with the hour, and at dusk an hour later the armoured cars leading the column reached the Via Balbia. The column turned on to the road and headed west. Its exact position was soon defined by a signpost which said, 'Derna: 3 km.' Nobody tried to stop the column passing on towards Derna and all other traffic on the road was moving in the opposite direction. It was Ponath who ordered a halt at the outskirts of the town, where a convoy of British vehicles which had run out of petrol was blocking the road. Ponath machine-gunners knew exactly what to do; within a flash a detachment manning a road block and another was hustling the astonished British drivers back towards Derna. Led by Ponath the main body doubled off towards the middle of the town on which vehicles bringing men and material falling back in front of von Wechmar were converging.

As the British vehicles pulled in to the town they were directed to a parking area where Ponath's men rounded up and corralled the occupants. In the dark amid the confusion the British trucks kept coming completely unaware of the presence of an Afrika Korps reception committee in Derna.

Next morning luck really seemed to have been on the German side when a patrol which Ponath had sent up the Via Balbia to try and contact von Wechmar's group met a tiny convoy travelling towards Derna. Three heavy lorries bristling with radio aerials were obviously signals trucks – although it turned out they were more than that: headquarters command vehicles in fact. But the occupants of the two staff cars travelling with the trucks were more important. Their occupants were none other than Generals O'Connor and Neame, two of the biggest fish in the Western Desert swim.

Objective Tobruk

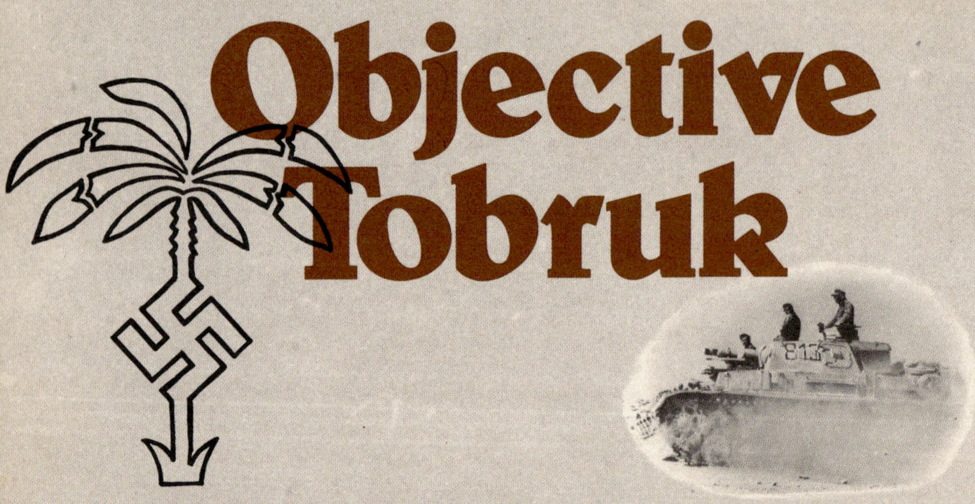

The story of the Afrika Korps in 1941 is really the story of Tobruk. After the capture of Derna Rommel was convinced there was nothing to stop the Afrika Korps reaching the Nile, provided the momentum of the offensive was maintained. In a letter to his wife on 9 April he wrote that the world was about to witness 'another Cannae' and at a staff conference the following day he announced that his objective was the Suez Canal. Von dem Borne, the Chief of Staff, quietly pointed out that there were a few obstacles to be overcome before the Afrika Korps reached the Canal, and Rommel agreed that Tobruk was the first of these. Supply problems were already bedevilling the Korps, for until one or other of the Cyrenaica ports could be put into working order all supplies for the Afrika Korps had to come by way of Tripoli, and Tripoli was now 750 miles behind the front. Benghazi had been a port of sorts and its facilities could be refurbished and brought back into service. But the harbour and facilities at Tobruk were preferable; moreover the Italians were not too keen on Benghazi being used; those who had villas there did not want to attract the further attention of the Royal Air Force.

The more immediate problem, however, was finding troops to maintain the momentum which Rommel believed was vital. At this particular moment the Afrika Korps was scattered over a 3750-square-mile triangle of desert bounded by Mechili, Derna and Benghazi. Floundering around in this wasteland also were large numbers of the enemy – stragglers from the 3rd Armoured Brigade, Indians who had escaped from Mechili and the bulk of Major-General Morshead's 9th Australian Division. The latter was falling back in good order towards Tobruk, but there was not much fire in the bellies of the remainder. Not that there was much fight in the Afrika Korps for that matter. Men were exhausted, and barely one of the tanks which had taken part in the 250 mile run from Tripoli was fit for action. Turret rings and carburretor air filters were clogged with sand, and even if an engine would run it was more than likely that the Panzer's gun could not be aimed properly. The vehicles needed maintenance and the men yearned for rest. Indeed many of them had been looking forward to a sojourn in Derna or Benghazi where there were green trees, pavements, a cool sea breeze and fresh clean water. But they were stuck in the desert, plagued by the *khamsin*; during the night of 9–10 April there was the worst sandstorm in the living memory of Italians who knew Cyrenaica. Meantime there was still plenty of mopping up to be done around Derna, Mechili and a score of other places where some of the more determined parties of enemy were trying to fight their way back to the coast and thence to Tobruk. Most of the action was confined to a fitful splutter of isolated engagements, except along the Via Balbia where the Australian rearguard was effecting a skilful withdrawal. Along this road and around Mechili a fantastic trail of wreckage – tanks, guns, trucks, weapons and the general rubbish of war – marked the path of the British retreat. The desert sand would soon cover it just as it had already half-covered the relics of the Italian retreat.

Two views of the 105mm Leicht Geschutz 42. This was a recoilless gun which could fire 32.6lb projectiles.

Rommel was not concerned with any of this. Just as soon as the storm had subsided he took off in 'YK' to seek his scattered units and having found them, to rally sleepy officers for the next phase of the operation. A few scathing remarks were addressed to Olbrich, whose Panzers were still at Mechili, and to Streich at Derna. The latter, tired and resentful of the remorseless Rommel was prepared to argue. His division had been driven too hard, he said, 'The men have been on the go for the past ten days and there is a limit to human endurance.' Rommel was furious, and if it had been feasible for him to dismiss Streich there and then no doubt he would have done so. In the event within a month both he and Olbrich were on their way to Germany on 'camel back' – the expression used when Afrika Korps officers were posted 'for incompatibility'. (The two officers complained bitterly when they reached Berlin and von Brauchitsch wrote to Rommel. His letter took the form of a mild reprimand, in which he stated that he thought that Rommel could have handled Streich and Olbrich – and others – in a more sympathetic fashion and that in future Rommel needed to temper his attitude. What he needed was more carrot and less stick in his approach to others.) With von Wechmar and units of the Brescia Division committed to rounding up enemy stragglers and clearing isolated pockets of resistance around Derna, the only battle group which Rommel could concentrate immediately consisted of von Schwerin's reconnaissance unit, one composite company of Panzers, and Ponath's Panzergrenadier battalion. (Von Schwerin was keen to go and the company of Panzers had seen no action so far; only the infantrymen were reluctant – they had been reckoning on rest and recuperation.)

To command this force Rommel appointed a newcomer to Africa, Generalmajor von Prittwitz und Gaffron. Von Prittwitz was as forceful and aggressive as Rommel himself and if fate had not decided otherwise it is likely that the two men would have fallen out eventually. Von Prittwitz had flown into Tripoli with his division's advance party on 9 April, and had straightway motored up to Derna. Rommel met him there, told him the objective was Tobruk, that the time factor was all important and that he had been unable so far to scrape up more than the battle group he now proposed to hand over to von Prittwitz. 'As we managed to take this place Derna with less than a battalion,' he added, 'You ought to stand a good chance at Tobruk.' Asked by von Prittwitz about what resistance to expect, Rommel replied, 'Very little for 62 miles – until you reach Tobruk itself which, so far as we know, is defended by an Australian brigade supported by the artillery that was in Benghazi.'

Neither Rommel nor any of his staff knew much about the defensive layout of the town. The Italians had failed to produce even a town plan let alone a diagram showing the fortifications they had constructed, but it was known that they had been digging a big anti-tank ditch when they were kicked out. (Nor

German troops approach Tobruk, April 1941.

was any town plan or layout of the defences forthcoming from the Italians until the Afrika Korps had suffered a costly repulse.) This ditch was on the eastern side of the town; behind it and continuing round the town in a rough semi-circle the Italians had built a series of strongpoints which had been wired in to form a continuous perimeter. In front of the wire the area had been liberally sown with anti-tank and anti-personnel mines.

A study of the maps of the area which the Italians had passed on to the Germans, together with aerial photographs provided by the Luftwaffe revealed little more except of a general nature. The Via Balbia, hugging the

coast ran straight through Tobruk and continued on to Bardia; another secondary road bypassed Tobruk, turning off the great metalled coast-road about 18 miles west of the town to circle south via Acroma, El Adem and El Duda before sweeping north again to rejoin the Via Balbia about 15½ miles south-east of Tobruk. At El Adem there was an airfield, fringed by the wrecks of Italian Capronis and from here another metalled road ran due north to Tobruk. From this von Prittwitz concluded that even if he was unable to capture Tobruk immediately the rest of the Afrika Korps could sweep past and continue their advance to the Suez Canal and the Nile.

The vanguard of the Prittwitz battle group reached the Acroma turn-off on the Via Balbia at about 1000 hours on 10 April, halted and waited for the main force. The sun was blazing down and it was scorchingly hot already. But there was neither sight nor sound of the enemy. A white-washed building with bullet-pocked mud walls which in happier days had been an Italian café was deserted. In the sandy compound behind the building there were four graves – in which were buried the casualties of the fighting three months earlier. Otherwise there was only sand, sea and the road; looking eastwards towards the horizon and Tobruk nothing moved on the Via Balbia.

Von Prittwitz saw no point in waiting any longer when his force had concentrated at the crossroads. Climbing into one of von Schwerin's armoured cars he gave the order to advance and the column of armoured cars and lorries carrying Ponath's Panzergrenadiers rolled up the Via Balbia. On its left flank the squadron of Panzers in arrow-head formation clanked along the strip of desert between the road from the seashore.

For half an hour and 10 miles the journey was uneventful, and Ponath's infantrymen were betting that Tobruk would be undefended. 'With luck,' said one, 'the Australians will have left their stocks of beer behind. So its just as well we're getting a thirst up.' Four shells which straddled the convoy terminated this and similar ruminations. As the vehicles pulled up and the troops leaped out a salvo of shells landed on armoured cars at the head of the column. Three cars, including that of von Prittwitz, which received direct hits exploded in a fire-ball of flame. General von Prittwitz und Gaffron was the 15th Panzer Division's first casualty and the first of the Afrika Korps to be killed in the battle for Tobruk.

It took von Schwerin over an hour to sort out the situation. At the time of von Prittwitz's demise the head of the column was about 8½ miles from the outer defences of Tobruk, and the shelling ruled out any further advance up the road. The enemy's guns were firing at the limit of their range, and if the vehicles attempted to drive on it was to be expected that the bombardment would intensify. So Ponath's men were ordered to debus, get off the road and disperse among the dunes while the trucks drew back out of range.

Meantime, urged on by Rommel, more of the Afrika Korps was moving up to the Acroma cross-roads. Streich's motorcycle battalion commanded by Major Knabe was the first to arrive; Knabe's orders were to take the Acroma road, bypass Tobruk and cut the Via Balbia at the El Duda crossroads. News that von Prittwitz had been killed and that von Schwerin was pinned down on the main road outside Tobruk was radioed to Knabe en route.

Rommel travelling in the black-painted Mk IV Panzer (black, it is said, because in Tripoli there had been no time to paint it khaki) – which was to become known to the Afrika Korps as 'The Black Mammoth', reached the Acroma cross-roads as the tail of Knabe's column disappeared down the bypass. In the next hour he was joined by both Streich and Olbrich – whose Panzers were coming up behind, the irrepressible von Wechmar, and the Italian commanders of the Brescia and Ariete Divisions. A brief conference followed during which Rommel expressed his disappointment with von Prittwitz's failure to get to Tobruk. 'We probably tried to do too much with too little,' he said. 'Anyhow, we are in a better position now.'

The trouble was that Rommel had assumed the problem of Tobruk was no different from the problems the Afrika Korps had faced at Derna and Benghazi. Tobruk's defences had been built by the Italians and they faced eastwards; its outer perimeter was a little longer, and its garrison was fresher perhaps – though lacking in experience. But the same treatment as had been applied at Derna and Benghazi should see the Afrika Korps through the back door into the town. But Rommel was wrong and if he had taken the time to spy out the ground properly and reconnoitre the defences of Tobruk he would have realised that he was wrong. What he did not know was that one of Morshead's brigades had been hard at work for the past month digging and wiring and extending the Italians' anti-tank ditch westwards, and that the ditch now formed a huge crescent-shaped girdle around Tobruk. Behind it the Australians, with the whole of Morshead's divisional artillery – four regiments of 25-pounders and all the anti-tank guns Morshead could lay his hands on – together with 23 tanks of the 3rd Armoured Brigade which had survived, were dug in and waiting. The original Italian strongpoints of Fort Pilastrino, Fort Airenti and Fort Solaro had been strengthened and look-out posts established there from which artillery observers could survey the countryside. Another high observation post, like a ship's crow's-nest had also been set up at the crossroads inside the perimeter where the El Adem road joined the Via Balbia; this became known as 'King's Cross'. The garrison was confident it could cope with the Afrika Korps. 'There'll be no Dunkirk here,' Morshead told them. 'If the Germans break in, we'll chuck 'em out again.'

The Panzerabwehrkanone 3.7cm gun.

Above: DAK men enjoy the cool evening. Below: The Messerschmitt Bf 110, which served as a long-range escort fighter, night fighter and bomber.

Before nightfall Rommel made a quick tour of the perimeter in the 'Black Mammoth', selected a spot on the south-west boundary as the point where the Panzers would break in, and returned to his command post to dictate his orders for an attack next day (12 April). The kernel of his plan was an armoured assault, spearheaded by the 5th Panzer Regiment on the western sector of the perimeter. As soon as Olbrich's tanks had breached the Australians' defences the Brescia Division would pour through the gap, fan out behind the perimeter and roll up the defences from the rear.

Shortly after first light next morning the Panzers deployed in a ravine below the outer barbed wire fence and at a given signal clattered up the slope, crushing a path through the barbed wire as they made for the trenches manned by the Australians. Behind them the Brescia's 'mobile coffins' moved up ready to crash through the gap into town. They did not get far. When the leading Panzers reached a point about half-way up the slope the enemy reacted and the battle began. Twenty-five pounders firing well above the official rapid rate of five rounds a minute opened up and a hail of shells crashed down on Olbrich's tanks. Some were knocked out in the first salvo, and the Panzers' advance degenerated into incoherent manoeuvring as the remainder tried to drive through the curtain of fire. The Italians behind them simply turned round and belted back down the slope out of range.

The battle continued for another two hours before Olbrich decided that his regiment was losing tanks and men to no purpose. The order was then given to disengage, and the Panzers drew back. Stretcher parties moved in to succour the wounded, and recovery units dashed out to drag back the disabled tanks which were accessible. For the first time since dawn the Panzer crews had a little leisure to wipe the grime and sweat from their faces, bathe their bloodshot eyes, moisten their parched throats and rest their deafened ears.

The first attack on Tobruk had failed, but Rommel had not given up. Back at his command post he embarked on a post-mortem of the battle as soon as he saw how the situation was developing. When Olbrich, just back from the battlefield, arrived to join the other senior officers called to the command post, Rommel addressed him angrily. 'We failed today,' he rasped, 'because we forgot one of the elementary principles of war – concentration of effort. Instead of concentrating everything on a single point and bashing a hole through the enemy's line, you let yourself be stopped half-way up the slope, waiting like a sheep for the slaughter. The day after tomorrow it's going to be different! Every man in the Afrika Korps that can be got up here will be used in an all-out assault.'

The time for the start of this 'all-out' assault was fixed at midnight on 14 April. Rommel opted for a night attack in the belief that it would bring incalculable advantages. In his view the men of the Afrika Korps were better trained, better motivated, tougher, and more disciplined than their opponents. What he underestimated was the toughness, independent self-reliance and indomitable determination of the Australians. Nor does he seem to have fully

A Panzer Mk III of the 15th Panzer Division

Weight 20 tons
Armament one 45cal 37mm anti-tank gun and three 7.92mm MG 34 machine guns
Armour 30mm, turret 30mm
Engine one Maybach HL 120 TRM V-12
Speed 11–15 mph (18–40 km/h)
Range 109–160 miles (175–257 km)

appreciated that a night attack in the prevailing conditions using only the information he had at his disposal, would present peculiarly difficult problems in visibility, control, direction-finding and fire-support – especially for his Panzers. The fact remains that Rommel was convinced that he could break through the line of the enemy defences. What he planned now was a conventional setpiece battle preceded by a massive bombardment to soften up the short sector of the Australian perimeter where the assault was to be delivered. Infantry and armour would then attack, a gap would be created, and – as before – the Italians would pour through this gap.

Throughout 13 April the troops on both sides rested, and the battlefield was strangely quiet. During the day Afrika Korps reconnaissance parties went forward to study the ground and familiarise themselves with the routes their units would take the following night. Sappers of the 200th Engineer Battalion would lead the way; their task was to clear passages through the enemy minefield for Olbrich's Panzers. Ponath's Panzergrenadiers advancing to the barbed wire fence marking the outer edge of the enemy defences would cover the sappers – each of the platoons moving independently on a predetermined route, starting from a line north of El Adem where the battalion was now concentrated. Sections of Olbrich's Panzers had been allotted to the Panzergrenadiers and these tanks were to move with their respective platoons. Panzers and Panzergrenadiers together would, everybody hoped, be able to deal with the enemy strongpoints and so clear a way for the remainder of the 5th Panzer Regiment to batter the gap in

the Australian perimeter.

The nearest vantage points which the recce parties could reach without attracting the Australians' attention were about a half-a-mile from the perimeter, and at that distance there was little to be seen. The enemy bunkers had been gouged out of the sides of the steep escarpment which ran parallel to the sea, a mile or so inland from the one-storey stucco buildings of the town. Under the scorching sun the bunkers looked like tiny yellow molehills, which – like the double apron of barbed wire that screened them – merged into the shadowless stony background. There was no movement to indicate the presence of the enemy. Nevertheless the Australians were there and waiting, as the Afrika Korps was to discover that night.

After dark both the Australians and the men of the Afrika Korps showed a common interest, which in the months ahead was to become a ritual. At 2100 hours every night Radio Belgrade opened its programme of news and propaganda with a nostalgic refrain sung by a husky-voiced female.

Vor der Kaserne vor dem grossen Tor,
stand eine Laterne und steht sie noch davor.
Da wollen wir uns wiedersehn, vor der Laterne wolln wir stehn, mit Dir
Lilli Marlene.

'Lili Marlene' was to become the hit tune of the war, as popular with British troops as with the Afrika Korps, and a sort of bond between the men who fought in the desert.

The night was black and moonless when Ponath's Panzergrenadiers took a last swig from their water bottles, stubbed out their cigarettes and climbed into the trucks that were to carry them from their assembly area to where they would launch their assault. At 2355 hours the leading vehicles moved off down the El Adem road, and there was the roar of engines and clatter of tank tracks as the Panzers supporting the infantry followed. In the darkness the noise seemed loud enough to wake the dead. Five minutes later on the stroke of midnight a series of cracks and a gentle hissing overhead signalled the start of the bombardment; seconds later there was a thunderous crash as the first salvoes of shells exploded way ahead over the enemy positions. The battle had begun.

Minutes later the trucks pulled up and the Panzergrenadiers leaped out to form up in their platoons along a line that had been taped by the reconnaissance parties earlier. The sappers were the first away. On hands and knees they crawled forward feeling for mines and taping lanes for the tanks; Ponath's Panzergrenadiers followed behind.

Punctually at 0015 hours the artillery lifted and for a moment or two the battlefield was silent again. In front of the Panzergrenadiers the enemy positions were shrouded in acrid smoke and seemed dead when Ponath gave the order to advance. With shouts of *Heia Safari* the infantrymen bounded forward, the tanks on their heels. It was then that the enemy responded. Machine guns opened up on the infantry, and the Panzers came under

Below left: Panzer Mk III.
Below: An Italian hairdresser on the Via Balbia near Gazala.

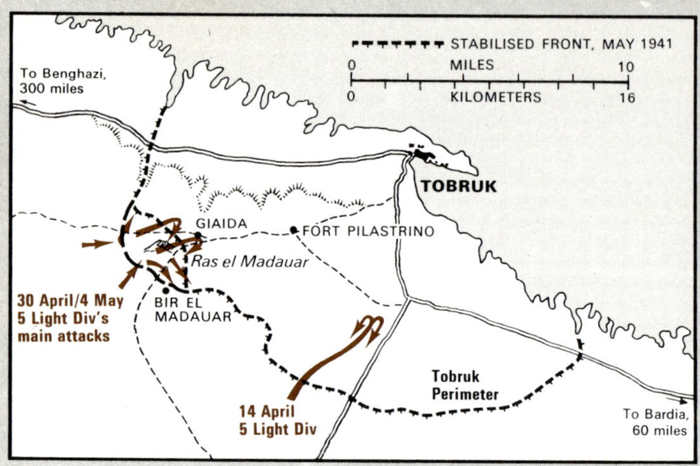

Above: The Tobruk perimeter.

heavy fire from anti-tank guns. Far from having been silenced by the artillery barrage the Australians were very much alive.

The attack proceeded on classical lines with Panzers and Panzergrenadiers supporting each other and although it was hard going some progress was made. By daybreak Ponath's men had penetrated the Australians' forward defences as far as the anti-tank ditch and had set about filling in a narrow section of the ditch. In the event this turned out to be a costly waste of time and effort, for Olbrich's tanks were pinned down on the slopes in front of the wire, 650 yards below the anti-tank ditch, where they were being pounded by all the artillery in Tobruk. The disaster of 12 April was repeating itself, and Rommel – realising the Panzers were in trouble – tried to throw in the Ariete Division. That was useless too because the Italians refused to move. (The Ariete would not be able to go into action for about ten hours, they said.)

Meantime the Australians had rus[hed] up reinforcements to straighten out [the] dent in their line by eliminating Po[nath] and the only four Mk III Panzers w[hich] had got as far as the anti-tank d[itch]. Anti-tank guns were rushed up fro[m] the nearby sectors and deployed [in a] corridor on either side of the salien[t] Panzergrenadiers had created. The [re]sult was that the Germans found the[m]selves caught in a blistering cross-fir[e].

The earlier model Panzerka[...] Ausf B, which was in fact a[...] light training tank, and wa[...] of service in 1942.

and by the middle of the afternoon – after 15 hours of continual fighting – more than half of the 400 Panzergrenadiers who had gone into the battle were either dead or seriously wounded. Ponath himself had been hit, but he had carried on, formed a defensive box around the four Panzers – which were now short of ammunition, and concentrated his casualties in the centre of the box.

About 1700 hours however the situation changed dramatically, when two squadrons of Stuart tanks arrived on the scene. Emerging from the town they drove straight through Ponath's position, halted under cover and proceeded systematically to shoot up Olbrich's Panzers. The Mk III Panzers and the Stuarts were both equipped with 37mm guns, and the Stuarts were lighter and less heavily armoured. But the armour-piercing ammunition fired from the Stuarts' cannons was devastatingly effective. Seventeen of the Panzers were hit, caught fire and blew up, and Olbrich ordered the remainder of the 5th Panzer Regiment to withdraw.

Ponath's men were now on their own, virtually surrounded and in desperate straits. They had three alternatives: to hold on where they were – fighting to the last man and the last round if

Messerschmitt Bf 109 Emil, the Luftwaffe's principal fighter.

necessary – in the hope that Olbrich's Panzers or the Italians would break through to them; to fight their way out and get back to the German lines; or to surrender. Ponath ruled out the last and for the time being the chances of fighting a way through the steadily contracting cordon seemed frail. So, as the only other option was to fight on, he decided to move to a position which could be more easily defended. As soon as darkness permitted a little movement, the dead were collected and buried, and the surviving combatants then withdrew from the anti-tank ditch to a rising ground nearby. The wounded were left behind in the ditch, to be collected and cared for by the Australians; Ponath knew they had little hope of remaining alive if he continued to hold out in his present laager. 'See you in Tobruk,' were the last words he said to them.

Despite repeated attempts to annihilate them the Panzergrenadiers stubbornly continued to hold out. During the first four days they even staged a couple of kamikaze-type raids to find food, weapons and above all, water. Tired, hungry and consumed by a raging thirst, they had crouched in their trenches sucking pebbles to assuage their thirst during the day. Nightfall, when the temperature dropped, brought relief from the sun. But it was then that Australian patrols were active. By 19 April when their water bottles had been empty for more than 12 hours the Panzergrenadiers were almost all in. That afternoon the Australians called on the Germans to surrender: 'Then you'll get water and food,' they said.

Ponath did not even reply. He was still hoping that relief would come and on 16 April it had almost seemed as if his mens' ordeal was nearly over. From their position the Panzergrenadiers watched the Brescia Division move in to attack. But their hopes were short-lived; the Italians faltered when the enemy artillery opened up and when British tanks appeared the Italian armour turned tail and made off. Abandoned by the tanks that were supposed to be supporting them the Italian infantry promptly threw down their weapons and ran towards the enemy lines with their hands in the air. Rommel in an observation post near El Adem saw all this happening, and a company of Panzers was sent to head off the would-be prisoners of war. The Italians won the race and got their wish. The nearer the Germans got, the faster the Italians ran and when the Panzers came under anti-tank fire they had to give up the chase.

On 20 April, after six days of fighting, Ponath's men were still holding out on the sandy mount; the Australians had failed to dislodge them, but the Panzergrenadiers all knew that the end could not be far away. None of them had more than five rounds apiece for their rifles; their three remaining machine guns were down to one belt, and their grenades had all been thrown. In an attack they would last no more than five minutes.

The expected attack came that night, and although the defenders fought on with their bayonets when their ammunition was exhausted the outcome was a foregone conclusion. Ponath refused to surrender when the Australians shouted for him to give up, and he was shot dead. By daybreak it was all over; only 20 men, under command of Unteroffizier Gleichmann, lived to tell the tale – 20 men out of 400, and they survived because they managed to slip away in the darkness and confusion and get back to the German lines.

On 21 April Oberst Max von Herff, commanding the 115th Panzergrenadier Regiment, reported to Rommel at El Adem. Von Herff's regiment was the first of the combat groups of the 15th Panzer Division to take the field, and von Herff himself was keen to make his mark in Africa. Like von Schwerin and von Prittwitz, his erstwhile commander, he was intelligent, ambitious, and a man of action. Within a matter of weeks he had amassed the wealth of experience that made him a superb desert leader. The rest of the world has heard little of him, but in the Afrika Korps, von Herff was almost worshipped.

The greater part of the 115th Panzergrenadier Regiment was sent on to Bardia and von Herff was appointed overall commander of the force operating there. Meantime the problem of Tobruk remained unsolved. The fact that it had not fallen had not prevented Rommel from thrusting ahead to Bardia, but it did effectively preclude the Afrika Korps marching on into Egypt afterwards. Tobruk was, according to Rommel, 'an ulcer in the side'. In two attacks – which admittedly had been quickly planned and quickly staged – the Australians had shown that the new 'mobile' warfare so well suited to the desert did not necessarily mean that the old-type positional warfare of World War I was completely dead. Yet the Afrika Korps was neither organised nor equipped for positional warfare. Moreover there was little hope of more men and more material being diverted to the

North African theatre. Hitler and the German High Command had expressed their satisfaction and congratulated Rommel on the conduct and success of his campaign in Cyrenaica. At the same time he was given to understand that he could not expect any more troops – German or Italian.

So far as the Afrika Korps, from Rommel down to the most humble *landser*, was concerned Italian troops were useless anyway; the recent fighting had highlighted this fact. But in positional warfare numbers are important and Rommel felt that he could not conduct a campaign in North Africa without his allies. For their part the Italians regarded the Germans as equally unsatisfactory partners and Rommel's relations with Gariboldi and General Roalta, Gariboldi's Chief of Staff, were distinctly strained. Apart from Rommel's high-handed way of running the war, the two Italian generals considered that their allies were prepared to sacrifice Italians needlessly. But an appearance of Axis solidarity had been maintained and on 23 April Rommel at a meeting with Gariboldi and Roalta: 'I was ceremonially awarded the Italian Medal for Bravery.' 'I am also supposed to be getting the Italian *Pour Le Mérite*,' he wrote to his wife. 'What a trivial business it all is at a time like this.'

Meantime the siege of Tobruk continued, and the pressure on the perimeter was stepped up. Battalions of the 115th Panzergrenadier Regiment were moved into the line to relieve units of the 5th Light Division and these newcomers to the Afrika Korps found the going tough. They had come to the Western Desert and the furnace of Tobruk where the thermometer read 35° C straight from Pomerania where

An eight-wheeled armoured car.

the temperature hovered around zero. Only a few of them had been in action before this, and their Australian opponents were magnificent soldiers who never missed an opportunity to strike at the Germans and Italians who were besieging their fortress. During the day they were rarely seen, but any movement on the German side invariably attracted a salvo of high explosive shells. From dawn to dusk the men of the Afrika Korps crouched in their trenches, waiting through the torrid day for evening to relieve them. As one said cynically, 'You look at your watch at ten o'clock and look again four hours later and it's ten fifteen.' Sandstorms, salty water and boredom were their most potent enemy in such conditions. Only at night did the front come alive. Water and rations were brought up, and it was then also that the Australians would emerge from their trenches – to harry and raid. This was the sort of activity to which the Australians were well suited and on occasions their patrols slipped through the cordon of German or Italian sentries around the perimeter to strike at units who, because they were far from the front, imagined themselves to be safe.

With the disembarkation in Tripoli of the rest of the 15th Panzer Division

A makeshift grave in the desert.

Rommel was determined to bring this state of affairs to a speedy end, and another attack was planned for 30 April. But now he encountered resistance from Berlin. Von Brauchitsch's Chief of Staff, Generaloberst Franz Halder was no friend of Rommel. Intelligent, precise and pedantic, he was an able staff officer but no fighting soldier, and he certainly had no notion of what command in the Western Desert involved. His prejudice is apparent from his diary in which he commented, 'Reports from officers coming from this theatre – one suspects that Streich and Olbrich were two of the officers concerned – as well as a personal letter show that Rommel is in no way equal to his task. He rushes about the whole day between the widely scattered units, stages reconnaissance raids and fritters away his forces. . . . By overstepping orders Rommel has brought about a situation for which our present supply capabilities are insufficient. . . . I am sending Paulus [to Libya] perhaps the only man with enough influence to head off this soldier gone mad.'

Generalleutnant Friedrich Paulus, the man selected to curb Rommel's ardour, was a tall, stern, precise puritan with an icy manner. He was the senior general staff officer in Berlin concerned with operations, a contemporary of Rommel and like him a product of the German middle class. In nearly every other respect however, the two men were the opposite of each other, and it was an odd coincidence that the one who was sent to Africa to bring Rommel to heel was in due course to surrender Stalingrad.

Rommel was waiting at the airfield when Paulus landed in Tripoli on 27 April, and he greeted his visitor cordially. He knew that the representative of the German High Command had the power to clip his wings and to cancel the attack scheduled to take place in three day's time. His reaction had been to step up preparations for the attack and to set the scene for his visitor. Paulus went from unit to unit in the Tobruk area and talked to the commanders. Then, at the end of two days he told Rommel that he thought another attack on Tobruk was almost certain to fail and that it would be best if the Afrika Korps withdrew to Gazala and took up a defensive position there. In the argument which developed Rommel pitted his not inconsiderable persuasive capacity against Paulus and the latter, seemingly convinced, ultimately agreed that the operation should go on.

This time the attack on Tobruk was to be made from the south-west with the main thrust at a point on the enemy perimeter where it was overlooked by a hill called Ras el Madauar. The hill would be the first objective. Once it was captured it would serve as an observation post for the 15th Panzer Divisional artillery. Some of the dual-purpose 88mm guns – if they could be manhandled up the slopes – would also have an ideal field of fire. Because Ras el Madauar was crucial to the rest of the plan Rommel proposed that a direct assault on it would be backed up by subsidiary attacks on either side. These attacks would converge and 'pinch out' Ras el Madauar. Combined with a hitherto unprecedented concentration of artillery and air raids to soften up the defences the weight of the three attacks should ensure the success of the all-important first phase of the attack. Thereafter the plan followed the pattern of the two previous attacks – an armoured break-in, followed by a roll-up of the defences from the rear.

Starting on 27 April layers of Luftwaffe Stukas and high-level bombers flew over Tobruk. Day and night the little white town rocked under the impact of explosions. (The planes had only about 15 miles to fly, and the Australians on the perimeter could actually hear the bombers warming up their engines at El Adem before they took off to bomb Tobruk.) Heavy artillery contributed to the racket. Siege-guns – long barrelled 15cm French guns – had been brought up to supplement the Afrika Korps' field artillery and the defences were pounded with shells and bombs. The defenders' response was negligible; they had no artillery capable of silencing the German heavy guns, and only a few anti-aircraft batteries to fight off the cascade of planes.

All according to plan the bombing and shelling reached its climax during the afternoon of 30 April, and at 1830 hours the attack went in. Panzergrenadiers in the centre charged forward, breached the forward defences and by 2000 hours they were on their objective, Ras el Madauar. The pincer movement was equally successful and while the leading assault troops consolidated their position on the hill more Panzergrenadiers moved in to mop up the triangle of ground that had been overrun. At first light next morning the Afrika Korps was still holding Ras el Madauar, enemy resistance had prac-

tically ceased on a 1½-mile front, and the Afrika Korps was within three miles of Tobruk town.

But the battle was not over yet. Phase two of the operation was scheduled as a break-in by the Ariete Division, and Rommel had ordered the division to move up as soon as the success signal marking the capture of Ras el Madauar went up. When dawn broke however the Ariete were seen to be stationary in front of the enemy perimeter. Petrified or paralysed, they remained there and Rommel noted in his diary, 'With British artillery sweeping the whole area, the Italians crept under their vehicles and resisted all their officers' attempts to get them out again.'

Fighting continued throughout the day, 1 May, but it did not bring any notable gains. From the observation post at Kings Cross the enemy gunners directed a murderous fire on parties and vehicles of the Afrika Korps which attempted to penetrate beyond the salient based on Ras el Madauar. Meantime Paulus had decided that he would not let the fighting go on. 'You must bear in mind,' he told Rommel, 'that there are other matters, greater matters than events in North Africa.' At that moment German divisions were moving into position for the invasion of Soviet Russia and it was this to which he was referring. North Africa was a sideshow, he stressed, and in consequence Rommel could expect only crumbs. Rommel should maintain his position, build up stocks of ammunition, petrol and supplies as best he could. But there must be no more attacks towards Egypt. Reporting to the German High Command Paulus reiterated what he had told Rommel and concluded that as it was difficult to get supplies across the Mediterranean, there was no point in reinforcing the Afrika Korps.

Meantime Tobruk, on the extreme right flank of a German front that extended from its own sun-parched patch of desert to somewhere on the Arctic Ocean, continued to be a problem for the Afrika Korps. More than 400 days were to elapse before they were done with it.

Below: A Panzer Mk IV.
Below right: Panzer Mk III passes a burning supply truck.

'Hellfire' Pass

For over a year the enclave of Tobruk was to be the thorn in Rommel's flesh, the sore in his side. As the year progressed, he became increasingly determined to root it out. But he was not a man to allow an obsession to mask opportunities and problems elsewhere. When the Australian 9th Division stopped inside the perimeter defences of Tobruk, Oberst von Herff's f[illegible] had pushed eastwards from Bardia, [illegible] the British in front of it as fa[illegible] Egyptian frontier. There they [illegible] dug in and von Herff, outrunning his supplies, had been unable to press on further. Consequently at the beginning of May the German 'front' extended south from the coast near Sollum, along the mighty escarpment which swings inland and continues across the desert as far as the white-domed tomb of the venerated Sidi Omar, about 21 miles to the south-east. It was terrain which had obvious defensive value from [illegible]ever side one viewed it.

Wavell, under pressu[illegible], thought he saw in the [illegible] month 'a fleeting opport[illegible] ing the enemy forward troops on the Egyptian border near Sollum in favourable circumstances.' In fact the circumstances could not have been less favourable. Rommel had his problems – the Afrika Korps was scattered and disorganised, its men were tired, the 15th Panzer Division needed training, the latest arrivals were not yet acclimatised, and a host of other difficulties occasioned by the swift advance still had to be sorted out. But such problems were more than matched by the ones on the other side of the hill. Wavell's resources were limited and stretched to the limit: the battle for Crete was in full swing, Raschid Ali was fomenting trouble in Iraq, first-class fighting troops were tied up in Tobruk and East Africa, the strength of the Royal Air Force was at an all-time low, there were German bombers in Syria and the Royal Navy was having a rough time in the Mediterranean. Nevertheless Wavell decided to try for a sudden bold coup in the desert.

It was an unhappy venture from the start. It came as no surprise to the Germans; they had monitored the British radio nets and were warned that Operation Brevity was about to begin. An armoured force under Brigadier William 'Strafer' Gott – von Herff's opposite

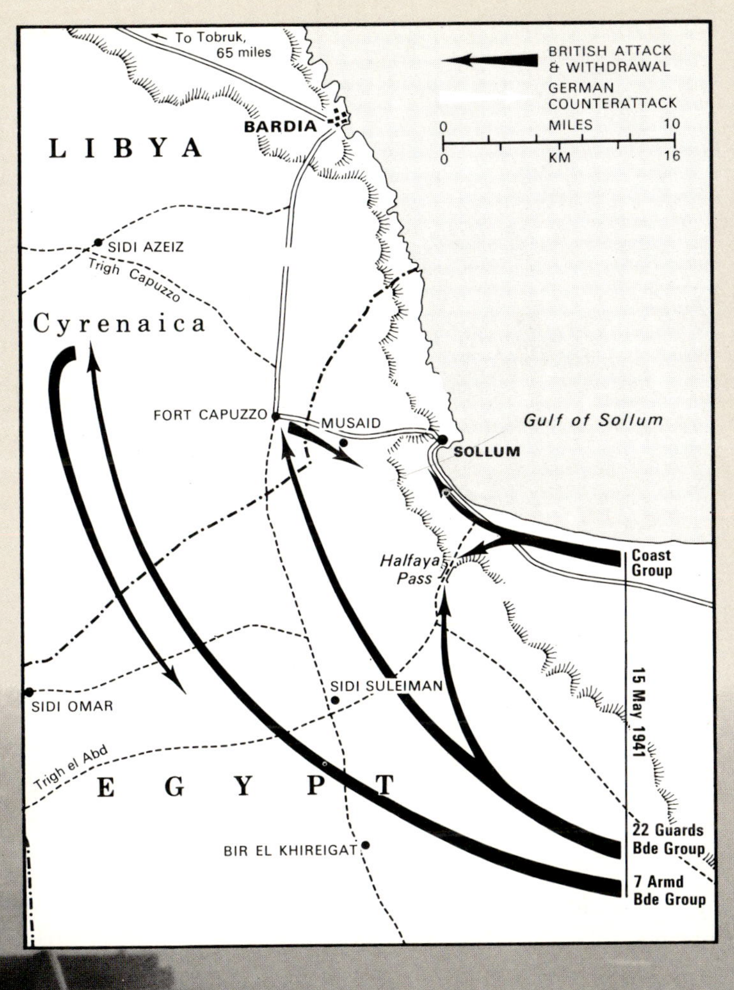

Top: A Panzer Mk III.
Above: Reinforcements on their way to Halfaya.
Left: Halfaya Pass.
Below: DAK gunners fire their 88mm anti-aircraft gun despite the sun in their eyes.

number – quickly captured Sollum, Fort Capuzzo and the Halfaya pass, but the Afrika Korps recovered Sollum and Capuzzo within 48 hours. 'We were,' according to Rommel on 18 May, 'except for Halfaya Pass, back where we started.' Operation Brevity had fizzled out, leaving the British holding the Pass through which wound the old Egyptian road to Bardia and Tobruk. Halfaya Pass, the scene of much heavy fighting in the days to come was the key to the door between Egypt and Cyrenaica. It was also a singularly unattractive place, with no house, no shelter, no water. 'Hellfire' Pass, as it came to be known, was in fact no more than a gap in the chain of hills between Sollum and Sidi Omar, but the only place where tanks could climb the 60yd or so escarpment. Strategically and tactically it was 'vital' ground in critically important terrain, and in 27 May von Herff's Panzers pushed the British off it. The Afrika Korps was back on form and according to Rommel the Coldstream Guards and the tanks that were with them fled, 'in panic to the east, leaving considerable booty and material of all kinds in our hands'. Rommel was exaggerating, though there is no question of the outcome of the battle being anything other than a German victory. Although British losses amounted to only 173 men, five tanks, four 25-pounder and eight 2-pounder anti-tank guns; the psychological effects of the defeat were far more important.

But the British had not given up and Operation Battleaxe which was launched 18 days later was an even more dismal failure than Brevity. The Afrika Korps, alerted again by radio intercepts, was ready. At Halfaya 12 88mm guns had been dug in on the hillside, with their barrels 'horizontal' as Rommel put it, to cover the approaches to the pass. Solid steel shells weighing 22lb – fired from these guns were to go through the armour of the British tanks like hot knives through butter. To back up the 88s the Afrika Korps had co-opted some Italian gunners under Major Pardi and hauled up a few 37mm Italian anti-tank guns recovered from the desert where they had been abandoned during the fighting seven months before. 'Parson' Bach had personally sited every gun position and his positions on Halfaya were virtually impregnable.

Above: The 3.7cm PAK was the standard German anti-tank gun at the outbreak of the war but by 1940 it was out of date.

Meantime, prodded on by Churchill, Wavell had rushed a large consignment of new tanks up to the desert straight from the quayside at Suez. Their recipients, the British 7th Armoured Division, had seen no action as a division since the campaign against Graziani, and the division's fighting capacity had suffered because its regiments had had neither the tanks nor the wireless sets with which to train. Furthermore some of the new tanks were of a pattern that had never before been seen in the Middle East; many of them needed to be overhauled; and all had to be fitted with sand filters and camouflage painted.

The operation had two main aims: to relieve Tobruk and to smash Rommel's Panzer forces. Moreover despite the logistical and technical problems associated with the new tanks and the fact that 'the crews were as strange to each other as their machines', Wavell was relying on the 7th Armoured Division for the achievement of both. The plan was for a

brigade of the 4th Indian Division to advance along the coast towards Sollum, between the sea and the escarpment, while the remainder of the division advanced towards Fort Capuzzo using the road through Halfaya as the axis of their advance. Meantime the 7th Armoured Division was to drive south around Sidi Omar, and then turn north to sweep in behind the Afrika Korps. It was hoped that this encircling move around the flank would lead to a clash with the Panzers, when everything would then depend on the new tanks.

Shortly after first light on 15 June the 4th Indian Division deployed in the plain before Halfaya and began to move up towards the Pass. Minefields at the foot of the Pass slowed the progress, however, and 24 hours later the Indians were still floundering around below Bach's outer defences. Further north however tanks of the 7th Armoured Division had stormed their way on to the escarpment above Sollum to capture Fort Capuzzo. Here they had been engaged by Panzers of the 8th Panzer Regiment and a stupendous battle had developed in the dust and heat. (It was 56° C in the shade, when there was any shade.) From midday until the sun went down the 8th Panzer's powerful black-grey Mk IIIs and Mk IVs, interlocked with British Crusaders and the heavily armoured Matildas careered back and forth across the top of the escarpment. (The Matildas were classed as 'I' tanks – infantry tanks. Although after this battle Rommel remarked it would be interesting to know why the Matilda was called an infantry tank when it was incapable of firing high explosives against his infantry.) Further south near Sidi Omar Matildas engaged Afrika Korps field artillery, and the German gunners – firing with the sun in their eyes – were unable to stop the tanks before the British tracks crunched over the trenches and emplacements. The British then edged forward towards Bardia.

They did not get far, for the Afrika Korps regained the initiative when the 5th Light Division moved down towards Sidi Omar to try to outflank the enemy. At Halfaya, Bach's 88s destroyed 11 Matildas as they tried to grope their way up through the minefield and four others were knocked out by mines. Much of the credit for the success of the anti-tank guns must go to the indefatigable Bach who dashed from one gun position to another throughout the action, smoking a cigar and seemingly oblivious to the shells exploding around him. The Knights' Cross he was awarded subsequently was richly deserved.

The British were suffering heavy losses, and by the end of the first day the 7th Armoured Division had been reduced to 48 tanks. Next day they tried to slog on, but they were gradually forced back off the escarpment. Threatened with encirclement by the 5th Panzer Regiment the British armour fighting around Capuzzo could retreat only in one direction – through the Halfaya Pass. But Bach's men had grimly withstood repeated assaults by the 4th Indian Division and although the British artillery pounded the German positions all that night the Afrika Korps was still firmly in control when dawn broke. Several shells had landed on the gun positions, causing a number of casualties. These were taken to a first-aid post set up in a dug-out which had served for a few days as a canteen and was decorated by some artistic wag,

A pilot of an Henschel Hs 123A prepares for a sortie. The Hs 123A was a ground-attack aircraft and was used against specific targets.

who had painted two alternative 'homecomings' of the Afrika Korps warrior: a soldier riding high on a camel loaded with gifts from the Orient, the other of a skeleton.

At first light on the third day the Indians redoubled their efforts to come to grips with the men on Halfaya, and they launched the first of a series of attacks. Many of them had trained and fought on India's north-west frontier and they advanced with skilful determination, working their way up the hillsides behind the rocks and across dead ground. But few of them had previously encountered that diabolical of all weapons, the mine. The Afrika Korps had cunningly laid minefield killing grounds into which the Indians were driven when men of the 104th Infantry Regiment counter-attacked. By nightfall on the second day the Indians were back at their start-line, having suffered appalling casualties.

Elsewhere the British had suffered more casualties from miscalculation and mistakes. One regiment of tanks had been left for ten minutes exposed to fire from Bach's guns while the commander hesitated about what to do next. When the leading troops of the 5th Light Division reached Halfaya during the morning of 17 June Battleaxe was as good as over. The British were pulling out, leaving the greater part of their tanks and many wounded behind them. In the last analysis they had been outfought.

'Dearest Lu,' wrote Rommel to his wife, 'the three-day battle has ended in complete victory. I'm going to go round the troops today to thank them . . . the joy of the "Afrika" troops over this latest victory is tremendous. . . .' He had good reason to feel pleased. Ninety-one of the 200 Crusaders and Matildas which had driven around Sidi Omar and climbed the escarpment had been knocked out or abandoned, at a cost to the Afrika Korps of only 12 Panzers. Nine hundred miles or so away in London the operation could be seen only as a major disaster, and Wavell's dismissal as Commander-in-Chief of the British Middle East followed on the heels of Churchill's receipt of the news on 18 June.

For the British it was indeed a moment of appalling seriousness; Egypt lay wide open, and there was nothing to stop the Afrika Korps. In the end what saved them was Tobruk, for Rommel remained extraordinarily sensitive about a threat to his flank. Tobruk was a millstone round his neck, and he could not bring himself to drive ahead into Egypt while Tobruk remained in British hands behind him.

June slipped into July without any further major operations being attempted on either side. A night-raid by British frogmen on Bardia never had any hope of success, for Rommel lived hard like his men, slept in the armoured caravan which was his tactical headquarters, and visited the town infrequently. Apart from this dramatic, but unsuccessful venture, operations on both sides settled into a routine pattern. The Egyptian frontier – symbolised for much of its length in the desert by a simple barbed-wire fence – constituted the front at this time, and it was watched by British and Afrika Korps patrols from respectable distances on either side. For the most part these patrols preferred to maintain a non-offensive, but cautious attitude towards each other. Only on a few occasions did they clash, for the desert bred an understanding that transcended human enmity. There were after all other enemies which British and Germans alike had to learn to live with – the broiling sun, the flies, the fleas, the scorpions, dysentery, sand fly fever and a score or more other ailments and pests. There was even some fraternising, though none of the football games associated with the chimera of clean and gentlemanly warfare in the Western Desert. More often than not the fraternisation evolved from the efforts of an Afrika Korps man wishing to test his knowledge of English (rarely the other way about).

One sequence of chats across the fence developed from a contact established when the commander of an armoured car from the 5th Light Division's Reconnaissance Battalion spotted a British armoured car in the dunes on the far side of the fence. Donning his head-set and tuning his radio transmitter to the frequency used by the British the Afrika Korps man spoke into the microphone: 'How are you over there?' Back over the ether came the reply: 'Not too bad. What about you?' The contact was renewed at about the same time and the same place over the course of the following week, and the conversation lengthened with both sides studiously avoiding any questions that might be construed as attempts to pump for information. Eventually the British operator asked what sort of cigarettes the Germans were smoking. 'Ration issue,' came the reply. 'We call them R6 and they're not bad. Would you like to try some?' An exchange for some British cigarettes and arrangements were worked out for the swop. Caution was still the watchword and while the German vehicle moved up to the place where the exchange would be effected the British armoured car pulled back a quarter of a mile. A packet of 'R6' was deposited and the Germans pulled back while the process was repeated by the British who substituted a packet of their own brand. Both crews were satisfied, and the arrangement might have continued indefinitely while the friendship blossomed if it had not been for a young Wehrmacht officer fresh from the Officers' Training School. Full of the Potsdam textbook ideas, he was given command of the troop of armoured cars which included the Afrika Korps fraternisers. Spotting the British armoured car awaiting the next chat session on his first patrol he asked sharply, 'What's that over there?' *'Englander, Herr Leutnant.'* The Herr Leutnant's immediate reaction was a string of orders which led to a 3.7cm shell whistling towards the British vehicle. As the latter sped away a surprised English voice was heard over the radio to query, 'What the hell is going on?' No reply was possible at the time, but two days later the original commander of the German armoured car was able to tell his opposite number that the incident had been caused by a new and over-zealous young officer. 'Not to worry,' came the response. 'We've got 'em like that too.' 'We're taming him,' said the German.

Back in Germany the propaganda fed

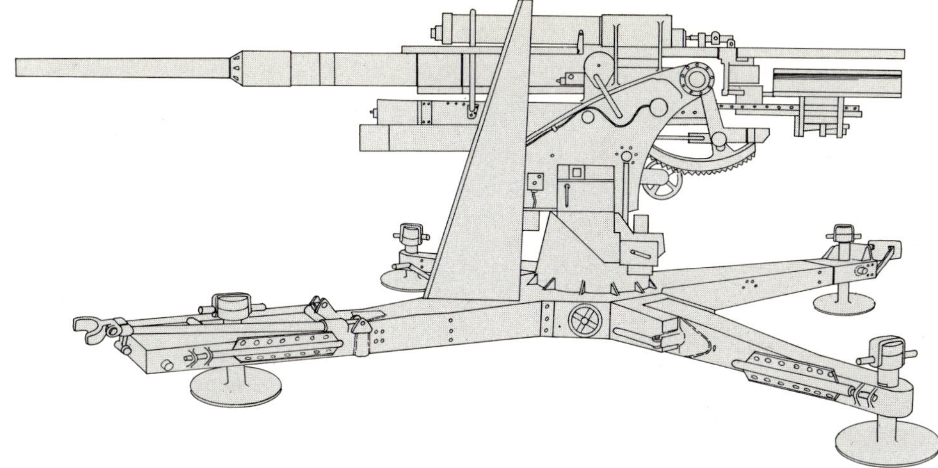

The adaptable 88mm anti-aircraft gun, with a range of 12,000 yards, was used as an anti-tank gun and inflicted heavy losses on British tanks in Brevity.

to the public depicted a carefree holiday existence in a Mediterranean setting. One picture in the *Berliner Illustrierte* showed sun-burned soldiers of the Afrika Korps strolling through orange groves and drinking Löwenbräu. Another which suggested that although the burning sun might possibly create some difficulties its heat could be put to practical purposes, and there was a photograph of soldiers frying eggs on the track-guard of a Panzer. (Needless to say the picture was faked. The cameraman put a petrol cooker on the tank's track underneath the metal guard.) Idealistic representation of this sort was far from the truth, and in Tripoli and Berlin there was considerable concern over the size of the Afrika Korps' sick list. There were approximately 50,000 Germans in Africa about this time, and some ten per cent of them were chronically ill. The Afrika Korps' medical facilities had been organised to cope with battle casualties; ravages by dysentery and infectious jaundice – the two most prevalent diseases – had not been expected, and consequently not catered for. In July a couple of high-ranking specialists were sent out to conduct an on the spot investigation. One of them promptly contracted dysentery, although he managed to cure himself. Their strongly-worded report drew an unfavourable comparison between the medical care enjoyed by the Luftwaffe and the lack of it in the Wehrmacht's field hospitals in Africa. No more field hospitals were forthcoming but the ration scale of the Afrika Korps was upgraded, and when the men in Cyrenaica got more eggs, butter and milk the size of the sick list diminished.

Throughout the summer of 1941 both sides were endeavouring to build up their strengths and prepare for another offensive. In this race the Afrika Korps was at a disadvantage, for while Hitler's eyes were focussed on Russia, Rommel's problems persisted. After Paulus's trip to Cyrenaica Halder, the OKW Chief of Staff in Berlin, was even more determined to curb Rommel's activities. When Russia was defeated Halder's staff opined, there might have to be an offensive in the Middle East. But the main drive would probably be directed through Turkey and the Caucasus, and the role of the Afrika Korps would be to support this. For the time being its activities should be restricted to the capture of Tobruk. Moreover should the attack fail, Rommel must pull back to Gazala.

To make sure that Rommel toed the line Halder decided to reorganise the command structure and to standardise the composition of the Afrika Korps. On the face of it, Rommel was gaining both prestige and power; in fact Halder's intention was to deprive him of direct command of the Afrika Korps. Henceforth the Afrika Korps and the Italian XXI Corps would constitute a new formation known as the 'Armoured Group Afrika'. Rommel would command the group; under him General-Leutnant Ludwig Crüwell (who had been sent to Africa as General von Prittwitz's replacement) would command the Afrika Korps, and General Navarrini the Italian Corps. Within the Korps the two existing divisions, the 5th Light and 15th Panzer, would be organised on a special establishment. The 15th Panzer was allowed to retain its title, but the 5th Light Division was renamed the 21st Panzer. A Special Service Africa Division (*Division Afrika zur besonderen Verfügung*, or *Div.z.b.V*) was also formed by combining a number of independent Wehrmacht units already in Africa and 'milking' the two Panzer divisions. This division, soon to be known as the 90th Light, had seven infantry battalions and supporting artillery, but no tanks. Under Generalmajor Richard Veith to begin with and subsequently under Generalmajor Ulrich Kleemann, it was quickly to estab-

Below: Operation Battleaxe was aimed at gaining control of the Halfaya Pass.

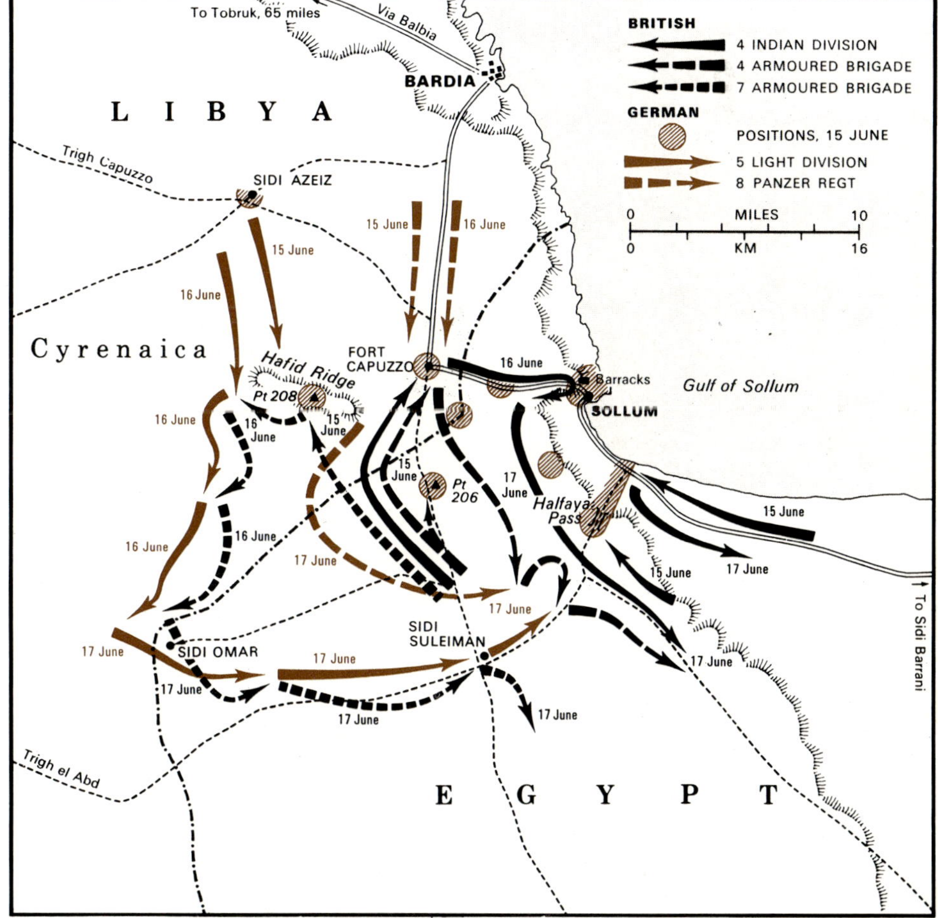

lish a reputation as a crack fighting unit. One of its regiments was the famous 361st Afrika Regiment. Composed of former French Foreign Legionnaires whose average age was much higher than that of the rest of the Afrika Korps, the reputation acquired by the Afrika Regiment reflected the independent devil-may-care attitude for which the pre-war Legionnaire was noted. When, soon after the regiment was formed the 'Afrika' men were issued with Italian-style tropical helmets and entrenching tools they ditched the lot and raided a Bersaglieri barracks to seize the spades and picks which Beau Geste experience had taught them was what they would need in the desert.

On a higher level, to coordinate the reorganisation and subsequently to observe and report on Rommel's activities Generalleutnant Alfred Gause, a former engineer, arrived from Berlin with a large staff. He had been told not to take orders from Rommel, but Rommel was not prepared to accept this arrangement and Gause became his Chief of Staff, answerable to him and not to Berlin.

Meanwhile on the Italian side General Gariboldi was replaced by General Bastico, a pretentious character who Rommel promptly nicknamed 'Bombastico'. Apart from Navarrini's XXI Corps in the Armoured Group Afrika, there was also the Italian XX Corps, containing the Ariete armoured and the Trieste motorised Divisions. After his experiences with the Ariete at Tobruk Rommel had little time for either of these divisions and to him the Afrika Korps was the teeth of the Axis army in Africa. But in order to refresh and train the German units for another attempt to take Tobruk Rommel was compelled to employ the Italians. So the Savona Division from Navarrini's corps was deployed along the Egyptian frontier, with companies of German infantry positioned at intervals among them as the bones of the defence. Between Sidi Omar and Sollum a formidable barrier of mines grew up and more minefields were laid around Tobruk to contain the garrison. The Achsenstrasse, a 40-mile bypass road around the town, was built so that the Afrika Korps could get through to Tobruk. Throughout this period, between July and October, the Luftwaffe continued to pound Tobruk's harbour.

Units of the Afrika Korps were rotated in the line, and those which could be pulled back to the coast between Tobruk and the front were put through a rigorous training course. The training was based on close cooperation between Panzers and anti-tank artillery in the assault. Battle-drills were evolved in which anti-tank guns were brought up to where the Panzers were threatened, and then emplaced and camouflaged in a defensive line on to which the Panzers would then lure the enemy armour. A siege artillery force of heavy and medium guns, under General Böttcher, was also formed, and well-meaning gunnery experts in Berlin sent out some 210mm mortars, which had been originally intended for the battering of the Maginot Line. In the event they were too heavy and are still lying in the sand outside Tobruk.

As the extra tanks, needed to convert the 5th Light to a Panzer division, started to arrive in Africa and stocks of spare parts, ammunition and food accumulated, Rommel began to plan another offensive. With or without encouragement from Berlin the commander of Panzergruppe Afrika was determined to attack, and his first objective clearly had to be Tobruk. As General Auchinleck wrote later, British 'freedom from embarrassment in the frontier area for four and a half months is to be ascribed largely to the defenders of Tobruk. Behaving not as a hard pressed garrison, but as a spirited force ready at any moment to launch an attack, they contained an enemy force twice their strength. By keeping the enemy continually in a high state of tension they held back four Italian divisions and three German battalions from the frontier area from April until November.' This sums up the situation: so long as Tobruk held out the Afrika Korps could not advance into Egypt.

Left: General Neumann-Silkow (left), commander of the 15th Panzer Division, talks to Captain Fromm. Neumann-Silkow was killed in action in November 1941.

Top right: Major Zwiessler (left) discusses water supply problems with an official from Munich. Right: Sergeant Major Schlund receives a Knights' Cross.

Rommel's plans for an attack on Tobruk in October or November were received with little enthusiasm in Berlin. Hitler and the High Command accepted that the British must not be allowed to relieve Tobruk because this would mean the situation in Cyrenaica had taken a turn for the worse, freeing British troops in the Middle East which might then be sent to the Caucasus to help Russia. If all went well on the Eastern Front an offensive in North Africa might be possible and even become necessary, but not before January 1942. The Italians, to whom Rommel was nominally answerable, were also against any move by Rommel. According to their intelligence, agents in Cairo and Alexandria had reported that convoy after convoy of ships which had travelled round the Cape had brought tanks, guns, trucks and several new divisions to Egypt and it was rumoured that the British were

preparing for a major offensive. Nor did all the senior German officers in Africa share Rommel's enthusiasm. They felt that the German High Command saw North Africa as a side-show, no more than 'picking the chestnuts out of the fire for the Italians'. Moreover they were concerned about air support. The Royal Air Force appeared to be in the ascendancy. Flying from Malta the losses they were inflicting on the convoys bringing supplies to North Africa were rising; raids from Egypt were also taking a heavy toll of Afrika Korps targets in the forward areas around Bardia and Tobruk. The Luftwaffe *Staffeln* were currently re-equipping with the ME 109F – the aircraft which was to finally establish German air superiority in the desert sky for months to come. (The Luftwaffe *Staffel* consisted of 12 aircraft organised in *Schwärme* of four or *Rotten* of two planes. A *Gruppe* had three *Staffeln* and a *Stabsschwarm* totalling 40 aircraft. Three *Gruppen* constituted a *Geschwader* of 120 aircraft. Italian equivalents were three *Squadriglie* to a *Gruppo*; three *Gruppi* to a *Stormo*.) But this was for the future; the effect was not to become apparent until the end of the year.

The situation came to a head towards the end of August. Anxious not to be caught unawares while the Afrika Korps was concentrating on Tobruk Rommel decided to find out just what the enemy was doing behind the frontier. Hans von Ravenstein, the commander of the 21st Panzer Division, was ordered to make a reconnaissance in force as soon as conditions favoured it, and 14 September was the date selected because there would be a full moon that night. The operation was called *Sommernachtstraum* (Midsummer Night's Dream).

At dawn on 14 September two of the 21st Panzer Division's battle groups, Schutte and Stephan, crossed the frontier south of Sidi Omar one driving east along the high plateau while the other thrust south into the desert. The Schutte force, searching east, made no contact, found nothing and turned back next day to report there was no sign of any enemy build-up. Nor was the Stephan group able to report having seen any signs of preparation for an enemy offensive, although they had had a more lively time than the Schutte force. On the first day of the sortie Stephan's Panzers had made contact with enemy armoured cars and a battery of 25 pounders near Fort Maddalena. The armoured cars had turned tail and run for it, but a truck that was with them had broken down and been captured. This vehicle turned out to be the orderly room truck of the 14th South African Armoured Car Regiment, and it contained documents and code books. (In the event neither documents nor the ciphers were important, and the Germans gleaned little from them.)

The Stephan group did not get back across the frontier unscathed. In response to a call by the armoured cars for air support two squadrons of South African bombers caught the Panzers while they were refuelling. When the South African aircraft flew away five of the Afrika Korps vehicles were burning and 27 others had to be abandoned.

By 17 September Operation Midsummer Night's Dream was over, and from what the two battle groups had seen Rommel concluded that the Afrika Korps need not fear an attack from Egypt; he could go ahead with his plans for the destruction of Tobruk. He could not have been more wrong.

This Stuka variant, Ju 87 R-a, had extra fuel capacity for long-range missions.

English prisoners of war take a rest during the long march to POW camps.

The Winter Battle

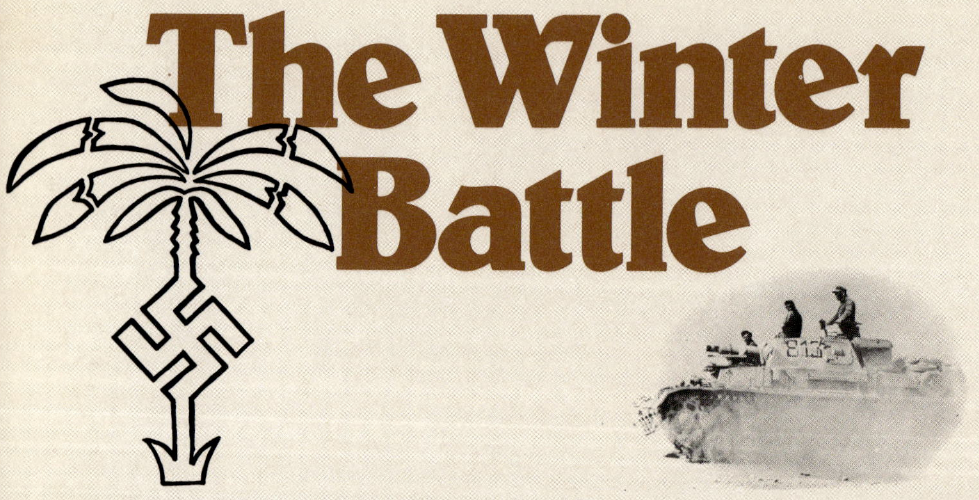

If Rommel's Midsummer Night's Dream had been staged a month later, the whole course of the war in North Africa might have been different. Although Rommel believed that the British were preparing for an offensive, he did not know how far the preparations had progressed; nor was he aware of the expansion of the enemy's land and air forces. In men, tanks and guns the British now outnumbered the Axis forces in the Western Desert; in the air they were on level terms.

General Sir Claude Auchinleck had regrouped his forces into two corps, and in Lieutenant-General W E Godwin-Austen's XIII Corps, in which the New Zealand and 4th Indian Divisions were lumped together, the 1st Army Tank Brigade had 135 Matilda and Valentine tanks, and the 2nd Army Tank Brigade another 126. Lieutenant-General C W M Willoughby Norrie's XXX Corps, consisting of the 7th Armoured Division and the 1st South African Division had another 477 tanks including 210 Crusaders and 173 of the American Stuarts – lanky, lightweight gangling vehicles, known in the Western Desert as 'Honeys'. (This picturesque nickname originated with an incident when the first batch of Stuarts issued to the Royal Tank Regiment in the desert was tested by Major R Crisp, a well-known South African commander. On being asked what he thought of it Major Crisp's driver, Whaley, beamed and said simply: 'It's a honey, Sir,' and the name stuck. Honeys were pretty fast, but equipped with the feeble 2-pounder gun which was useless against the thicker armour and more powerful armament of the Panzers.) With about 200 other tanks in reserve this meant the British had a total of about a thousand while the 15th Panzer and the 21st Panzer between them could muster only 250 medium and light tanks. (Of the German Panzers 150 were Mk IIIs and 55 Mk IVs. Additionally General Gambara's Ariete Division had 146 medium Italian tanks and 52 light.) During September the two British corps were placed under the command of General Sir Alan Cunningham and the whole force became known as the Eighth Army.

In Tobruk the garrison was relieved. All the Australians came out, except one battalion, and were sent back to Palestine and Syria. They were replaced by the British 70th Division and the Polish Carpathian Brigade; the 32nd Army Tank Brigade was also shipped in and the caves holding Tobruk's reserve supplies became stuffed with petrol and food. Tobruk was being groomed for offence as well as defence.

Throughout September Auchinleck steadily built up his supplies and prepared for the offensive, which, if Churchill had had his way, would have been launched before the onset of winter in November. Auchinleck's first objective was the same as Rommel's – Tobruk, and the plan adopted was similar to that of Battleaxe. However the forces and resources to be employed were far larger and the whole operation was on a much bigger scale. Up in the coastal area the 4th Indian Division was to contain the Afrika Korps in case of a retaliatory incursion into Egypt. South of the Indians the New Zealand Division would cross the frontier wire opposite Bir Sheferzen and make for Fort Capuzzo, and wheel north towards Sollum and Bardia. Further south still, the 7th Armoured Division would pass through Maddelena and strike in a wide arc northwestwards to Tobruk, swinging in on the Tobruk road by way of Sidi Rezegh and the broken ground around El Duda, less than 12½ miles from the Tobruk perimeter. At the appropriate moment the Tobruk garrison would break out of its fortress and join up with this force at El Duda, so cutting the road along which the Afrika Korps was expected to retreat. After this Tobruk would be relieved, and the Axis armies would be driven out of Cyrenaica once and for all. The ultimate objective would be Tripoli.

The details all appeared straightforward enough at a distance. In Tobruk it was appreciated that the break-out and link-up with the Eighth Army was not going to be easy. Rommel had seen to that. Between Tobruk and El Duda there were several strongpoints which would have to be captured. So, in great secrecy ammunition was dumped in the forward area in readiness; the dumps were carefully camouflaged. Six wooden bridges were also made to allow the British tanks to sally across the anti-tank ditch; the routes to be taken through the desert to the start line were also taped.

All was ready by the middle of November. Both Auchinleck and Cunningham believed that the Afrika Korps Panzers would counter-attack when Rommel realised the British were advancing towards Tobruk, and they were confident that the British armour would triumph. Both of them would have liked more time for training and preparation, but with Churchill insisting on an early offensive, Auchinleck ultimately set the date for the launching of Operation Crusader as 18 November.

On the other side of the hill Rommel had also set the date for his offensive – and then postponed it. Originally the first Afrika Korps attack was to be launched on 14 November, Rommel's 50th birthday. But the weather at the beginning of the month caused him to put it back until 23 November. A warm and sunny October had merged into a warm and sunny November, and then it suddenly was very windy, very wet and very cold. The African summer had given way to the coastal winter, and with it the thermometer dropped 30° C. Greatcoats and extra blankets were issued to the Afrika Korps, and around Tobruk the dust turned into mud. Men of the 115th Panzergrenadiers manning front-line positions close to the perimeter wrapped old sacks round their legs and soldiered on, sharing their trenches with desert rats – real ones, sleek, grey and gluttonous monsters. The weather also favoured scorpions and scorpion-baiting developed as a minor sport. (Petrol sprinkled in the sand around one would be ignited with a match. When the heat got too fierce the scorpion would try to charge out of the flaming ring, but would invariably draw back baffled by the fire. Meantime he would lunge about with his tail, until in a final frenzy, he would stab himself and sink down dead.) Conditions at the Halfaya Pass were worse. Bach's men were shrouded in thick fog for at least four hours a day, and refrigerator-type cold replaced furnace-like heat. Rain cascaded down the hill-sides and filled the gun-pits with muddy, ice-cold water. Among the men coughs, colds and sneezing were the order of the day.

Accompanied by von Ravenstein, Rommel flew to Rome on 14 November to submit his proposed plan of attack to the *Comando Supremo* and to discuss his supply problems, for the bad weather was limiting the use of Derna and Benghazi. Some 63 per cent of the ships bringing supplies and reinforcements to the Afrika Korps had been sunk during October and reports had just come in that another two Italian convoys had been wiped out by British warships. In any event Rommel was anxious that some reserves of both armoured and soft-skinned vehicles should be available to him in North Africa. Having been briefed by General Bastico, *Comando Supremo*'s Marshal Ugo Cavallero received him coolly. 'Is there not a strong possibility of a massive enemy offensive?' he asked politely. Rommel, who knew very well from reports compiled by the Afrika Korps' radio intercept service that there was indeed every possibility of such an offensive, said he only foresaw action by small forces. Cavallero indicated that he was not convinced; it would be best, he said, of the Afrika Korps were deployed in a defensive role; General Enno von Rintelen, German military attaché in Rome since 1936, sided with him. Rommel was furious. Having called von Rintelen a 'coward' and 'a crony of the Italians', he seized the telephone and spoke to Generaloberst Alfred Jodl, the Wehrmacht Chief of Operations and Hitler's confidant. 'I gather you want me to give up the attack on Tobruk,' he said. 'I'm absolutely disgusted.' Jodl asked about the rumoured British offensive. Rommel said he would arrange for the 21st Panzer Division – whose commander (von Ravenstein) was in the office with him – to hold the British off while the attack on Tobruk was in progress. 'Can you guarantee there'll be no danger?' asked Jodl, according to Rommel. 'I will guarantee it personally!' Rommel shouted, and Jodl gave in.

Rommel took advantage of his visit to Rome to celebrate his birthday. Frau Rommel and the Countess von Ravenstein joined their husbands and did the social rounds. But Rommel saw few of the sights of Rome: tourist attractions had no interest for him; he was concerned only with soldiers and soldiering. (However he did see the Italian film *On From Benghazi*. This managed to depict the Afrika Korps victory in the spring without showing a single German soldier. 'Very interesting and instructive,' he is reputed to have commented sarcastically, 'I often wondered what happened.')

Meantime back in Africa, while Rommel's health was being toasted in Rome, 30 British commandos, led by Lieutenant-Colonel Geoffrey Keyes were being put ashore from two submarines on a deserted beach near Beda Littoria. Their task was to raid the house said to be Rommel's command post. The raid had been planned for midnight on 18 November so as to coincide with the opening of Operation Crusader; Rommel was to be taken 'dead or alive'.

To get to the house from the beach necessitated a difficult climb up a cliff and an 18-mile walk. It was bitterly cold and raining, and for most of the way the party was walking ankle-deep in mud. At the top of the cliff the commandos rested for a while before setting out to find the track where they were to meet the man who was to guide them to their objective. (The guide was in fact a

Below: Crusader was Auchinleck's first operation in the Desert War. Below right: DAK men bury a dead comrade, Lieutenant Borchout, before Crusader opened.

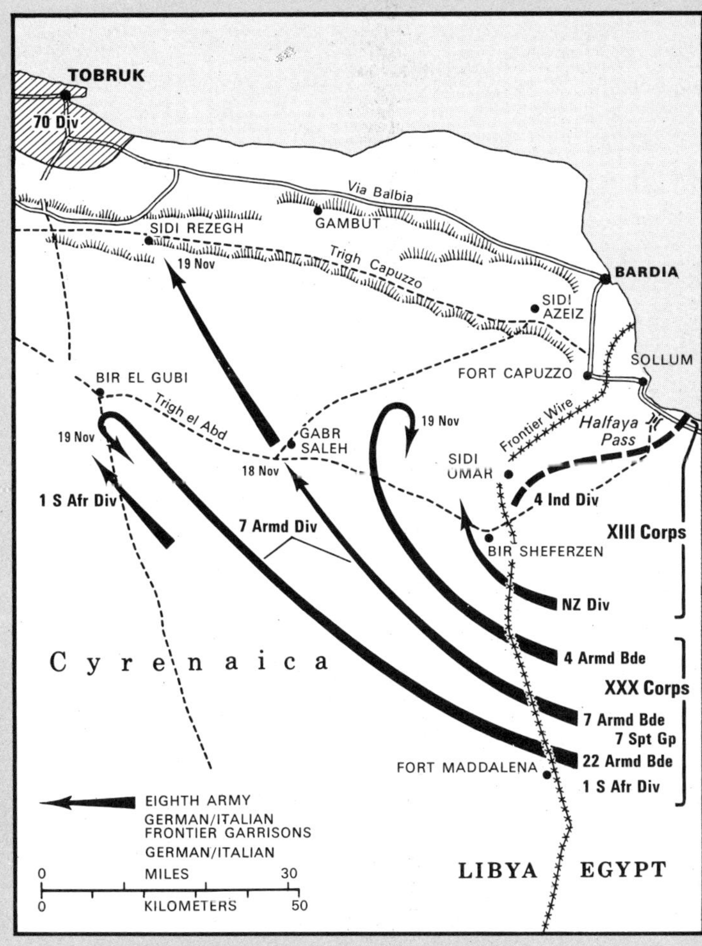

gallant British officer, John Haseldon, who had been living behind the German lines disguised as an Arab.)

Their guide was waiting and although there were several anxious moments during their walk to their objective they eventually located it and the party split up to block the approaches. Keyes himself with two other men dashed boldly up to the front door and kicked it open. Inside they were confronted by a German officer who grappled with Keyes while trying to wrest from him the machine-pistol Keyes was carrying. One of the other commandos shot the German, the light went out, and another guard who came down the stairs was mown down by a burst from Keyes machine-pistol. However, when Keyes flung open the door to one of the rooms opening off the hall he was shot almost immediately. His two companions carried him outside and laid him on the grass by the front door, but he was already dead. The raid had failed. It could never have succeeded because their guide's information had been incorrect. The Arabs who had supplied it had either seen Rommel there by day or had confused him with someone else. The house was in fact the office of his 'Q' staff; Rommel's own headquarters were in the desert west of Derna. (Keyes was buried at Benghazi with military honours by the Afrika Korps, the chaplain of the garrison church at Potsdam performing the ceremony.)

If the commandos failed to surprise Rommel in his headquarters, the opening of Crusader took him and the Afrika Korps completely by surprise. On the eve of the operation the 15th Panzer Division had closed up to the south-east corner of the Tobruk perimeter and the Afrika Division had moved up to the area from which they would launch their assault. Apart from Bach and his gunners at Halfaya the front was held by a thin screen of Italian infantry. First indications that something unusual was happening came with a surprising diminishing of radio activity; the British had ordered wireless silence and the ether was strangely

Below: The commander of the 'Fortress' Bardia, Generalmajor Schmidt, inspects defensive positions during the Crusader Operation.

quiet. But it was impossible to discover if anything was afoot. The heavy rain which had fallen during the previous week had turned the Luftwaffe's forward airfields into bogs, or a reconnaissance flight might have detected that the inertia of the desert life on the enemy side of the front had given way to nervous alacrity. In the absence of any definite information von Ravenstein was apprehensive: Rommel had promised Jodl that the 21st Panzer could cope with enemy activity while Tobruk was being reduced and von Ravenstein was responsible for seeing that it did cope.

Rommel was still in Rome when the blow fell. Exactly as planned the Eighth Army swept through the frontier wire (Mussolini's great fence was generally known simply as 'the wire') at dawn on 18 November, and drove through the empty desert. The first clash came about 1000 hours when armoured cars of the 11th Hussars met the reconnaissance screen provided by the 21st Panzer. Half-an-hour later Crüwell was told of a 'British reconnaissance in force', and similar reports were repeated throughout the day. It was clear that a large number of enemy vehicles had crossed the frontier.

Above: Generalleutnant Ludwig Crüwell in November 1941.

'Parson' Bach's men at Halfaya were the first to feel the shock of the British offensive. For three hours their positions were bombarded by the concentrated artillery of the entire British XIII Corps, and over 3000 25-pounder and 80-pounder shells (from the British 5.5ins medium guns) fell on and around their positions. The worth of their work to improve and strengthen their strongpoints and shelters was now apparent.

The barrage stopped at 1800 hours and the New Zealanders moved in to the assault. They covered about 200 miles to the edge of the minefield before they were pinned down by fire. The Halfaya road-block held, and its hard-pressed garrison was to continue to hold out until the middle of January. Meantime Halfaya was outflanked from the south. The British 7th Armoured Division advanced in what was for the most part a leisurely and uneventful fashion during the first day, and by next morning its advance guard was at Gabr Saleh, halfway to Tobruk. 'The Axis forces have been cut in two' a jubilant English journalist cabled prematurely to London.

In actual fact the entire Afrika Korps was intact; it had not yet left its positions around Tobruk when Crüwell reported to *Panzergruppe* HQ late in the afternoon soon after Rommel's return. Von Ravenstein, Crüwell said, was 'unhappy' about the current situation and wanted to move one of the 21st Panzer's battle groups towards Gabr Saleh. He, Crüwell, had agreed that it would be wise to do so and he had also warned Walter Neumann-Silkow to be ready to move his 15th Panzer Division if the need should arise. Rommel was not pleased. 'We must not lose our nerve,' he said tartly. 'No troops should be moved . . . for fear of discouraging the enemy too soon.'

Next morning Crüwell returned to ask Rommel to reconsider von Ravenstein's proposal to send a battle group south to engage the enemy. The enemy was reported to be advancing on Tobruk and excited signals from units of the Ariete Division south of the village of Sidi Rezegh claimed the Italians were under attack. Better, opined Crüwell, to seize the initiative and hit the British in the open desert around Gabr Saleh. A good deal of discussion followed before Rommel accepted his subordinate's view and agreed to a battle group being sent off. Orders were issued about noon, however, and a force of some 120 Panzers under command of the redoubtable Oberst Stephan (commander of the 5th Pz Regiment of the 21st Panzer Division)

Final preparations in Sollum, November 1941. DAK men dig up the desert to lay telephone lines for improved communications.

was assembled. Soon after 1430 it was on its way and before nightfall the Panzers had met and halted the advance of the British 4th Armoured Brigade.

Meantime Crüwell had concluded – correctly as it turned out – that the enemy armour around Gabr Saleh was one component of a much larger British armoured force spearheading a drive towards Tobruk, and whether this was able to concentrate outside Tobruk or not depended on it being stopped in the desert near Sidi Rezegh. With this in view the 15th Panzer was ordered to be ready to move from its positions around Tobruk.

The next development came that evening, shortly after von Ravenstein had telephoned Crüwell proposing that the 15th Panzer should join the 21st Panzer around Sidi Azeiz and for the two divisions to operate together. Crüwell's Chief of Staff, Oberst Fritz Bayerlein, spoke to Panzergruppe HQ. Rommel in his turn had decided the enemy south of Sidi Rezegh was only a reconnaissance force and had made up his mind that the main British force was further east in the Gambut area, halfway between Bardia and Tobruk. So Bayerlein was given the go ahead for the move of the 15th Panzer and told that Crüwell's job was to 'destroy the enemy in the Bardia-Tobruk-Sidi Omar area before they can offer any serious threat to Tobruk.' So at daybreak the 15th Panzer moved off down the Trigh Capuzzo, the road across the plain on which the white tomb of the venerated Bedouin Saint Sidi Rezegh was a prominent landmark.

Up to now the 7th Armoured Division had met no serious opposition, and General Cunningham with growing confidence ordered its armoured brigades to secure a number of widely dispersed objectives on the road to El Duda – where the advancing British column were to link up with the troops breaking out of Tobruk. One of these objectives was Bir el Gubi, held by the Ariete, where the Italians put up a much stiffer fight than Italian units usually did. In consequence the British were compelled to withdraw when a battalion of the Afrika Korps arrived to reinforce them. Another Panzergrenadier battalion was deployed near the Sidi Rezegh airfield which was in a lozenge-shaped bowl between two escarpments – one rising to the south, the other to the north beyond the Trigh Capuzzo. Here the British were able to achieve their

Two senior British officers after being taken outside Tobruk.

objective. The airfield was taken without the Afrika Korps contesting its occupation, and 19 grounded planes, including 12 of the yellow-nosed gullwinged Stukas, were destroyed.

The reason why the 7th Armoured Division's columns around Sidi Rezegh had encountered virtually no armoured opposition is easy to explain. Rommel's two Panzer divisions had been sent on a wild goose chase which took them first to Sidi Azeiz and then to Gabr Saleh in pursuit of the 4th Armoured Brigade. Time was wasted at Gabr Saleh because the Panzers had to refuel and replenish their ammunition supplies. However by the evening of the 20th Rommel had appreciated where the real threat to Tobruk was building up, and Crüwell was sent an urgent message ordering him to fetch the 15th Panzer Division back to 'destroy the enemy force which has advanced to Sidi Rezegh'. Having sent this order it seems that the Panzergruppe commander had doubts as to whether Crüwell realised the urgency, and would drive the Panzers fast enough or strike sufficiently hard when they met the enemy. So at 0400 hours on the morning of 21 November a second radio message was sent to Crüwell; '. . . the situation in this whole theatre is very critical . . . the Panzer divisions must get going in good time.' The stage was now set for the tank battle which started at Sidi Rezegh on 21 November and raged for three days; and which – if awards of gallantry on both sides are an index of its intensity – was the fiercest armoured clash the desert had witnessed to date.

The Panzers travelled fast. Shortly after daybreak the morning of Friday 21 November they were speeding from Gabr Saleh towards Sidi Rezegh. The British who were expecting an attack from the direction of Tobruk were surprised when the 15th Panzer approached from the south-east. The 7th Armoured Brigade and the 7th Support Group – mostly riflemen and gunners – was caught between von Ravenstein's Panzers in the north and Neumann-Silkow's 15th Panzer Division in the south. The men of the British units were seasoned veterans, but they were outnumbered, outgunned and outmanoeuvred. Cunningham's plan had been for the 7th Armoured Brigade to hold the Afrika Korps and for the other two armoured brigades (of the 7th Armoured Division) to strike them. But the 4th and 22nd Brigades failed to arrive and Crüwell's Panzers systematically savaged the 7th Armoured Brigade and the Support Group. Tanks of the 7th Hussars were destroyed squadron by squadron, and by 1000 hours, when nearly all of their tanks were in flames and the commanding officer and many of his men had been killed and wounded the unit had virtually ceased to exist. During these actions the Panzers and their prey careered backwards and forwards across almost four square miles of desert. It was an area covered with a greyish-bluish-yellowish fog shot with flame, inside which men lay in agony, waiting helplessly for it to stop with the acrid stench of high explosives in their nostrils and the deafening clamour in their ears – waiting until nightfall, hoping that an ambulance would find them. Tanks went up in flames or exploded, and men ran or crawled from the wreckage and tried to get off the battlefield before they were run over by other vehicles or caught in the cross-fire. After the initial charge it became a free-for-all, with all rules forgotten. The odds, however, were weighted in favour of the Panzers.

That was the story of the first day's fighting at Sidi Rezegh though it would not be complete without mention of the British brigadier, commanding the Support Group, Jock Campbell. Three times, when the Afrika Korps attacked the airfield from the east Campbell leaped into his staff car – a station-wagon minus its roof – collected every British tank he could find and then led them in a charge against the Panzers. Three times the Panzers and infantry of the Afrika Division fell back before him. But this sort of resistance could only delay the inevitable and the rest of the Support Group suffered a similar fate to that of the 7th Hussars.

Rommel saw none of this butchery. He had sensed the possibility of the garrison in Tobruk bursting out of their prison and was watching for it. (It is unlikely that his Intelligence officers had interpreted the single word 'Jam' picked up by the Afrika Korps wireless intercept section as the code signal telling the garrison to stand by and be ready to execute the agreed break-out plan 48 hours later.) The perimeter was under constant observation; at night when Tobruk came to life searchlights swept the ground, making it difficult for the British to lift the mines in front of their wire.

When tanks sallied out of Tobruk and rumbled over the bridges that had been laid across the anti-tank ditch the Afrika Korps was waiting. Right from the first minute the fighting was bitter. The Germans already had plenty of guns in position ready for Rommel's assault and they laid down a thick, accurate barrage. Four main objectives had been assigned to the assault force – Afrika Korps positions about two miles from the perimeter which air photographs had revealed. On the ground these camouflaged positions, to which the British gave meaningless names – 'Tiger', 'Jack', 'Butch', and 'Twogun', went almost unnoticed among the jumble of knolls and wadis until one was on top of them. But they were formidable strongpoints, well dug in and well wired.

For the British things started to go wrong from the beginning. Their tanks had difficulties getting across the anti-tank ditch; so the assault started late and the softening up barrage fired by the guns in Tobruk was already half-way through. To complicate matters further they advanced in the wrong direction and Panzergrenadier machine gunners located in a strongpoint not included in the British plan of attack, cut swathes in the ranks of the attacking British infantry.

Despite very heavy casualties the Black Watch stormed 'Tiger' making their final assault to the skirl of bagpipes – to the utter astonishment of those of the Afrika Korps who witnessed the scene. The Scotsmen were the only ones to capture their objective that day, the other battalions taking part in the attack were pinned down before they got to the wire surrounding the German positions. However the tanks edged round behind the defences and about 500 odd men of the Afrika Korps and roughly the same number of Italians were taken prisoner. Some of the wounded were taken to a British field dressing station where the Black Watch casualties were being treated. The rest of the prisoners were marched back to Tobruk through the barrage laid down by General Böttcher's heavy guns, and one of his 210mm shells fell slap in the middle of the column. (Those who survived this march were to undergo further hazards when they were embarked by sea for Alexandria. For six months the Luftwaffe's Stukas had been making the journey between Alexandria and Tobruk the most perilous in the world and many Afrika Korps prisoners who were transported below decks in the British troopship *Chakdina* were drowned when she was dive-bombed four hours out of Tobruk.)

During the fighting the Afrika Korps commander himself joined the *mêlée*. As soon as he heard that the garrison had launched the break-out attempt, he had been expecting, Rommel assumed command of a tiny scratch force consisting of von Wechmar's Reconnaissance Abteilung and two troops of 88s. With these he hurried off to the 'bulge' which the Tobruk garrison was creating, and sealed it off. His 88s were also turned with devastating effect on to the one British armoured regiment, the 6th Royal Tanks, which tried to push north to El Duda from the Sidi Rezegh area. Like the 7th Hussars, the 6th Royal Tanks were shot to pieces.

Further afield there was confusion unassociated with battle. While Wavell was commanding the British forces in the Middle East, he had decided that the vast interior desert of Libya had to be patrolled and, as the British could not afford to use long range aircraft, small mobile columns capable of being self-contained for weeks and capable of travelling 2000 miles without refuelling came into being. Operating from a base at Siwa, an oasis on the edge of the great Libyan sand sea 187 miles south of Sollum, these columns of the 'Long Range Desert Group' patrolled deep into Libya and Cyrenaica. At the beginning their missions were restricted to reconnaissance, but with the passage of time they went on to the offensive, laying mines on desert tracks, charging into desert outposts and attacking convoys way behind the Axis lines. One such column penetrated to the coast between Derna and Tobruk at the time the battle for Sidi Rezegh was raging. It was near Derna that a luckless Afrika Korps *gefreiter* ran into them.

The *gefreiter* was from a supply unit located just off the Via Balbia near Gazala. Water was scarce in the camp and such as there was tasted brackish. So the *gefreiter* had been told to load a truck with empty water containers – 20-litre jerrycans on which a white cross, the sign for drinking water, was painted. He was then to drive to Derna and fill up with fresh clean spring water. The truck was an old Fiat abandoned long ago by the Italians, but recovered and repaired by the Afrika Korps workshops. All went well until the *gefreiter* was on his way back with the full cans. Trying to take a short cut, he lost his way and when he attempted to turn back the vehicle's rear wheels spun and sank into a soft patch of sand. At this point a British armoured troop carrier arrived on the scene, and the Afrika Korps *gefreiter* found himself surrounded by bearded and dishevelled British soldiers and menaced by half a dozen rifles. To the German's surprise they seemed quite friendly, although they helped themselves to half his jerrycans of water. 'Get the spades,' said one British Tommy, and when a couple of spades were unstrapped from the sides of their vehicle the British soldiers set about digging the Fiat out of the sand. A tow rope was then hitched to the Fiat and the British vehicle pulled the German truck back on to the road. From the time of their arrival until the Fiat was back on the road no one had said anything about war, or hinted that it might be over. Indeed the conversation had been mostly about cigarettes, for the *gefreiter* had lit one of the Africa Korps ration issue during the recovery operation. 'What on earth's that you're smoking?' asked one of the British. 'One of our ration cigarettes,' replied the *gefreiter*. 'They're very good for keeping flies away.' 'I should bloody well think so,' coughed the Englishman. 'You'll kill yourself with those things, no need for us to fight you; your bloody tobacco will fix you.'

'What happens now?' the *gefreiter* asked. 'Well, we've got no room for you. You'd better be on your way,' said the Englishman. 'Anyway, you're not going to get far in that thing,' gesticulating at the Fiat. Then, pointing towards the noise of battle which could be heard in the distance, 'Tobruk's over there. Look after yourself!'

In the combat zone water was so scarce and replenishment such a chancy business that in the ding-dong of the battle men were forbidden to wash. During daylight the battle swayed backwards and forwards across the top of the escarpment. At nightfall, however, the forces on both sides drew apart and in the illumination provided by the fires of burning tanks ambulances and stretcher parties German and British alike would move out to succour the wounded who had been lying there while the fighting stormed around them; recovery units went out to drag back the knocked-out tanks and do running repairs. Petrol and ammunition columns appeared on the scene.

Sidi Rezegh airfield on the right of the 21st was littered with burnt-out tanks, overturned guns and corpses. Some of the dead were lying on the runways where they had fallen, crushed by tank tracks. Hundreds of dazed, unwashed, unshaven, hungry and thirsty prisoners had to be rounded up, and on the morning of 22 November they were sent back to Benghazi, the first staging post on their journey to prisoner of war camps in Italy and Germany. The story is told of an Afrika Korps *feldwebel* sneeringly addressing the prisoners singing the opening bars of the song popular with British troops: 'We're going to hang out the washing on the Siegfried Line.' The prisoners responded by taking up the song and singing it.

The US light tank Stuart Mk I, 'Honey' met with mixed success in Crusader.

The battle reached its climax on 23 November the last Sunday in the Protestant Church year and traditionally celebrated as *Totensonntag*, Germany's 'Sunday of the Dead'. (*Totensonntag* dates back to 1816, when it was declared a solemn day of remembrance for those who had lost their lives in the Napoleonic Wars. It falls on the last Sunday in the Protestant Church Year which was 23 November in 1941. South of Sidi Rezegh on the southern escarpment Crüwell led the tanks of the 5th and 8th Panzer Regiments and a mass of motorised infantry in a fantastic charge against the 5th South African Brigade and what was left of the 22nd Armoured Brigade. The charge carried the position, but Afrika Korps losses were not light; the 5th Panzer Regiment which came under fire from 25 pounders firing over open sights lost about a dozen tanks, and most of the officers and NCOs of the motorised infantry were killed. Crüwell himself was almost captured at one stage, but managed to escape. For the British the battle was even more costly; by nightfall the 5th South African Brigade had completely disintegrated. Their anti-tank gunners had used up every round they had and then stood helpless as the Panzers thundered past – picking up the South African brigade commander as a pris-

Above: A German armoured car heads down the Via Balbia to Bardia.
Below: A 2cm Vierling anti-aircraft gun doubles up as an infantry gun.

oner on the way. Tanks from 22nd Armoured Brigade had tried to come to the rescue of the South Africans and there had been a period of utter confusion when the Panzergrenadiers dived for the South Africans' trenches. However the British tanks were too few and the Germans had gained the upper hand.

When the time came for a reckoning it was found that 45 Panzers and 11 Italian tanks had been knocked out during the day. But many of the 'knocked out' tanks only needed a couple of hours work on them to make them usable again. The Afrika Korps recovery services worked well and the mobile workshops effected repairs at breakneck speed. The result was that all four Panzer regiments were able to field no less than 75 tanks apiece through the critical three days of the Sidi Rezegh battles, and while the British were claiming to have inflicted staggering losses, the Afrika Korps invariably turned up with more tanks than the British thought they ought to have had.

Rommel with Panzergruppe HQ at El Adem was in a stage of 'excited exultation' when reports of Crüwell's action began to trickle in to the HQ. It was not clear what had happened south of Sidi Rezegh that day, and it was the early hours of 24 November before any sort of picture of the day's events around Sidi Rezegh began to emerge. No clear picture was ever really possible, the 'Neapolitan Ice sandwich' was even worse after dark than it had ever been in daytime – with Afrika Korps and British units and straggling detachments from both sides hopelessly intermixed and often laagering on the same slice of desert. Men were tired, too tired to care what happened next. Feldwebel Joachim Saenger, the commander of a Mk III Panzer of the 5th Panzer Regiment, recalls that it was a pitch black night and he and his crew were dozing when there was a peremptory rap on the side of his tank. 'Hey you,' said a gruff voice, 'get this Panzer ready to move.' 'We're out

of petrol, and these things won't move without petrol,' Saenger snapped back. 'Then get going and get some.' 'Petrol comes to us; we don't go for petrol. Anyway, the motor's just about *kaputt*, so . . .' 'How many miles have you done with it?' 'About 2000.' 'Good heavens, man! In Russia we never had any mechanical trouble under 3000 miles!' 'Look you fool,' said Saenger sarcastically, 'you may not have noticed, but we're in Africa not Russia. So stick it!' At this the unknown voice exploded, 'How dare you speak to me like that. I'm General Crüwell. What's your unit?' 'Fifth Panzer Regiment, Herr General.' 'I might have known – a proper bunch of idiots!'

The foregoing anecdote serves to illustrate the informal relationship which existed between all ranks of the Afrika Korps – all ranks except perhaps Rommel, who was a law unto himself. Crüwell's ire may well have been roused during his verbal exchange with Feldwebel Saenger, but his bark was worse than his bite. The men of the Afrika Korps knew and respected him as the bluff, hard-headed and experienced Panzer leader that he was. Crüwell believed there was no sense in being killed unnecessarily for the fatherland, and he applied this maxim both to his men and to himself. For this reason he would not tolerate wireless aerials being erected anywhere near him. 'They attract the RAF,' he said, 'and we don't want them. Any messages I've got to send can go by runner.' Crüwell liked his food and his beer – his portly frame testified to that, and the crew of his Panzer kept a step ladder handy to ease his climb into the vehicle. In the evening when the vehicles laagered they would dig a special slit-trench for the 'old man', and when he'd retired for the night the Panzer would be driven over the top of the trench so that Crüwell had no need to stir in the event of an air raid.

Unlike Papa Streich, his predecessor, Crüwell was ready to stand up to Rommel when the need arose and on a number of occasions he and his Chief of Staff, Fritz Bayerlein, were both threatened with a court-martial for daring to argue with the Afrika Korps commander. Of Rommel Crüwell is reputed to have maintained that his commander was 'one who wins an action and loses the battle,' adding in a resigned fashion on one occasion, 'not that it matters whether he wins a battle or not. Every success brings the day nearer when the Americans will come into the war.'

Rommel was out of touch with Crüwell until the two men met at 0600 hours next morning (24 Monday) on the *Achsenstrasse*. Six hours earlier Rommel

had sent a signal to Berlin stating it was his intention on 24 November: (a) to complete the destruction of the 7th Armoured Division, (b) to advance with elements of forces towards Sidi Omar with a view to attacking the enemy on the Sollum front.' Intention (b) was the prelude to a most controversial operation which military historians still argue about.

Rommel had sensed that he was now in a position to swing the battle round and turn Crusader to his own advantage by repeating the manoeuvre which had been so successful in June. What he proposed was to make a huge turning movement around the British flank, encircling and isolating the bulk of the enemy's army in a vast pocket. Von Wechmar's Reconnaissance Abteilung was told to keep open the coast road east from Tobruk, while Rommel with the rest of the Afrika Korps and the Ariete Division (which had now been put under his command) would sweep south and eastwards to Sidi Omar – relieving the frontier garrison, destroying the fragmented remnants of the British XXX Corps, and finally encircling and destroying Godwin-Austen's XIII Corps. 'This will be the end of the campaign. I shall finish it with a single stroke,' Rommel told Siegfried Westphal, his Chief of Staff. Westphal was to stay back at El Adem; he, Rommel, hoped to be back there by the evening (24 November) or the next morning (25 November) at the latest. It should then be possible to deal with Tobruk, only a few days later than had been intended.

'You have the chance of ending this campaign tonight!' Rommel repeated to von Ravenstein when he issued his orders some time later. The 21st Panzer was to drive fast to the frontier wire and beyond 'looking neither to the right nor to the left', then turn northeast and make for the coast near Sollum. Meanwhile a battle group, comprising a Panzergrenadier battalion and a company of tanks detached from the 15th Panzer, advancing independently, would aim for Fort Maddalena where they would attack Eighth Army Headquarters. Another battle group from the 15th Panzer following up would then go on to capture Bir Habata, the terminus of the railway line from Egypt, where there were known to be large stocks of petrol. If, as the Afrika Korps commander rightly suspected, the enemy was thin on the ground between the frontier and Alexandria, the 21st Panzer would join the battle group at Bir

British infantry look on Tobruk as they wait to enter the town following the German retreat.

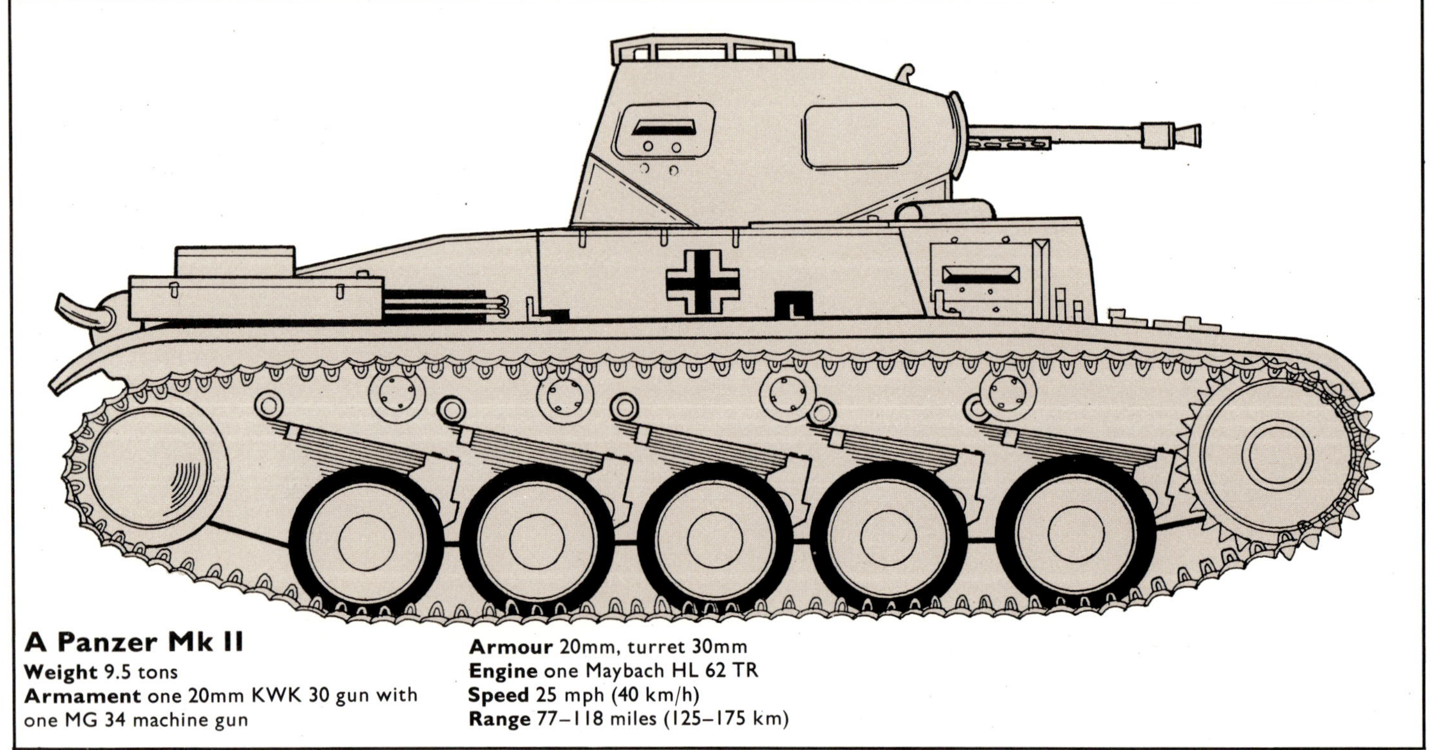

A Panzer Mk II
Weight 9.5 tons
Armament one 20mm KWK 30 gun with one MG 34 machine gun
Armour 20mm, turret 30mm
Engine one Maybach HL 62 TR
Speed 25 mph (40 km/h)
Range 77–118 miles (125–175 km)

Habata and strike down into Egypt. (There was in fact one brigade of the 4th Indian Division and the raw, unblooded and badly equipped 2nd South African Division to stop the Afrika Korps if Rommel had pushed on beyond the frontier.) The Western Desert War would then be over.

Rommel's plan was unquestionably a bold one; unfortunately it went wrong from the beginning. Von Ravenstein set off at dawn (24 November) and drove south at full speed; by noon his long column of Panzers and tractor-drawn artillery, flanked by motorcyclists, had reached Sidi Omar where the ground was still littered with the debris of the June battle. Rommel, driving a station wagon, and accompanied by Generalmajor Alfred Gause, moved with the leading Panzers of the 5th Panzer Regiment. His command vehicle had stuck in a soft patch of sand soon after starting out from El Adem. Consequently the commander and the Chief of Staff of Panzergruppe Afrika were out of touch with their rear headquarters for the next 24 hours – a fast-moving period during which at least one crucial decision had to be taken by Westphal.

On the way to Sidi Omar von Ravenstein's column passed close by the Eighth Army's two main supply dumps, one 15½ miles south-east of Bir Gubi and the other 15½ miles south-east of Gabr Saleh. Together the two held enough petrol to carry the whole of the Afrika Korps to Egypt and back again; petrol without which all the Eighth Army's vehicles would have been stranded. The huge dumps each covered an area of about 6 miles square, but they were well camouflaged and although von Ravenstein saw the defences around them he did not choose to stop and investigate. His orders were to press on to the frontier, and Rommel was with the divisional vanguard. At the time nobody knew how close the Afrika Korps had come to capturing the Eighth Army's stocks of petrol, water and stores. There were other more immediate disappointments and it seems the Afrika Korps was out of luck that day.

As the German columns cruised down towards Sidi Omar they met and passed enemy columns and drove through countless static installations. Sometimes a British convoy would get mixed up with a German formation before its members realised what they had run into. A brisk action would then ensue while the two sides disentangled themselves, and the British vehicles scattered, running off into the desert like stampeded sheep. Static installations like supply dumps, workshops and field hospitals could not move of course and medical posts simply carried on. During the afternoon of 24 November Rommel stopped to inspect one such medical centre, a field hospital near Sidi Omar.

'Five pairs of socks!' 'Here!' An anti-aircraft unit on the Sollum Front gets a thorough inspection. Their commander satisfies himself that all their equipment is up to scratch.

A mixed bag of British and German wounded occupied the beds, but the hospital was still in British hands, and the British medical officer who showed Rommel round did so under the impression that the latter was a Polish general. This situation seems absurd, but the prevailing situation was chaotic. For the past five days, from soon after the start of Operation Crusader, there had been no fewer than five fronts running down inland from the coast between the west of Tobruk and the east of Sollum. Now the two sides were also interlocked in layers running east and west; the Afrika Korps' use of British vehicles and the fact that some of the British were driving around in German trucks added to the confusion.

That Rommel was not apprehended by the British during his visit to the field hospital could be considered a stroke of luck. After this his luck changed. Somehow or other the combat group which was to attack Fort Maddalena failed to catch Eighth Army Headquarters, so that part of the grand plan miscarried. Rommel rejoined von Ravenstein's column when he had finished inspecting the hospital, and at one stage in the operations that afternoon the two men spotted a group of staff officers conferring on the far side of the frontier wire. 'That's Cunningham,' Rommel said excitedly, turning to von Ravenstein. 'Go and get him,' Von Ravenstein rushed off calling for a troop of Panzers, but Rommel – never a patient man at any time – shouted after him, 'Never mind, I'll go myself,' and he roared away in his staff car with his escort of half a dozen motorcyclists. Whether or not Cunningham was in the group Rommel was intent on capturing is not known. Seeing the car and motorcyclists heading towards them the enemy promptly jumped into their vehicles and made off.

Rommel's next piece of luck – bad in some respects, but good in the end – came after dark. In the late afternoon he, Gause, Crüwell and Bayerlein, driving without escort in two British-made armoured signal trucks, had crossed the frontier through a gap in the wire which indicated there was also a gap in the mine belt. They had turned back after dark, but failed to locate the gap in the wire through which they had come. To make matters worse the two trucks became separated, and at one stage Rommel kicked his driver out and took over the driving himself. He could do no better however, and to halt and wait for daybreak was the only course open to them. So in their separate vehicles the commander of the Afrika

Above: A Junkers Ju 87 Stuka has been completely covered by camouflage paint and is ready to go on another bombing mission.

Above: German soldiers have a quick wash outside the Tobruk perimeter. Right: English prisoners of war, captured in December 1941 near Tobruk, wait to be transported to camps behind the lines.

Korps and its most senior officers spent the night of 24 November on the frontier of Egypt, in an area bristling with enemy. Next morning Crüwell found Rommel's truck with Rommel and Gause inside, shivering with cold. Carefully they drove back across the wire and at 0700 hours on 25 November were found by an Afrika Korps patrol near Fort Capuzzo.

The 25 November was a day of growing confusion. Auchinleck had seen his opportunity and decided to open the road to Tobruk. With the Afrika Korps Panzers absent the New Zealanders recaptured the ridge at Sidi Rezegh and pushed on to El Duda. Meanwhile Rommel had ordered Crüwell to attack eastwards with the 15th Panzer between Sidi Omar and Sidi Azeiz, and to send the 21st Panzer through Halfaya; the Ariete Division was still too involved with the 1st South African Brigade at Bir el Gubi to be of any use. Throughout the day the two Panzer divisions fought a series of disjointed actions, during which the artillery of the 4th Indian Division and the Royal Air Force inflicted heavy losses. By the evening the 5th Panzer Regiment had only 12 tanks in action and the 8th Panzer Regiment 53. This time few of those which had been knocked out could be recovered or repaired. Rommel raced to and fro between his formations – looking for people to send into battle among straggling parties of Panzergrenadiers searching for their units and groups of stranded vehicles awaiting trucks bringing petrol and ammunition replenishments.

Oberst Westphal, running Rommel's main headquarters back at El Adem knew nothing of this confusion on the frontier, but he did realise that the Afrika Korps was over-extended. The agitated Italians had been telling him this since Rommel had torn off to the east with the two Panzer divisions, and they were pressing Westphal to do something to correct the deteriorating situation around El Duda. Rommel had specifically laid down that nothing was to be done which would interfere with his grand coup and advance into Egypt. But Westphal at El Adem saw what his commander could not see on the Egyptian border. By the evening of 26 November, after all attempts to contact Rommel and Crüwell by wireless had failed, Westphal decided that he must act. Thus in defiance of Rommel's orders, a signal was sent recalling the 21st Panzer to Tobruk.

Von Ravenstein, 36 miles inside Egypt and less than 12½ miles from the British railhead breathed a sigh of relief when the signal was handed to him. The 21st Panzer was exhausted and von Ravenstein himself – having watched his precious tanks dissipated and destroyed – had no confidence in the ability of his division to strike into Egypt. The 5th Panzer Regiment could muster only seven battleworthy tanks that night and as one of the Panzer commanders sarcastically commented, 'We shan't get very far with them.' With grim humour the troops had been issued with a field postcard apiece. This may be the last chance you'll get to write home they were told. Westphal's order changed all this. 'We're saved!' said the signaller when he handed the message to von Ravenstein. Normally he would never have dared venture such a comment to the divisional commander.

Above: Fieseler Fi 156 Storch.

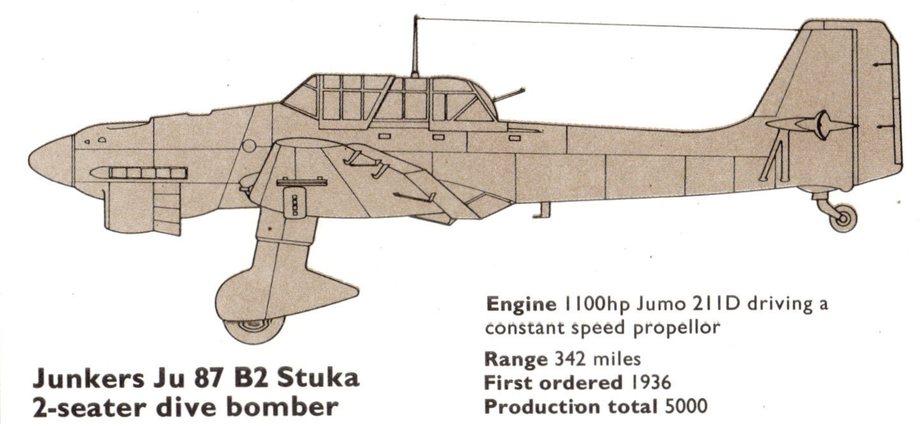

But he and the rest of the division all sensed that time had run out on this operation.

The 21st Panzer was soon on the road, moving back to Bardia through the Halfaya Pass where the vehicles were loudly cheered by 'Parson' Bach's men. At Bardia von Ravenstein was met by Rommel. 'What the hell are you doing here,' he asked von Ravenstein. 'I expected you to be halfway to Alexandria.' Von Ravenstein produced the signal recalling his division to Tobruk. Rommel exploded. 'It's a fake,' he shouted. 'It has come from the British; they must have our code.'

Some hours elapsed before Rommel could be convinced that the situation at El Duda was critical. From Bardia he drove to Gambut where Crüwell was waiting for him, and from there he was able to speak by wireless to Westphal at El Adem. The latter tersely explained how the Tobruk front had crumbled, and that the Italians were panicking. That night, after a discussion with Crüwell, Rommel flew to El Adem where his staff were awaiting his return with considerable apprehension. How, they wondered was he going to react to Westphal's decision to take matters into his own hands. Leutnant Voss, one of Rommel's aides, has described what happened when he arrived at El Adem: 'At first Rommel was furious that the 21st Panzer had been called back. . . . On returning to headquarters he greeted nobody, but stalked silently into the command vehicle and looked at the situation maps. Behind him stood Gause. We tried to signal to Gause that he should talk to Rommel and explain Westphal's decision. But it was not necessary, for Rommel suddenly left the vehicle, saying that he was going to lie down. Nobody dared to go to the vehicle where Rommel was sleeping, to report on the situation. Next morning, however, to everybody's relief, the general made no further mention of the incident. He was as friendly as ever and work at headquarters continued smoothly.'

That night the Afrika Korps Commander wrote to his wife: 'I'm very well. I've just spent four days in a desert counter-attack with nothing to wash with. We've had a splendid success. . . . It's our 25th wedding anniversary today. . . . I need not tell you how well we have got on together. I want to thank you for all the love and kindness through the years which have passed so quickly. . . .'

Clearly there were at least two sides to Rommel's character: the sentimental side reflected in the correspondence with Frau Rommel, and that which provoked fear among his subordinates – none of whom was safe from the lash of his tongue. In the Eighth Army Rommel was something of a hero, 'Wish we had one like him' was the wistful wish of many who served in the Western Desert; and this hero-worship has been perpetuated and developed by British military historians in books published after his demise. In Germany, however, Rommel is less popular, for the men of the Afrika Korps knew him as an ambitious and ruthless driver, a hard man who placed more reliance on the whip than on the carrot. In all fairness, however, it must be noted that Rommel lived frugally and almost as hard as any Afrika Korps Schütze. In the desert he lived simply on rations cooked on the issue cooker called rather pompously a *Sicherheitsfeldkochgestell*, swilled down with water. At his headquarters the standard was only marginally better; certainly there was none of the *grand château* life-style that is often associated with the generals of previous wars, especially World War I.

Messerschmitt Bf 110s take off on the Cyrenaican front.

German gunners man a rather exposed position in the Halfaya Pass.

At first light on the morning of 29 November the Afrika Korps advanced on El Duda in three columns – from the south, the north-east and the west. During the afternoon of Friday 28 November the tanks and motorised infantry of the 15th Panzer had climbed on to the escarpment from the south-east; it was this force which provided the main thrust. Sweeping through the British machine-gun and anti-tank gun positions, Neumann-Silkow's troops cut the tenuous British corridor to Tobruk, the 21st Panzer was still slowly moving towards Tobruk, but von Ravenstein had motored up to see for himself what the situation was around El Duda. He reached the battlefield in the middle of a counter-attack to restore the corridor and was promptly picked up by New Zealanders and taken to Tobruk (where he was put on board a ship for Alexandria which was sunk by the Luftwaffe. Von Ravenstein, who was washed up on the shores of Egypt wearing only his pyjama jacket was eventually interned in Canada and repatriated to Germany in 1948).

Revenge came next day when the 21st Panzer attacked the New Zealanders at Belhamed. During a bitter and bloody battle the New Zealanders suffered heavy casualties, and the corridor to Tobruk was closed once more. But the men who had sallied out of Tobruk still held El Duda, and although the Afrika Korps battered away incessantly, the British could not be dislodged. Realising that his troops were getting nowhere Rommel pulled them back to regroup, and for three days the Sidi Rezegh battlefield was strangely silent. It was the calm preceding a storm.

The storm burst on 4 December, when the Afrika Korps made another desperate bid to overrun El Duda. Once again the British, entrenched among so many derelict tanks that most of them were now being charted as landmarks on maps, held firm. Auchinleck had rushed up reinforcements and the 7th Armoured Division which had been so severely mauled a fortnight before had been reformed. By contrast the Afrika Korps was feeling the effects of its exertions. The two Panzer divisions had only 34 tanks between them, and they could not hope to beat an enemy four times as strong in men and equipment. So Rommel ordered his troops to pull back west of Tobruk. As a result, on 6 December, patrols sent out by the British in Tobruk suddenly found nothing opposite them but Italian stragglers. The defenders of El Duda moved on to Sidi Rezegh and made contact with the rest of the Eighth Army and by 9 December they had seized El Adem with its vast airfield. On 10 December the relief of Tobruk was complete and General Godwin-Austen made his famous wisecrack, 'Tobruk is relieved, but not half so relieved as I am.'

Meantime the Afrika Korps had moved back in good order, despite the fact that it was no easy matter extracting the men and material east of Tobruk. Rommel asked the *Comando Supremo* to evacuate the mixed German-Italian garrison in Bardia and Sollum by sea, but the Italians said that it would be impossible to do so – however they did promise to do what they could to send in supplies by submarine. Bach's men at Halfaya were doomed from the start, but Rommel considered that all the abandoned outposts would still be performing a useful purpose in pinning down large British forces. Furthermore he thought that they might even become the basis of a big counter-attack – as Tobruk had been for the British. Much equipment had also had to be abandoned and the desert around El Duda and Sidi Rezegh was speckled with derelict vehicles. The odour of death brooded over the battlefield. It was quiet now, and the sand was sifting gently in to cover the waste of twisted wreckage and fill the ruts made by tank tracks. In some places violent action had frozen little groups into grim silent tableaux, and the Afrika Korps had not had the time to remove many of the corpses from the blackened hulls of their vehicles. Down by the sea north of Tobruk, the British found a complete Afrika Korps workshop and the fact that 38 Mk IV Panzers had been left behind is an indication of the speed with which the positions around Tobruk were evacuated.

On 2 December a succession of drenching showers heralded an ominous change in the weather. Rain was to fall unceasingly in the weeks to come and men huddled in their greatcoats in trenches or crouching in the cold damp cabs of vehicles realised that the winter was going to be as hard as the summer had been arduous. The rain turned the dust into a pasty mud through which convoys of vehicles churned ruts 12ins deep. On occasions British vehicles drove through the convoys of the retreating Germans, and Afrika Korps vehicles cut through advancing British columns without a shot being fired. Both sides were using captured trucks and tanks and although the Afrika Korps hoisted red swastikas as a recognition sign over their vehicles, a few

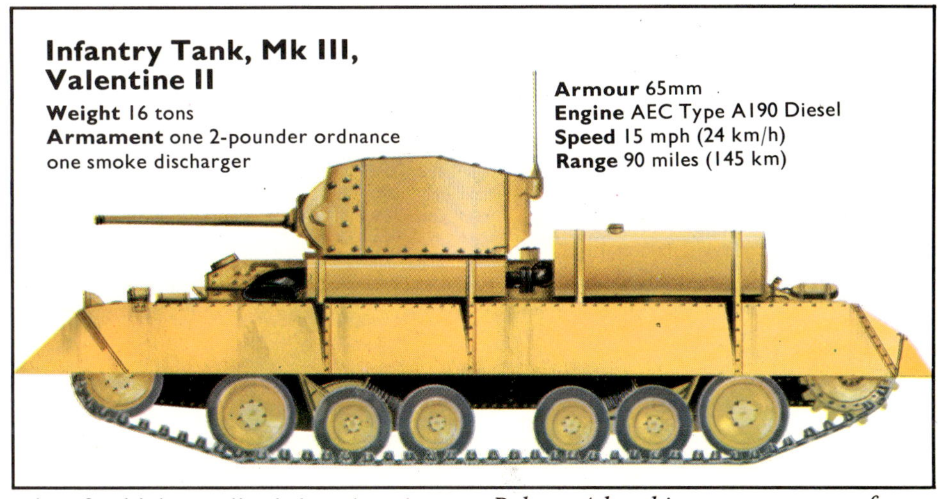

Below: A bombing crew prepares for a mission to delay the British advance.

A Junkers Ju 88, the German tactical bomber. It had two 1200hp Jumo 211B engines and a bomb load large enough to carry 3690lb in an internal bay and on four large innerwing racks.

miles through the mud and the flags were dark grey-brown rags and British troops waved as they passed. Similarly Italian tanks salvaged by Indian troops drove through German lines without being challenged.

On 6 December Rommel decided to halt the retreat and make a stand at Gazala. Here a strong force of Italians stiffened by Afrika Korps infantry had been preparing a formidable defence line, with concrete gun emplacements nearly ten feet deep and cleverly planned machine-gun posts. Contrary to whatever its name might suggest, Gazala is not a town or a village, or even an oasis. It is another of those geographical fictions so common in the desert, springing from the necessity of giving names to places where things happen. At a point where a long inlet of the Mediterranean almost touches the foot of the escarpment the Turks had built a little fort and the Italians two airfields; that was Gazala. The so-called Gazala line began at a point where a track spirals up to the top of the cliff from the Via Balbia. From here it ran south, threading along a series of barely perceptible rises and ridges, sweeping away in a big curve until it finally disappeared into the desert.

Sidi Rezegh had marked the end of a phase of massive tank battles, and the current phase was one in which Rommel was anxious to conserve his Panzers. Up to and beyond Gazala they would sit hull down just over the skyline, taking pot-shots at British tanks and retiring swiftly when the latter came too close; by virtue of their superior gun power the Panzers were easily able to keep out of range. But such tactics could not save them from the enemy air force, and on 6 December planes of the South African Air Force bombed and strafed the 15th Panzer. Several of the Panzers were knocked out and Generalmajor Walter Neumann-Silkow was mortally wounded. (All three Afrika Korps divisions lost their commanders within a month: von Ravenstein captured, Neumann-Silkow killed on 6 December, and Summermann killed in an air raid on 10 December.)

By the night of 7 December, when the bulk of the Afrika Korps and the Italian mechanised units were back behind the Gazala line, Rommel had changed his mind about standing there. The Afrika Korps was desperately short of petrol and ammunition, the British seemed to be at the receiving end of endless supplies and reinforcements, and it was reported that a British armoured force had worked its way round the southern flank of the Gazala line and was already half-way to Tmimi. Rommel did not intend to have the battered remnants of his army caught in a fatal trap, so he decided to pull back still further and on 9 December the Afrika Division (renamed the 90th Light Division on 5 December) fell back to Agedabia, 125 miles south of Benghazi. This move was made to protect that area from the 29th Indian Brigade which had captured Jalo and was threatening to cut the Afrika Korps' lines with Tripoli.

In flight the Afrika Korps proved to be every bit as skilful as it had been in attack and what the British press was describing as 'only the handful of Panzers that remained of the German armoured units which had been more or less annihilated' fought a skilful rearguard action – leap-frogging back, never

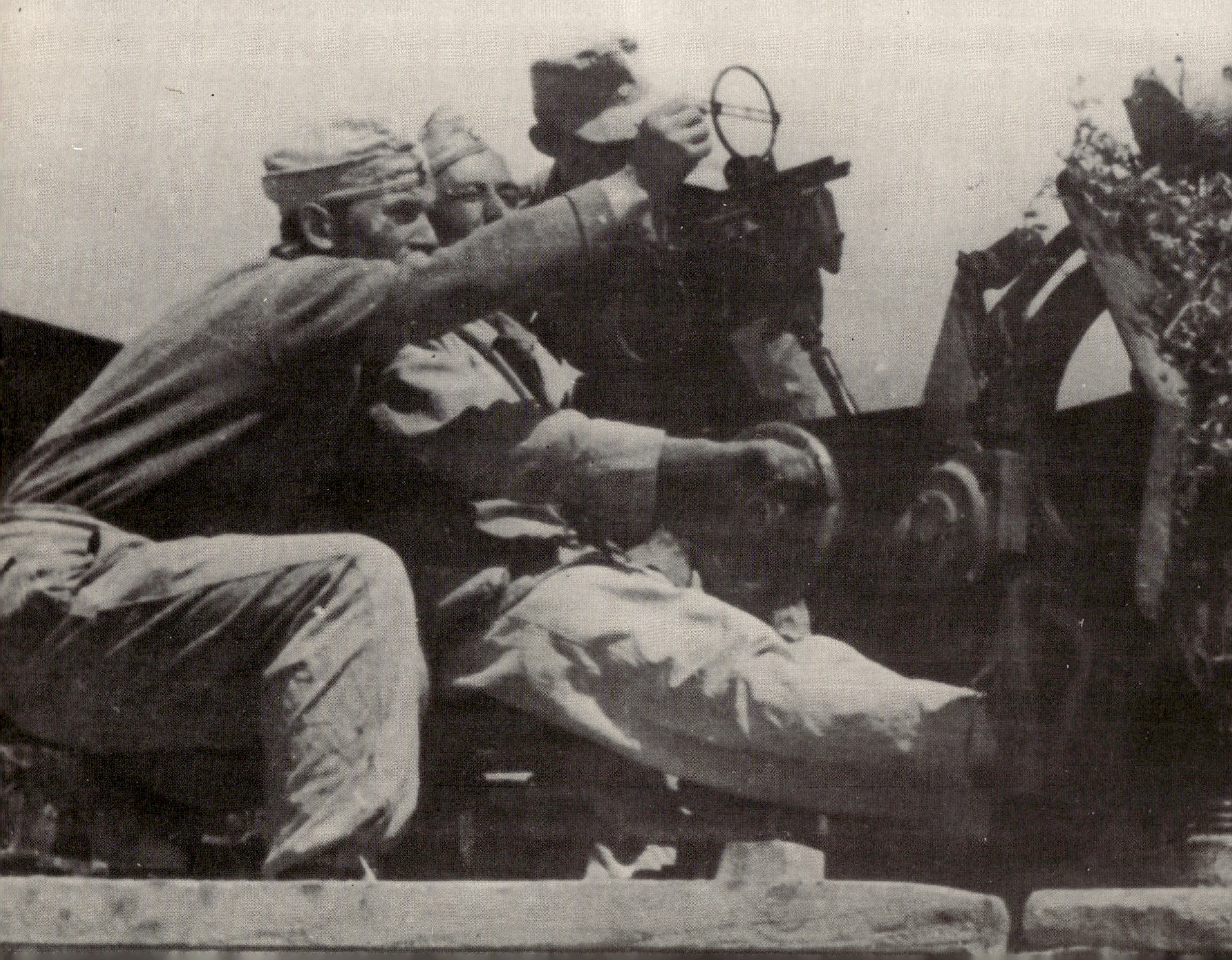

letting the British tanks get within range with their two-pounder guns, and generally playing for time until the British ran out of petrol. Then, when the British tanks fell back to refuel, the Panzers and the whole Italian holding force would fall back on another bound. It was cleverly done, and the men of the Afrika Korps never had the feeling that they were beaten. Their retreat was definitely not a rout; they were withdrawing but it was a fighting withdrawal which preserved morale.

Orderly withdrawal or controlled rout, it was still a retreat and the Italians did not like it. At a meeting with Rommel on 8 December General Bastico announced that the withdrawal must stop, and there was a heated argument during which both generals indulged in undignified recriminations. The argument ended with Rommel flatly refusing to comply with Bastico's orders. A week later Marshal Cavallero arrived from Rome with Feldmarschall Kesselring, whom Hitler had recently appointed 'Commander-in-Chief South' (Kesselring had no operational authority over Rommel, but he was responsible for supplies and air support for the Afrika Korps); their purpose was to arbitrate and during the next three days there were meetings and separate and joint consultations and discussions with both Bastico and Rommel. The Italians demanded that Rommel should halt and stand at Derna, since the loss of Cyrenaica would have unpredictable political consequences for Mussolini. Rommel insisted that this was impossible. If his army remained in Cyrenaica it would be cut to ribbons, he said; the ability of the Italians to resist was almost non-existent, and the men of the Afrika Korps needed to rest and re-equip. He must pull clean out of Cyrenaica and reorganise in the Mersa Brega bottleneck. Kesselring and Cavallero reluctantly agreed but Bastico seemingly remained unconvinced. There will be no further retreat, he declared. Bastico was related to Mussolini by marriage, and was more afraid of the Duce's wrath than of the consequences of disaster at Derna. He was supported by his deputy Gambara, who had his eye on promotion. The argument ended when Rommel asked Bastico how he would set about holding Derna and saving Cyrenaica. 'After all,' he said, 'you are the Commander-in-Chief North Africa; you should be the one to produce the plan.' Bastico was taken aback, but after a moment's hesitation he replied, 'It is not for a Commander-in-Chief to get involved in detail. I am merely telling you that it is essential the enemy be stopped at Derna.'

Next day, as planned, the retreat continued, and on Boxing Day the vanguard of the Eighth Army was drinking a Christmas beer ration in what was left of the Afrika Korps canteen in Benghazi – a canteen which once had been fitted up as a Bavarian *Bierkeller*. The Germans had not left any beer and the town had been gutted. But the Afrika Korps' rearguard had left a defiant message for the incoming British. Scrawled on the once white walls of villas in the Europeans quarters were the two words, 'Back soon.'

Below: A 2cm anti-aircraft crew practise sighting their gun.

Riposte

Two days before Christmas 1941 Rommel was writing to his wife '. . . It will be a proper Christmas gift if I can get our troops back. . . .' His troops were certainly doing their best to see that their commander's wish was fulfilled, and on 19 December Britain's *Daily Mail* commented, 'The German Afrika Korps is defending itself tenaciously. From all points of view Rommel is worthy of the grave dug for him by the British Army.'

For the German soldiers a full-blooded retreat was a new experience and one which brought unexpected hardships. The men of the 99th Motorised Pionier Battalion, for instance, suddenly found that shortage of petrol meant they had to retreat on their feet and like the majority of soldiers accustomed to driving into or out of battle they did not care for walking. However, the Afrika Korps was doing more than 'defend itself tenaciously'; every now and then its units would turn and give their opponents a bloody nose. On 23 December, for example, as Rommel was penning his letter to 'Dearest Lu,' the 8th Panzer Regiment led by Oberst Hans Cramer cut British confidence to size. The 8th Panzer was covering the retreat of Italian infantry trudging wearily westwards back along the Via Balbia from Benghazi, and tanks of the 22nd Armoured Brigade were harrassing the German rearguard. When it seemed they were concentrating for an assault Cramer turned about and counter-attacked. Twenty-two Mk III Panzers which had arrived at Benghazi four days before had been hastily unloaded, and sent straight up to Cramer, augmenting his strength to 60. (Another 33 Mk IIIs and Mk IVs reached Tripoli on the same day, 19 December. Forty-five others were lost on 13 December when the *Carlo del Greco* and the *Fabio Filzi* were sunk in the Mediterranean.) Advancing in an arrowhead formation these 60 tanks drove straight for the middle of the British force. When Cramer pulled out of the battle 17 Matildas were in flames and 20 more which had received hits were in difficulties; the cost to the 8th Panzer was seven Mk IIIs of which five were dragged from the battlefield and subsequently repaired.

Meantime the remainder of the Afrika Korps and the Italian armoured divisions, with Crüwell in overall command, were moving back by way of Antelat and by Christmas Eve the whole of the Korps was concentrated near Agedabia. The men dug in, put up barbed wire and laid minefields, but offensive operations were conducted in

Below: A forward reconnaissance unit runs into a heavy dust cloud.

a low key; ammunition was none too plentiful and Rommel was anxious to build up stocks for the offensive that was already in his mind. For their part the men of the Eighth Army were glad of the respite resulting from this relative inactivity on the German side. The speed of the Afrika Korps retreat and consequently the speed of the British pursuit had surprised General Neil Ritchie, the Eighth Army Commander. He had expected things to move more slowly, and the Eighth Army's organisation and supply system was not geared to the sudden and rapid extension of the line of communications. The Afrika Korps was now again reasonably close to the ports through which their supplies came and Rommel was beginning to benefit from the pendulum's swing.

On Christmas Day he wrote to his wife: 'I opened my Christmas parcel in my caravan yesterday evening and was very pleased with the letters from you and Manfred [Rommel's son, currently the Mayor of Stuttgart] and the presents. Some of them, like the bottle of champagne, I took straight across to the Intelligence truck where I sat over it with the Chief, the Ia and Ic. The night passed quietly, but the Italian divisions give us a lot of worry. . . . German troops are being forced to go to the rescue everywhere. . . .'

The Deutsche Afrika Korps strikes back. Right: A temporary gun emplacement prepares to hit British positions. Inset: A Messerschmitt 110 ready for take-off.

The German troops were actually doing very well. On 30 December one of Crüwell's battle groups gave the British another sharp lesson, when 23 British tanks were knocked out at a cost of seven Panzers. But the fighting rarely flared into armoured actions of this scale; it was mainly patrols and skirmishes in appalling conditions.

The dawn of 31 December was cold and grey and during the day a bitterly cold wind swept across the Agedabia plain. Apart from a few patrols, Germans and British alike huddled in their trenches and vehicles; after dark, when the moon had set, the front seemed more silent, more desolate and more inactive than usual. In the forward area on this New Year's Eve there was little to celebrate. Shortly before midnight, however, when the sky suddenly cleared, revealing a few cold and distant stars, Oberstleutnant Schmidt of the 115th Panzergrenadier Regiment of the 90th Light Division said to his troops, 'That's the end of 1941.' He was going on to say that like everybody else in the Afrika Korps he hoped 1942 would bring victory, when the front suddenly erupted. Over the whole nine-mile line held by the Afrika Korps rose a gigantic firework display, as nearby every type of automatic weapon fired into the air – light anti-aircraft guns and machine guns popping off tracers, mortars sending up illuminating flares, while the rattle of fire from rifles and submachines added to the cacophonous chorus of explosions. For approximately three minutes this defiant display and waste of ammunition continued; then, as suddenly as it had begun, the din ceased and silence reigned once more. But not for long, for the British responded with a similar display.

To both sides it was a mutual and spontaneous gesture which in retrospect

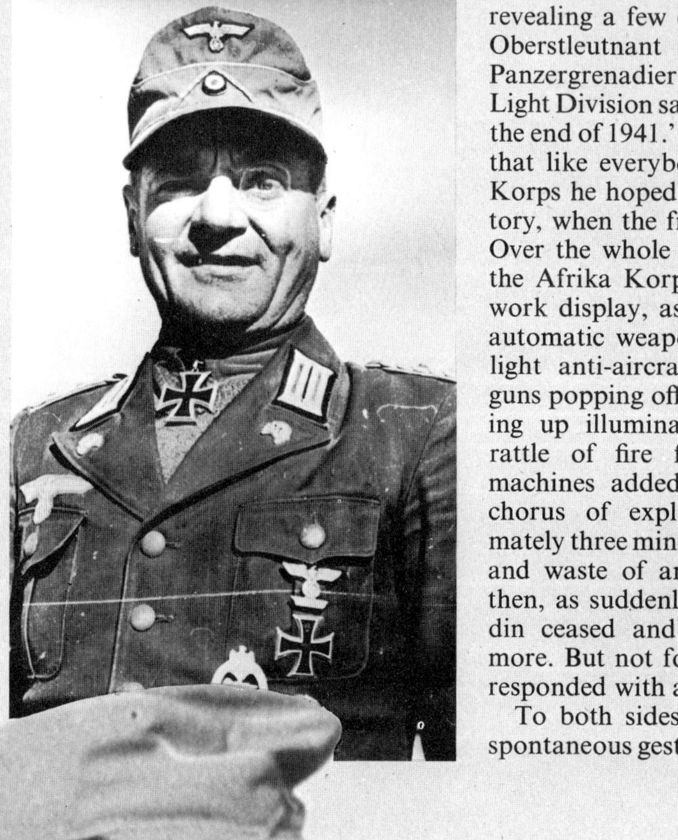

Right above: Oberst Kramer, a Pz regiment commander. Right: General Crüwell (left) congratulates Oberst Michel, who had escaped from captivity.

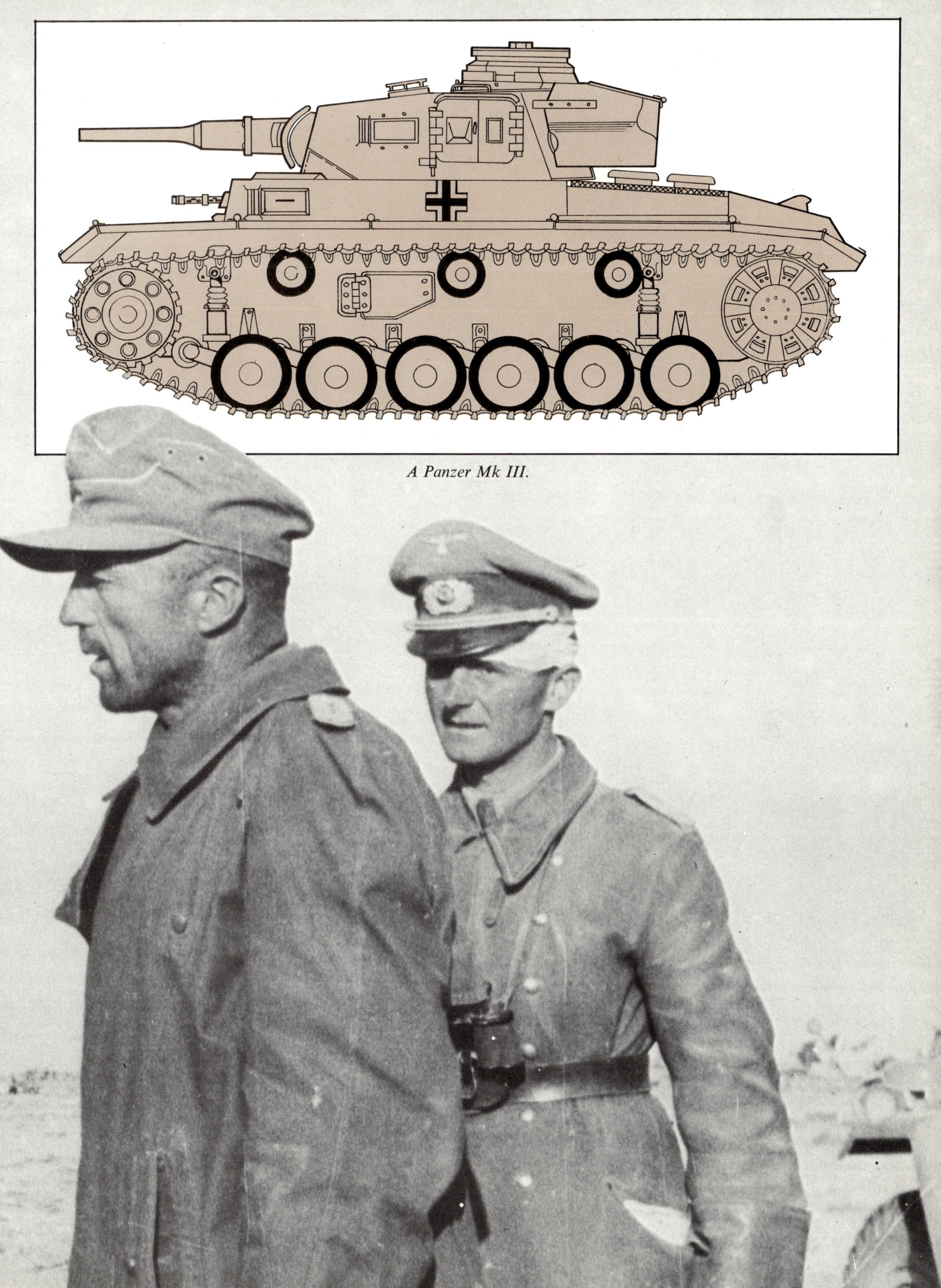

A Panzer Mk III.

could be seen as a fitting salute to the end of one round of hostilities and the start of another. In the winter battles the British had lost about 18,000 men, two-thirds of whom had been captured. But Cyrenaica was now in their hands. Afrika Korps casualties totalled about 15,000 – about one-third of the total German force, and the Italians had lost about 22,000 men – also about a third of their total strength in North Africa. On the material side losses had been high too; the Afrika Korps had lost 220 tanks (85 per cent of its strength) and 48 guns, and the Italians 120 tanks and 181 guns. Two hundred and seventy-five Axis aircraft had also been destroyed. But contrary to the hopes of the men who had to do the fighting the campaign was not yet over. The game of military ping-pong was about to begin again,

and Rommel was to sweep forward and re-engulf most of the territory that he had lost. For the fourth time in little more than a year the unhappy bewildered inhabitants of Cyrenaica were to change their masters yet again.

Meanwhile isolated Axis garrisons were holding out behind the British front, awaiting the return of the Afrika Korps. The war had swept past Sollum and Halfaya, some 500 miles from El Agheila. But the men there, and at half-a-dozen other outposts between Capuzzo and Halfaya were of considerable nuisance value. Straddling the coast road they compelled the Eighth Army's supply columns to make a depressing detour south along desert tracks which sorely tried the springs of vehicles and the physical endurance of the drivers.

In Bardia Generalmajor Artur Schmitt commanded a combined force of about 8000 men – 2200 of them Germans, cut off during the retreat. Apart from a company of the 104th Infantry Regiment (the rest of the regiment being at Halfaya) and two composite Afrika Korps battalions whose tanks and vehicles had broken down, most of the Germans were not from 'teeth' units. The Italians on the other hand were nearly all front-line soldiers and in addition to a collection of individuals from three infantry regiments, there was a machine-gun battalion, a company of light tanks – the 'mobile coffins', and a large contingent of gunners. Indeed Bardia's 19-mile long perimeter was bristling with artillery. This included some 155mm German field pieces as well as an Italian naval battery of 105s, and for anti-tank protection 14 anti-tank guns had been positioned in concrete emplacements to cover every avenue of approach. Mines and entanglements embodying hundreds of miles of barbed wire girdled the

DAK men with an 34s.

Staff officers prepare battle plans.

entire perimeter. Unlike most of the other isolated garrisons Bardia's defenders had plenty of water, plenty of food, plenty of petrol and ammunition and until the British decided they must be eliminated anything they needed urgently came by plane from Crete. Bardia itself – one street of single-storey sun-bleached ruins tottering on the brink of a cliff above a tiny harbour, was really of little strategic significance militarily. Nevertheless it was a thorn in the enemy's side. Troops of the 2nd South African Division had tried to capture it on 16 December, but they were repulsed and it was the end of December before they tried again. By then the weather was appalling. As preparations for the attack went ahead between 27 and 30 December blinding choking duststorms alternated with squalls of rain during the days and the nights were bitterly cold. It was obvious that something was about to break and during the afternoon of 28 December Schmitt signalled Panzergruppe HQ, to report that the British had been shelling the town and harbour continuously since 0800 hours that morning. This, in fact, was only the beginning of the softening up process. Worse was to come; airraids on Bardia were stepped up and on 30 December a British warship stationed off the coast added its guns to the thunder of the landward barrage.

'Michael of Augustusburg', mascot of the Afrika Korps with his personal attendant.

The South Africans attacked at 0600 hours on New Year's Eve. It was bitterly cold and a biting wind was driving in from the sea as the troops moved up to their start line. Off shore the British cruiser *Ajax* – remembered best for her role in the epic action against *Graf Spee* – was steering towards the coast with four destroyers to bombard Schmitt's positions. Throughout the night, working in the cold and dark, sappers on the south-western side of the perimeter had been carving corridors through to the perimeter defences for tanks of the 1st British Tank Brigade to go in. Worming their way through the harsh prickly camel scrub, dragging tools and explosives with them, they had blown in the sides of the anti-tank ditch, levelled shallow causeways for the tanks and opened gateways in the line of barbed wire entanglements. Then they had made safe paths through the minefields. By first light everything was ready and the tanks clattered forward followed by two battalions of South African infantry. Meanwhile north-west of the town more South Africans were creating a noisy feint to draw off Schmitt's artillery fire. The diversion worked, for while the British tanks were crashing through the perimeter in the south-east, Schmitt was rushing guns and troops in the opposite direction to counter the menace there. Many shells were expended by bewildered gunners who directed salvo after salvo on to rows of empty petrol tins, which the South Africans had laid out in front of the perimeter during the night and whose sole purpose the defenders failed to appreciate was to draw their attention away from where things were really happening. Meantime the assault force in the south was systematically clearing strongpoints and moving towards the town. Within an hour the perimeter had been punctured; the South Africans had achieved their initial objective and there came a lull, for the next phase of their attack was scheduled for dusk. In this interval an incipient sand storm began to blow in fierce cruel gusts.

As soon as he discovered that the assault in the north was a feint Schmitt reacted skilfully. Everything was swung round and rushed to the south-east again. First, every available gun and all the men he could muster were flung into building an impromptu defensive line to stem the enemy's advance from the south-east. Then, under cover of a formidable artillery barrage, Schmitt hit back with a counter-attack. The garrison's only two 88s had been dragged to the new line and their shells ripped through the armour of the British Matildas. Within minutes eight of the British tanks caught fire and exploded, and Schmitt's men were able to advance and recover some of the strongpoints which had been lost. The sandstorm was still raging, but the Germans and Italians continued to hammer the South Africans with every sort of weapon, while Panzergrenadiers supported by Afrika Korps armoured cars which blasted a passage with their automatic cannons in an attempt to get round behind the South Africans. Steadily the South Africans were forced to give ground and when they had been pushed back almost to the edge of the old perimeter it was decided to postpone the night attack which was to consolidate their earlier success.

There was little fighting during the night. Both sides, huddled in greatcoats, sought shelter in their trenches while icy rain swept across the stony plain. At first light 1 January 1942 was bleak and raw, and another violent sandstorm raged throughout the day; when this blew itself out the icy rain returned. Despite the weather, however, both sides tried to consolidate their position, while the Axis gunners exchanged fire with their South African counterparts. During the morning Allied planes bombed Bardia, and Schmitt sent another signal to Panzergruppe HQ: 'The enemy has resumed his attack. I cannot hold out much longer without reinforcements,' he said. But if German airborne troops and anti-tank weapons were flown in from Crete, he thought the garrison might be able to hold out. The problem was to stop the British tanks, and the only serviceable weapons remaining to do this was a single 5cm anti-tank gun and an 88.

Panzergruppe HQ replied curtly. There were no German airborne troops available, Bardia was beyond the range of aircraft operating from Crete, and it was regretted that no air support would be forthcoming because of the bad weather. The message ended with a query as to why Schmitt could not use his field artillery in an anti-tank role. To this Schmitt replied with equivalent curtness. His guns could not be moved and they were fully engaged on other tasks.

At 2200 hours (on 1 January) the South Africans returned to the attack and Bardia's defences were smothered in a thunderous artillery barrage. Above and between this background of exploding shells, however, a more ominous noise emerged – the clatter of tracks and the high pitched whine of tank engines. For psychological effect the Matildas' exhausts had been removed and they were making all the noise they could. Schmitt's anti-tank guns went quickly into action, but the tanks surged ahead with the South African infantry following closely behind. The Italians and the Afrika Korps men fought with great tenacity and the South Africans had to struggle for every yard of ground and storm every position they took. But they were gaining ground, and Schmitt knew that Bardia's fate was sealed. Shortly after 1300 hours in the morning (2 January) his radio tapped out a message to Rommel to tell the Afrika Korps commander that further resistance in Bardia would entail the useless sacrifice of brave men. The enemy had penetrated his defences, his ammunition and supply dumps had been overrun; the German and Italian soldiers had done their duty and he was going to send a *parlementaire* to negotiate a surrender. Meantime the senior Italian officer was wirelessing his own message to the Italian HQ at Sirte: 'We are lost; give greetings to all.' A reply to this signal came an hour later: 'Courage, we will conquer. Will not forget to send your greetings.'

Having warned Panzergruppe HQ that he proposed to surrender, Schmitt now turned to the practical implications of what this meant, and orders were issued for the destruction of the stocks of ammunition and stores that still remained. At first light the fighting died down, and when the sun rose a desolate scene was revealed. A pall of black

A badly injured British prisoner of war receives medical attention from other prisoners.

Above right: DAK men inflict heavy losses on the Eighth Army with their heavy MG 34s.
Right: A Messerschmitt Bf 110 circles over the Jebel Akhdar as it patrols the sky to shoot down British bombers.

Right: *Unloading much-needed supplies from a Junkers Ju 52 transport aircraft.*

Left: *The DAK men used binoculars to pinpoint their targets.*

smoke hung over the town and harbour and where the fighting had been fiercest the battlefield was like a combination of Dante's *Inferno* and an *abattoir*. Amid the corpses and exhausted men who had just flopped down to rest, the German Red Cross personnel were tending the wounded of both sides.

About 0700 hours a car bearing a white flag and carrying Schmitt's *parlementaires* left his headquarters and drove down the tarmac road towards the South African lines. The car was stopped at a road block and two officers got out; one was an Italian and the other a German. Both saluted when they were taken to a South African officer, Lieutenant Innes, and the Italian said in English, 'We have come from General Schmitt to see your general, as he wishes to discuss terms for the surrender of Bardia.' South Africa's Major-

General I P de Villiers, commander of the 2nd South African Division was not one to stand on ceremony, and when the two Axis emissaries were taken to him they were told that he expected Schmitt to report to him by 1000 hours or he would 'blow Bardia to pieces'.

The meeting took place on the road just inside the perimeter wire, and War Correspondent Alexander Clifford witnessed the surrender. 'Schmitt was punctual, faultlessly turned out, meticulously correct,' he wrote and continued:

> The morning was cold and blustering and the South African and German generals climbed into a station-wagon and discussed terms sitting together on the back seat. The Italian officers thrust their heads through the windows, making excited comments and suggestions, but Schmitt took not the least notice of them. He alone was surrendering Bardia. He scanned the list of conditions and accepted the lot. But he put his finger on one point and said, "It is no good my signing that – I have already given orders that everything inside the perimeter be destroyed. It's too late to stop it now." Then he drove off to pack his bag for captivity. (*Three Against Rommel* p. 216.)

After the fall of Bardia, the South Africans turned their attentions to Sollum and Halfaya. Together with several outposts – the most important being 'Cirener' (Pt 207) (so called after Oberleutnant Willi Cirener who had won the Ritterkreuz in France and was killed during the first attack on Tobruk) about five miles from the top of Halfaya, and 'Faltenbacher' (Abiar Abu Talaq) – named after the garrison commander – three miles south-west of Halfaya. The garrisons of these places controlled a semi-circle of strategically important terrain extending from the cliffs just north of Sollum to the coast about six and a quarter miles further south-east. At Halfaya Pass, important because it was the only way up the escarpment at the coast and consequently across the British supply line, about 5000 German and Italian troops had barricaded themselves into the area they had fortified in the cliffs and ravines around the Pass. The redoubtable, cigar-smoking pastor and commander of the 300th Oasis Battalion, Major Wilhelm Bach, was still in command despite his being outranked by half a dozen senior Italian officers. During November the Savona Division had pulled out of the positions it had been holding on the Egyptian frontier and part of it had settled in Halfaya. Bach, isolated and out of touch with Rommel's headquarters since the Panzers had retreated west of Tobruk, welcomed the long range wireless transmitter which the division's headquarters brought. Unfortunately a crop of new problems went with it. An Italian major-general and his staff were nuisance enough, especially as relations between the Major-General, Fedele

Left: An armoured car, which was used as a mobile firing unit.
Below: An anti-aircraft gun emplacement on the edge of an airfield.

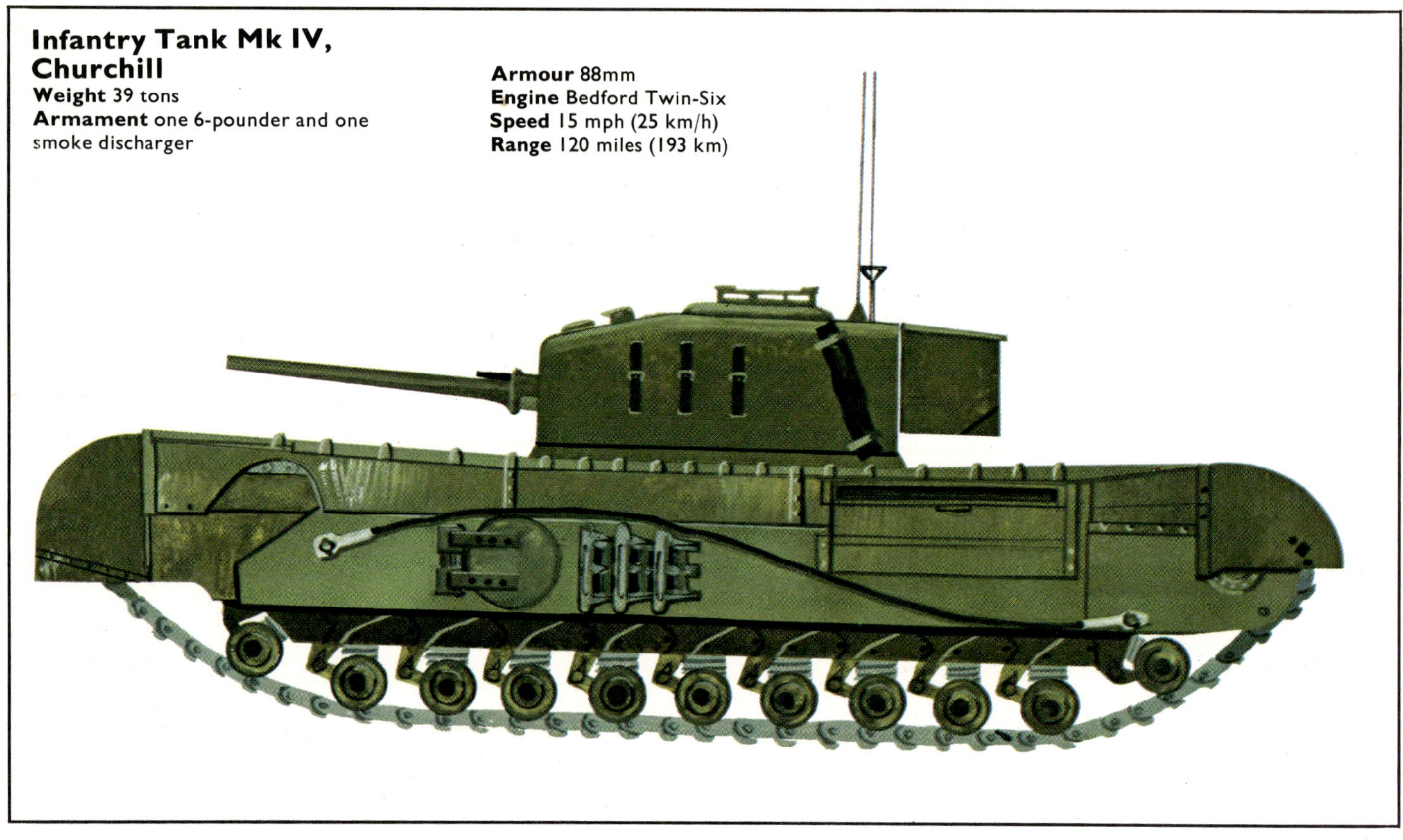

de Giorgis and Bach were not exactly cordial. More serious was the effect of the Italian influx on Halfaya's carefully hoarded supplies, since doubling the garrison also doubled the rate at which the stocks of rations were devoured. British bully beef, raisins, boiled sweets, chocolate – were dropped on the garrison by Luftwaffe transport planes flying from Crete. As the activities of RAF and SAAF fighters prevented the drops being made in daylight the planes would fly in after dark – aiming the cannisters containing the food packages at target areas ringed with tins of burning oil. No parachutes were used and many of the cannisters burst on impact, so that the amount of food which was dropped never came anywhere near the quantity that was needed to feed 5000 men on more than a starvation ration. Early in December the anti-tank gunners tried to augment the ration by shooting up a herd of gazelle which was moving up the wadis, away from the fighting towards the more peaceful desert. Men trained to kill tanks a 1000 yards away could hardly fail to kill gazelle at half the distance with 37mm weapons. But the meat which the dead animals yielded was not enough to restock Halfaya, the gazelle did not return, and the garrison was back on starvation rations. On this Halfaya diet some wag among them quipped, 'life could only be borne lying down'.

The crew of a Messerschmitt 110 prepares for a mission.

Water was in even shorter supply than food. Halfaya and Sollum's water had originally come by pipeline from Bardia and when the South Africans closed in on Bardia on 7 December they promptly cut the pipe. Subsequently, when they discovered that the section of pipe between where it had been cut at Sollum and where it terminated at Halfaya still held thousands of gallons of water, the South Africans sent out patrols to blow it up in three more places. For the garrison there were only now two alternative water points available – four '*birs*' or underground water cisterns hollowed out of the rock centuries before to collect surface water, and Fig Tree Wells. But both sources were outside Bach's defensive perimeter, and when a South African patrol discovered the *birs* on 8 December and found they contained about 80,000 gallons of water a guard was put on them. Bach's men tried to recapture the *birs*, but were unable to do so. Fig Tree Wells, the other source was near the coast just south of Sollum and when Sollum fell on 12 January the South Africans quickly seized the ground overlooking the wells. Because of this the men at Halfaya welcomed rain because it was possible to collect water in groundsheets suspended over the trenches. Efforts were also made to set up primitive distillation plants to convert seawater into a potable liquid. However this seawater possibility went when the South Africans captured Sollum, for then they lost access to the sea.

Over Christmas Bach reverted to his role of padre, going round his positions, talking of Christmas and forecasting better times ahead. 'There is always hope,' he told the troops. 'Pray, my friends; hope and sing.' Sing they did. A westerly wind wafted the refrain of *Stille Nacht, Heilige Nacht* down the Pass and the singing was heard by men of the 4th Indian Division blocking the road below.

The shelling and bombing which was now a daily feature of life at Halfaya did not stop for Christmas. But the work which Bach's men had put in digging deep trenches and scooping shelters out of the rocks paid off, and their casualties were not high. Fleas which had found homes in the dug-outs and shelters were more troublesome than high explosives, for there was no way of getting rid of them.

The South Africans attacked Sollum on 11 January, Hauptmann Ennecerus, the commander of the German garrison, had just handed out the daily ration of 200gms of bread, a handful of rice and a spoonful of currants per man when the South African artillery, mortars and machine-guns opened up. Morale among the garrison was said to be 'not high', although, if the ensuing battle is anything to go by, this does not seem to have been so. When the barrage lifted and the South African infantry moved in towards the village they immediately came under intense artillery mortar and machine-gun fire and they were pinned down in rocky terrain where digging was almost impossible. Progress was feasible only when the South African artillery put down another intense bombardment, and even then some of the South Africans were compelled to spend a bitterly cold night where they had taken cover behind the rocks.

Hauptmann Ennecerus and his men held out for 24 hours, during which they were without food and water. When they surrendered soon after 0800 hours on 12 January, they had used up all their ammunition. It had been a fiercely fought engagement, in which the South Africans suffered 100 casualties – of whom 28 were killed; in turn they had killed 30 of Ennecerus's men, captured 334 and secured a few ruined houses with a picturesque view over a sparkling blue bay. But the possession of Sollum meant that the South Africans had now drawn a complete noose around Halfaya.

Germans fill up their water cans at a supply post at Al Agheila.

With the *birs* denied to them and the pipeline from Sollum in enemy hands, the garrison at Halfaya had to rely mainly on Fig Tree Wells for water, and it had to be fought for. 'We were running short of water. Once Lower Sollum fell, the British occupied our waterhole,' one of Bach's men wrote. 'Our lips began to crack, our throats were dry. Something had to be done, and on 13 January Papa Bach ordered a Storm troop to recapture the waterhole for a short time so that we could replenish our supplies.' The task went to Leutnant Eicholz, and that night as soon as it was dark, he set off for the wells with a fighting patrol and an empty water truck. Near the wells Eichholz split the patrol into two, sending the two sections in to approach from the right and left; on the way, however, one of the German parties bumped into a South African patrol. In the darkness there was considerable confusion during which the other section of Eichholz's patrol fired into the *mêlée*, killing one of its own men and wounding another. But in the general chaos the German water truck managed to get down to the wells, fill up, and get away again. Unfortunately this was an exploit that could not be repeated. Eichholz tried again the following night, but the South Africans were waiting for him and the Afrika Korps men could not get anywhere near the wells.

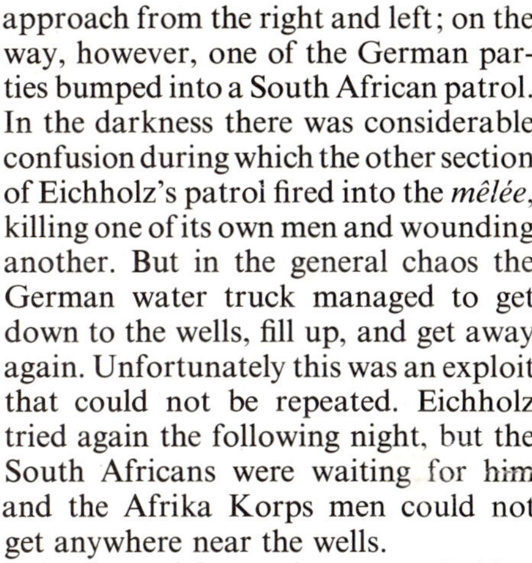

In the end it was hunger and thirst that defeated the Halfaya garrison, and there was never any need for the British to launch an attack that would almost certainly have proved costly. At 0730 hours on 17 January Colonel Martinelli, one of the senior Italian officers at Halfaya, and Hauptmann Voigt, Bach's second-in-command, crossed into the South African lines in a car flying the white flag. Surrender terms were quickly agreed and the German emissary nodded to his driver, who then changed the white flag from one side of the car to the other as a signal to the garrison to destroy their weapons. Major Bach, General de Giorgis and a posse of senior Italian officers formally surrendered at midday. Soon afterwards South African troops moved in to take over, release Allied prisoners of war who had been held at Halfaya garrison, and marshal their former captors – 2126 Germans and 3400 Italians.

Parson Bach went back with them, to point out the minefields and supervise the evacuation. (Bach was sent to a prisoner-of-war camp in Canada, where he died in 1944, and he was buried in the cemetery at Gravenhurst, Ontario.) An unfortunate incident now occurred. While the South Africans were issuing

A British forward defence line, comprising a tank ditch and minefield.

food and water and No 1 Oasis Company under Leutnant Dr Gehring was preparing to be marched off, the artillery of the Free French Brigade deployed south of the Pass opened fire and shells crashed down on them. The Free French had not been told of the surrender and having spotted movement up the Pass were making the most of the target it afforded. South Africans and Germans alike took cover, but Bach's men suffered a number of casualties before the bombardment could be stopped.

Above: Oberst Crasemann (left), shares his copy of Die Woche *with a subordinate.*
Below: Generals Crüwell (left), Bayerlein (centre) and Hauptmann von Pilsach go through their plans.
Inset: Lieutenant-General Fritz Bayerlein.

While the South Africans were tightening the noose around Halfaya General Ritchie was planning an offensive that would take the Eighth Army to Tripoli. The code name Acrobat was given to it, and the date on which it was to start was fixed as 27 January. But Rommel struck first. On 19 January he issued orders verbally for an operation which would begin two days later. It was short notice, but Rommel did not divulge his plans until the last minute for fear the Italians would veto them. Nor did he trust some of the senior German officers; by 'leaking' information to Berlin they were just as capable of provoking a veto from the High Command.

Zero hour on 21 January had been set at 1830 hours and punctually at that time two battle groups rolled across their start lines. The first – a specially constituted force, consisting of units from the 90th Light and the 21st Panzer, commanded by the able and experienced Oberst Werner Marck – advanced north-east along the Via Balbia, while the second, comprising virtually the whole of the rest of the Afrika Korps also moved off in a north-easterly direction, but straight through the desert. Behind them the Italians were left to hold the old defensive line at El Agheila. In front the British had only a thin protective screen to stop the Germans. The 2nd Armoured Brigade, supported by some armoured cars and a few 'Honey' tanks were scattered over an area covering 1875 square miles; the 200th Guards Brigade were deployed south-east of Agedabia; the 7th Indian Brigade was across the road south of Benghazi and the rest of the 4th Indian Division further north round Barce. That was all the fighting troops that Ritchie had in the area. The Eighth Army was trying to solve its supply problems, consolidate its lines of communication, and build up supply dumps in readiness for the proposed thrust into

Junkers Ju 87 Stukas fly in formation over the desert.

Tripolitania. Benghazi could not yet be used as a port, the main roads were still being repaired, heavy rains had turned the desert route to mud, many of the British vehicles were in poor condition. Thus Rommel had launched his offensive at a propitious moment, and what he may well have intended originally as a full scale tactical reconnaissance was swiftly reshaped into an offensive.

The 2nd Armoured Brigade, inexperienced and untried, was no match for the veterans of the Afrika Korps. Leutnant Heinz Schmidt who was with the Marcks Group has described the Panzers' tactics:

> We had our first skirmish with British tanks on the second day of the march [22 January]. . . . We sighted about 30 tanks stationary at the foot of a rise in hilly ground. When we received the order to attack, we were certain we had not yet been observed. We brought our 50mm anti-tank guns into position in a hollow. The enemy was totally surprised when we opened fire, and a dozen Panzers raced down against the tanks. He decided his position was untenable and pulled out hurriedly with the loss of a few tanks.
>
> We had now developed a new method of attack. With our 12 anti-tank guns we leap-frogged from one vantage-point to another, while our Panzers, stationary and hull-down, if possible, provided protective fire. Then we would establish ourselves to give them protective fire while they swept on again. The tactics worked well and, despite the liveliness of the fire, the enemy's tanks were not able to hold up our advance. He steadily sustained losses and had to give ground constantly. We could not help feeling that we were not then up against the tough and experienced opponents who had harried us so hard . . . .
>
> We were not entirely happy about our petrol position. Yet one young officer, who said to Rommel, 'Herr General, we need more fuel,' received the brisk answer: 'Well, go and get it from the British.'

The advance on the day of this action was facilitated by a blinding sandstorm which screened the Panzers from air reconnaissance and, as usual, Rommel managed to create a confused tactical picture. The initiative was firmly in the Afrika Korps' hands.

With Rommel in one of the leading vehicles the Marcks Group arrived at Agedabia at 1100 hours on 22 January, and pressed on up the Mechili track. It reached Antelat about 1530 hours and spent the rest of the daylight hours 'rommeling' (in Afrika Korps parlance) south-east towards Saunnu. Marck's Panzers had nearly bagged the whole of Godwin-Austen's corps headquarters at Antelat; they compensated for not doing so by the capture of the 2nd Armoured Brigade's supply column that night. All in all, 22 January 1942 was a good day for Rommel, for that was the day also that his command was elevated to Panzer Army and his own rank to Generaloberst.

Rommel's new status made it more easy to cope with the Italians, to whom the new offensive was as much a surprise as it was to the British. The first Bastico heard of it was on 21 January and *Comando Supremo* in Rome received a bitter signal from him protesting about the way Rommel launched operations without either consultation or permission from his superiors. Cavallero flew to Tripoli, and on 23 January the two Italian commanders and Feldmarschall Kesselring arrived at Rommel's headquarters near Mersa Brega. Rommel's diary records: 'Cavallero brought directives from the Duce for future operations. Everything indicates that Rome is anything but pleased with the Panzer Army's counter-attack, and would like to put a stop to it as soon as possible by issuing orders. During the discussion Cavallero said, "Make it no more than a sortie and then come straight back." I was not standing for this and told him I had made up my mind to keep at the enemy just as long as my troops and supplies would allow; the Panzer Army was getting under way and its first blows had struck home. We were first going to drive south and destroy the enemy south of Agedabia; then we would move east and later north-east. I could always fall back to the Mersa Brega line if things went wrong, but that was not what I was after; my aims were set much higher. Cavallero implored me not to go on with it. I told him that nobody but the Führer could change my decision, as it would be mainly German troops who would be engaged. Finally, after Kesselring had made some attempt to back him up, he went off growling.'

Kesselring's own recollections reflect some of the tension and also some of the Germans' disdain: 'I myself flew Cavallero to the conference in my Storch, as this was the only aircraft on the tarmac and Cavallero insisted on my accompanying him. The meeting was longer than expected, so that we

Rommel's mobile headquarters was affectionately known as 'Moritz' by the Afrika Korps.

had to take off on the return flight when the sun was already setting to land in the dark at El Agheila. So a General field-marshal flew the senior *Maresciallo d'Italia* over the desert in an aircraft unsuitable for night-flying and safely delivered his very suspicious passenger into the arms of his numerous generals. The *abbraci* [embracing] and *bacci* [kisses] that followed our landing are no flight of my creative imagination. . . .'

By 25 January the fighting had moved further north. On the 2nd Armoured Brigade's petrol, won from its supply column, Crüwell with the 15th Panzer swept on to Msus, an old Turkish fort sited where desert tracks converged 75 miles south-east of Benghazi. At Msus the Panzers paused while Rommel decided on his next move. There were at that moment three courses open to him: he could turn back and retire to El Agheila as the Italians wanted him to do – satisfied with the success of his reconnaissance in force; he could push on eastward to the key track junction at Mechili; or he could turn west and aim for Benghazi. Rommel had no intention of pulling back to El Agheila until he had probed all the possibilities of the situation, and although the route to Mechili appeared to be clear, he felt certain that the British would try to stop him along the track. Nor, for that matter would it be wise to advance towards Mechili with Benghazi still in British hands on his flank. Inevitably, therefore, the choice was Benghazi and another newly constituted battle group, centred on the 90th Light Division and spearheaded by the 190th Panzer Battalion, was sent off up the Via Balbia towards Benghazi. Meantime, with Rommel still in the lead, the Marck's group and the 3rd and 33rd Reconnaissance Abteilungen battered its way up a difficult track running north-west from Msus through the hills of the Jebel El Akdar range. The emergence of this

Below: Two views of Rommel's advance through the desert – an endless plain broken up by the debris of war.

force above Benina on 28 January surprised the Benghazi garrison – the surprise being the more complete because Crüwell's force had distracted the Eighth Army's attention by a fake move towards Mechili.

There was one clash with the 7th Indian Brigade south-east of Benghazi before the brigade commander decided that his men could not cope with the Panzers. Most of the Indians managed to slip away and their sappers blew up some of the more important installations in the town, but a large quantity of supplies and 1300 British lorries in perfect working order were left behind. For the Afrika Korps, both supplies and trucks were a welcome gift. 'These will keep us going for quite some time,' one 'Q' officer is reputed to have said cheerfully.

That evening Rommel moved into Benghazi and set up his headquarters in the town. There he received orders from the *Comando Supremo*:

... In the event that Benghazi should be inadequately defended by the retreating enemy and be on the point of falling, you should seize it with your reconnaissance forces alone and without calling upon the covering forces for Tripolitania. . . .

Rommel's reply was brief and to the point. The orders had been carried out to the letter, he reported, adding, 'before I had even received them.'

From Benghazi the Afrika Korps pushed on towards Derna, reaching Martuba a few miles south of it on 2 February, after brushing the 5th Indian Brigade aside. Behind the Germans the Ariete and Trieste divisions were brought up to occupy Barce and Maraua which the Eighth Army had evacuated ahead of the Panzers' advance. On the right flank Mechili was captured on 3 February, and on 5 February – a month to the day after withdrawing into Tripolitania – Rommel was able to announce that he had recaptured the entire Cyrenaica 'Bulge' and was back at Tmimi and Gazala.

But now he had to stop, for the British had done exactly what Rommel had done to them. They had withdrawn so fast that they had run the Panzers to a standstill, and the Afrika Korps now had all the problems that the British had had at El Agheila. The Germans had got Benghazi back as a supply port and they had recaptured nearly all the big Cyrenaican airfields from which the Luftwaffe could raid Egypt. More important still they had gained tremendous prestige and had humiliated the British at a time when they could ill afford to be seen in a poor light. The winter fighting, however, for the moment was over, and both sides began to prepare for the decisive battles which would come in the summer. Rommel himself was exalted. To Lu he wrote on 4 February: 'We have got Cyrenaica back. It went like greased lightning. I hope to be home in ten days time for a bit of leave . . .'

The Cauldron

By February 1942 Paris radio was pointedly referring to Cyrenaica as '*La Promenade des Anglais*'. Since August 1940 the pendulum had swung five times across the Western Desert. Its terrain was now scarred with trenches, shell-holes, ruts and rubbish and it was littered with the fire-blackened bodies of thousands of vehicles which had been brought thousands of miles. Thousands of men had died and thousands more had been led into captivity while defending it. Yet nobody appeared to have achieved anything. The truth was neither the Germans nor the British wanted the desert they were fighting for. A few thousand square miles – room enough for airfields along the Mediterranean coast – was all the British needed; the Germans did not need it at all – to Rommel it was merely terrain through which the Afrika Korps must pass on its way to the Nile. Now the pendulum had come to rest at what was probably its point of equilibrium, with the two armies symmetrically deployed. (Each side had two ports: Tobruk and Alexandria equating to Benghazi and Tripoli, each had a single tarmac road and a few hundred miles of coast. The Axis seaborne supply line was shorter than that of the British, but it was more dangerous because the British had Malta in the middle of it.)

Above: Major Brandt follows the overall situation in North Africa. Below: The German column advances on the Via Balbia. The gun is a 5cm PAK 38 which replaced the 3.7cm PAK 36.

Traditionally generals and armies rarely have a second chance to fight their battles over again. But in the Middle East it was different. Every new offensive in the Western Desert started in almost the same circumstances as the last one, but at a higher level of sophistication. So that by March 1942 certain trends and principles were beginning to emerge and it was possible to predict what would almost certainly happen in any set situation. Thus the typical desert campaign could usually be separated into two main phases. In phase one the victors would emerge after intense fighting, in which the decisive weapon would be tanks; in phase two the victors would pursue the vanquished across Cyrenaica. On three occasions – once by Graziani and twice by Rommel – the Axis troops had gone into phase three and advanced with no preliminary phase one because the British had not stayed to fight. On two occasions Wavell and Auchinleck had won phase one, but neither could pursue his opponents far enough in phase two because they outran their resources and the Axis troops were able to make a quick recovery.

Thus, during the spring of 1942 both Rommel and Auchinleck had their minds on two things: first, being able to win the opening battle when the conflict re-erupted, and secondly to be able to continue the pursuit to the bitter end. In material terms this meant tanks and supplies.

A great armaments race now started and huge quantities of war material began to accumulate on the Gazala plain. From the Ruhr, over the Alps, down through Italy and across the Mediterranean came Panzers and other equipment to reinforce the Afrika Korps. (At the beginning of March the Afrika Korps had only 139 tanks and one-third of its man-power establishment.) From Britain and North America tanks and supplies flowed in a steady stream around the Cape, up the Red Sea to Suez, to revitalise the Eighth Army. The quantities shipped by both sides would have been greater and the race consequently more intense, but for the fact that the desert campaign was subordinated to wider strategic issues. On the German side, preparations for the second summer offensive in Russia were taking precedence over Rommel's demands on behalf of the Afrika Korps because of the setback received that winter at the very gates of Moscow. But the British had their problems too, and Auchinleck started with a triple handicap. First there was the length of his supply route; secondly, Singapore had fallen on 15 February and British reinforcements originally destined for Egypt were diverted to the Far East; thirdly, there was the question of the *quality* of equipment, for it was all too evident that British tanks and anti-tank guns were inferior to those of the Afrika Korps.

For the new tanks the British had to apply to the Americans, who provided some hundreds of M-3s – known then as the 'General Lee', rechristened 'General Grant' by the British and called 'ELH' (Egypt's Last Hope) by the Eighth Army. The Grant was a heavy cumbersome leviathan, but it was better than anything else the British had in the desert if only because its 75mm gun was as powerful as that of the Mk IV Panzer. As regards anti-tank guns the Eighth Army clearly needed something bigger and better than that outmoded two-pounder, and Auchinleck was promised copious supplies of the new six-pounder which was just going into production. This, he was told, packed a deadly punch.

An improvised shower provides welcome refreshment during the dusty advance.

While he was waiting for the new equipment Auchinleck set about reorganising his army and trimming its tail. New techniques and battle drills emphasising greater cooperation between tanks, infantry, artillery and the Royal Air Force were worked out and practised. Efforts were made to simplify administration procedures and supply systems, and the now familiar Afrika Korps 'jerrycan' was officially taken into service. Unofficially for some considerable time the Eighth Army had been using these robust containers rather than the four-gallon petrol tins – those 'flimsy and ill-constructed containers' which Auchinleck reported were responsible for 30 per cent of petrol being lost between 'base and consumer.' Apart from the petrol that was wasted, supply trucks carrying them over rough terrain in the forward area became dangerously inflammable as petrol slopped out of the leaking tins.

Rommel was also busy with his reinforcements, but he had none of the British problems of new techniques and new battle drills. The doctrine he had worked out for the Afrika Korps Panzer divisions still held good; the German tanks, anti-tank artillery and fighter aircraft were still better than anything the British had in North Africa so nothing better was needed in that line either. Rommel's problem was merely that of bringing shiploads of replacements across from Europe. As the island of Malta dominated the Axis supply lines across the Mediterranean, it was intimately linked with the North African fortunes of both Afrika Korps and Eighth Army. To deal with it a formidable German-Italian air force was concentrated in Sicily and week after week Malta's airfields were reduced to a state at which it was almost impossible for aircraft to operate from them. Rommel knew that with Malta neutralised his preparations would go ahead faster than those of Auchinleck, and in the short run he would have the advantage: that was the moment of attack. In the long run, however, time was on Auchinleck's side – time to get reinforcements and equipment around the Cape of Good Hope.

At the beginning of April, Churchill, in London, urged Auchinleck to start a new offensive in the desert to ease the pressure on Malta. By the end of the month he was demanding that an offensive should be launched by the end of May; with good reason the

Well-needed supplies and new equipment, including an anti-aircraft gun (above), arrive in Tripoli.

British Prime Minister feared that the Germans might attack before then. Meanwhile Rommel and his masters were also discussing Malta. The German arguments centred on the question as to whether Rommel's plan for another offensive in the desert could ever be really viable as long as a hostile Malta lay across his Mediterranean supply route. If the answer was no, then clearly the capture of Malta should take precedence over the proposed desert campaign. In the event the outcome of a conference chaired by Hitler at Obersalzberg in late April was that Rommel would be permitted to go ahead with his offensive on the understanding that once Tobruk was taken he was to go over to the defensive while the main Axis effort was concentrated against Malta. (Two airborne divisions under command of Generalleutnant Student were to invade Malta, following an intense aerial bombardment to neutralise AA positions and coastal batteries. Hitler called off the invasion in June 1942.) With the capture of Malta supplies would flow to North Africa relatively unhindered and the Panzer Army would be able to advance to the Nile – and, eventually, on to Syria and Iraq to join hands with German armies driving

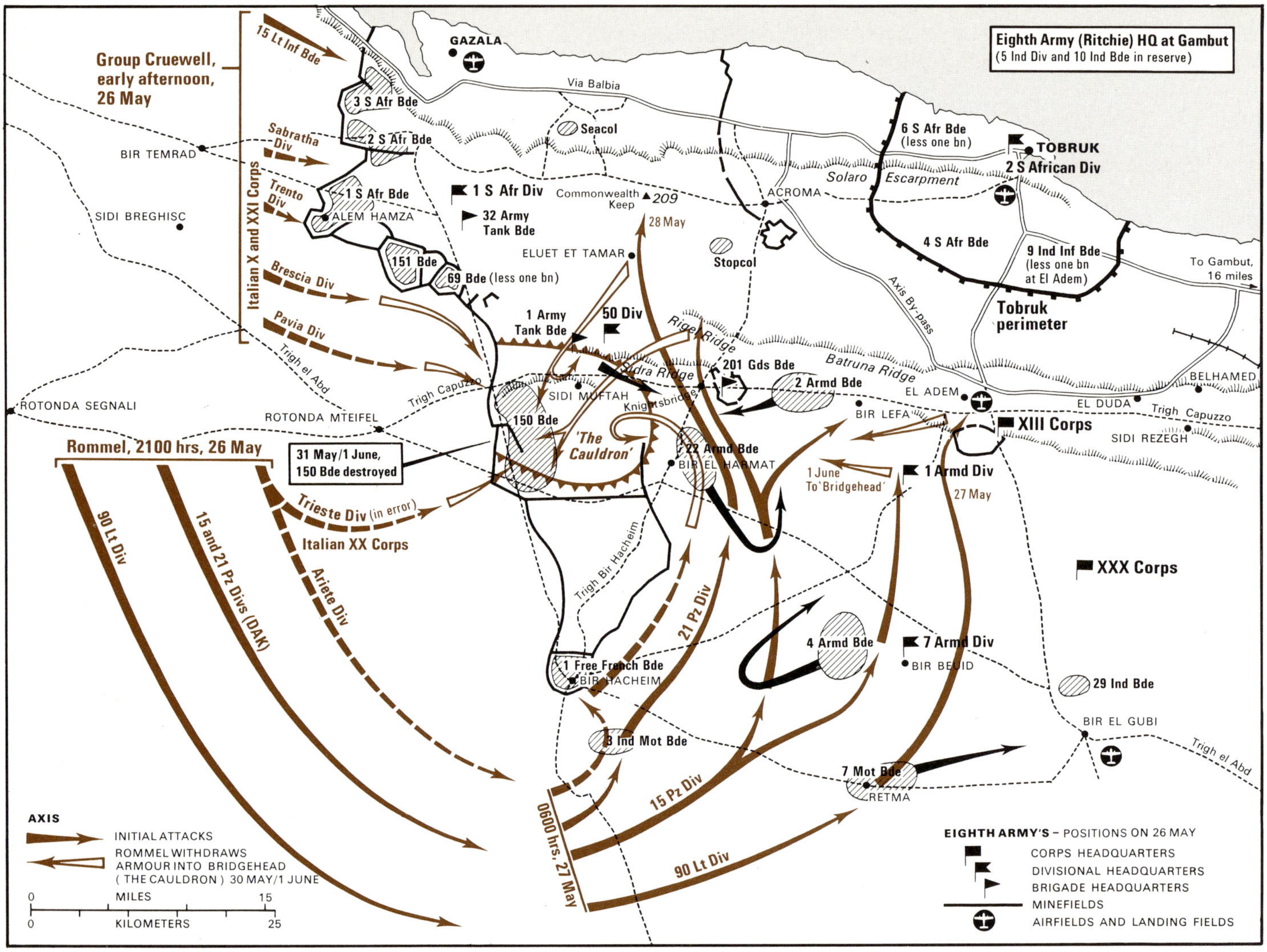

Above: The Gazala line was a series of minefields running to Bir Hacheim. Right: British POWs on the long road to the German camps.

down through the Caucasus to meet them.

Appreciating that the Eighth Army was also preparing for an offensive, Rommel was anxious to get in first without waiting for Malta to fall. But he had to conform to the great strategic plan approved by the Führer, and so the proposals he submitted for operations during early June were limited to the destruction of the British forces on the Gazala line. He added, 'the capture of Tobruk (as a continuation of the same action), possibly by a surprise attack or otherwise by means of a prompt assault.' From his proposals a relatively simple but daring plan emerged which some of those who were to carry it out were inclined to classify as simple enough but daring to the point of suicide. 'Attack at 1400 hours, in broad daylight?' Obergefreiter Bruno Preuss of the 361st Infantry Regiment is reported to have remarked, 'I don't like it. The whole thing stinks.'

Preuss's condemnation was based on what he had seen of the defences which the British had constructed when the Panzers stopped in February. Known as the Gazala line, these defences comprised a number of strongpoints – 'boxes' manned by infantry, established behind a vast carpet composed of a million mines and a thick curtain of barbed wire. From Gazala Bay the line stretched inland for some 200 miles, fading out at an old disused Bedouin well called Bir Hacheim (Dog's Well) where the entrenched Free French Brigade manned the last of the 'boxes' on the southern flank. Back behind the Eighth Army's fixed defences and slightly to the south, the British 1st and 7th Armoured Divisions waited as a mobile counter-attacking force. It was a pattern reminiscent of Waterloo, where the cavalry waited behind the squares of infantry.

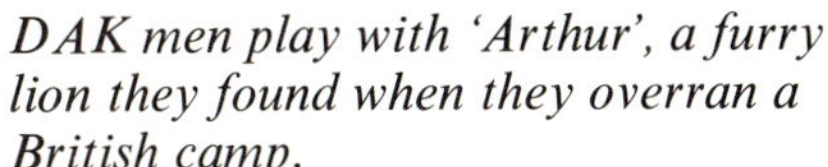

DAK men play with 'Arthur', a furry lion they found when they overran a British camp.

Auchinleck believed that Rommel had two courses open to him – to attack the Gazala line frontally, or to go round it to the south. He also reckoned that the Afrika Korps commander would almost certainly opt for a frontal attack – perhaps combined with a diversion to give the impression the real attack was coming round the Bir Hacheim flank. In the event Auchinleck's forecast proved to be wrong. Rommel chose the second course – a sweep round the desert at the southern end of the enemy line and feint attack along the 'front'.

Rommel issued his orders on 20 May. Under Crüwell's overall command, four Italian infantry divisions, Pavia, Brescia, Trento and Sabratha, and three Afrika Korps battalions of Panzergrenadiers would hurl themselves on the Gazala line at 1500 hours in the afternoon of 25 May. This was the attack which had no appeal for Obergefreiter Preuss, and the diversion which Rommel hoped would screen his real intention. He himself would move with the Afrika Korps (now under command of Generalleutnant Walter Nehring) which – with the two Italian mechanised divisions Trieste and Ariete – would set off after dark on 26 May and drive round the British left flank. Towards the limit of the British front Ariete and Trieste were to veer off eastwards, force a passage through the wire and minefields (which would ultimately serve as a shortened supply route) and bypass Bir Hacheim to the north. While the Italians were doing this the Afrika Korps would overrun the French position. Rommel was counting on a blitz decision. His troops would be carrying only three days petrol and water with them and he reckoned that this plus any stores they might capture would see them through. It was another example of his bold blitz tactics, and this was one occasion when they failed.

The battle started at midday on 26 May, when the Luftwaffe began pounding the Gazala line. A strong *khamsin* whipped up a sandstorm – generally known as *ghiblis* to the Germans – which greatly helped the Afrika Korps' preparations and concealed the initial concentration of the armoured force. Promptly at 1500 hours Crüwell's attack was launched, and the Italian and German infantry fought throughout the day without making much headway. Nor did their activity along the front draw the British armour north and away from Bir Hacheim as Rommel had hoped. Meanwhile travelling at a good speed the Afrika Korps Panzers and the two Italian divisions moved steadily south-east towards the open British flank beyond Bir Hacheim. They advanced in three great columns with the Ariete and Trieste on the left, the 21st Panzer in the middle and 15th Panzer Division on the right. The force totalled about 10,000 vehicles; armoured cars escorted by motorcyclists were in the van, a great black phalanx of tanks followed, then came the artillery, and finally the petrol and ammunition trucks. Moving with the columns also were trucks mounting aircraft engines with propellers which, roaring at full blast, created additional cover of artificial sandstorms and, hopefully, caused the enemy to believe that a vast armoured armada was descending on him.

A full moon enabled the advance to continue during the night and it was daylight (on 27 May) before the columns halted to rest for an hour some 3 miles south-east of Bir Hacheim. The three columns had been spotted long before this – at 1600 hours on the previous afternoon to be precise – and the 4th South African Armoured Car Regiment had shadowed the advance throughout the night, wirelessing hourly reports back to Eighth Army headquarters. (The first of these reports, according to the German operator monitoring the enemy's radio traffic was to the effect that the South African armoured cars had 'run into a bloody great German Panzer division'.) At one stage, in the dark and after midnight, some of the German armoured cars and motorcyclists actually drove through two of the South African squadrons without realising who they were.

During the night Rommel changed his plan and issued fresh orders to the Italians. The subjugation of the 'rebel' French at Bir Hacheim would now be done by Ariete and Trieste. 'Clean up Bir Hacheim by the day after tomorrow,' Rommel ordered. Trieste never saw Bir Hacheim; taking too much of an easterly course this division ended up facing the British box at Sidi

The 88mm anti-aircraft gun crew are ready to challenge British armour.

Muftah – one of the strongest of the whole front. But Ariete's 'mobile coffins' drove bravely at full speed towards Bir Hacheim and at about 0630 hours the Italians ran into the 3rd Indian Motor Brigade. Literally out in the open desert, having only just moved, the Indians fought with desperate fury, but they never stood a chance and after 40 minutes their resistance collapsed – and then only when Panzers from the 21st Panzer had been called in to help.

Having brushed aside the Indian regiments, the Italian column moved on to attack Bir Hacheim. The 132nd Regiment, which was the Ariete's advance guard, was commanded by a Colonel Prestissimone, a man anxious to distinguish himself in battle. Prestissimone led the initial assault which went wrong from the start. Some of the 'mobile coffins' were blown up by mines, among them Prestissimone's. Climbing on to another tank, the gallant *colonnello* rallied the rest of his force and took the lead again. When a French '75' knocked out the second tank, Prestissimone transferred to a third and charged forward again. However the third tank went up in flames when it was hit by anti-tank fire, and although Prestissimone escaped, he was taken prisoner by Foreign Legionnaires. This was enough for the Italians and the Ariete turned away leaving 32 of their mobile coffins on the battlefield.

Rommel had changed his plan to give the Afrika Korps more latitude in the sweep around Bir Hacheim. Unaware of the difficulties the Italians were experiencing, the armoured columns pressed on. The 90th Light on the right was the first into action. About 0730 hours the 90th ran up against the motor brigade of the British 7th Armoured Division, scattered it and continued on towards the objective which Rommel had set, El Adem. Half-way there armoured cars of the 90th fell on the headquarters of the 7th Armoured Division and captured the divisional commander and three other officers. (The divisional commander was Major-General Frank Messervy, a man des-

tined to play a decisive role against the Japanese in Burma. Ripping off his badges of rank, Messervy told his captors he was a batman. 'What a bloody war this is,' the German doctor dressing Messervy's 'officer' (in reality one of his staff) said to Messervy. 'Thank God I'll be out of it in a month or so as nobody serves in the DAK over 33.' Then, looking more closely at Messervy he said, 'But you must be a good deal older than that. What are you doing in the desert?' Messervy replied with an ingratiating grin, 'Well, you see, sir, I'm an old soldier who joined up again for this. Of course I'm not much use, so they made me a batman.' Messervy and his companions escaped that afternoon and after two days walking through the desert got back to the British lines.

Meantime the 15th Panzer had clashed with the British 4th Armoured Brigade and forced it to withdraw to El Adem, pursued by the 90th Light. As the 15th and 21st Panzer resumed their advance north across the Trigh el Abd towards Tobruk, another little drama was taking place on their right flank.

Among the reinforcements the Afrika Korps received during April was the unit known as the 288th *Sonder-Verband* (literally 'Special Force'). Formed for service in Iraq it had originally been composed largely of scientists and technicians detailed to resolve scorched earth and other problems in the oil fields in the event of a German victory. As the likelihood of this happening receded and the Wehrmacht was scraping the bottom of the manpower barrel, the 288th Sonder-Verband was an obvious choice for service with Afrika Korps. Shorn of its scientists and most of its technicians it was thought that the unit could perform a useful function with Rommel's Panzers, especially as it had an unusually high number of powerful wireless sets and highly-trained operators to man them and interpreters. On arrival at Tripoli a

detachment of the 288th was sent up to Rommel and in the current operation it moved with the advance guard of the 90th Light. Its job was to monitor the enemy's radio traffic, and when one of its vehicles was captured by the 4th South African Armoured Car Regiment near Bir el Gubi, the German wireless was found to be tuned to the regiment's frequency.

Had it not been for their truck breaking down, it is unlikely that the detachment would have been taken prisoner. The vehicle concerned was a Citröen 3-tonner – a lorry which had never been intended for use in desert terrain. Bouncing along trying to keep up with the armoured cars of the 90th Light, the sump was damaged and it was clear that the vehicle could not continue until a new one was fitted and the oil which had leaked out replaced. The men in the truck waited, hoping that a recovery vehicle would show up. But nobody came; they were alone in the desert. Realising that they were on their own, one of the *unteroffiziers* in the party volunteered to seek assistance; so, carrying half a jerrycan of water, he set off towards the coast, 50 miles or so from where the truck had broken down. Two days later, the *unteroffizier*, half dead with thirst, was picked up by a German patrol and taken to Rommel's headquarters. A replacement oil sump was produced and he was flown in a Storch to where he had left the truck and the rest of the detachment. The pilot had some difficulty locating the spot; according to the *unteroffizier* '. . . everything looks different from the air'. When at last they spotted it the two men in the Storch were just in time to watch the crews of a couple of South African armoured cars hustling the luckless Germans towards the enemy vehicles and setting fire to their Citröen.

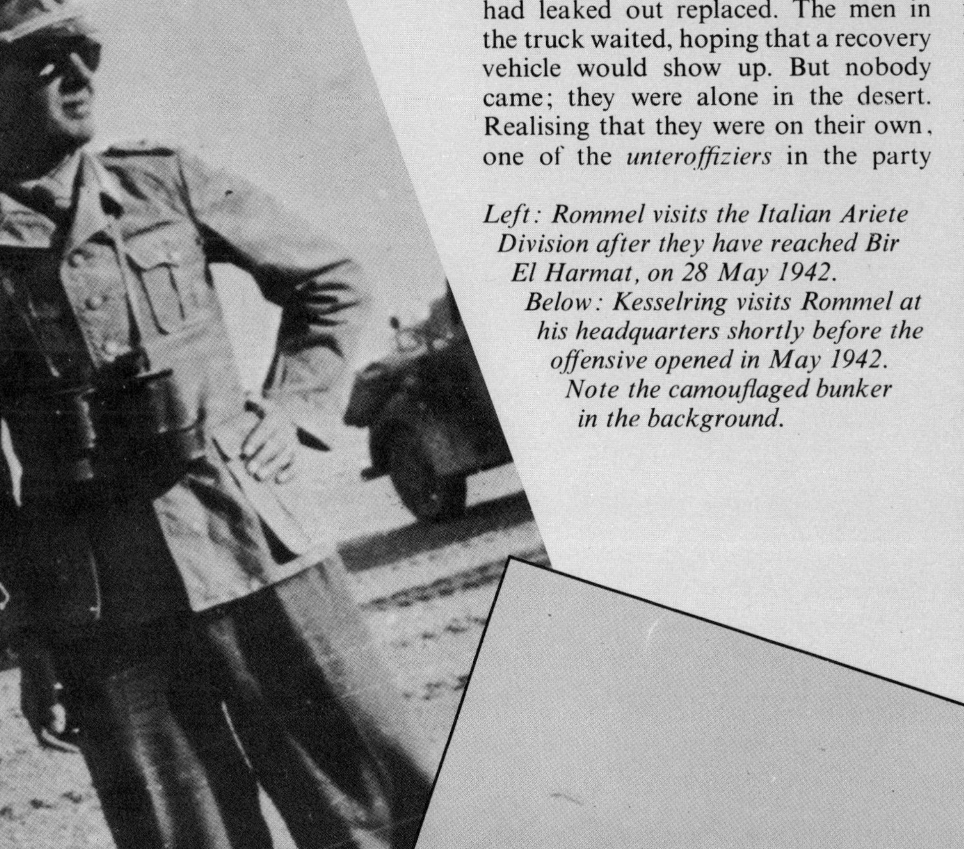

Left: Rommel visits the Italian Ariete Division after they have reached Bir El Harmat, on 28 May 1942.

Below: Kesselring visits Rommel at his headquarters shortly before the offensive opened in May 1942. Note the camouflaged bunker in the background.

Things started to go wrong for the Afrika Korps around mid-day (27), and neither of the two Panzer divisions achieved their objectives. The 21st Panzer was going for Knightsbridge, a fortified rectangular compound surrounded with barbed wire and minefields which the British had planned would be the pivot of their defence; the 15th Panzer was aiming for the airfield at El Adem where it was to link up with the 90th Light. But British tanks intervened. Unaware of what had happened to the brigades of the 1st Armoured Division, Lieutenant General Norrie ordered the 2nd and 22nd Armoured Brigades into action. Both were equipped with American Grants, and although their crews had not had time to fully master the new tanks, their performance was to give the Germans a nasty shock. Although Rommel had included a description and the specifications of a Grant in his operation orders for 20 May 1942, in his *Krieg ohne Hass*, he stated that: 'The appearance of the Grant was an unpleasant surprise.'

The two brigades had been standing by in battle formation on the plateau overlooking Knightsbridge since 0500 hours. It was almost noon when the Panzers came over the horizon and rolled cautiously forward on to the plain. The Grant squadrons had been told to hold their fire until the Panzers were within a thousand yards or had halted. When they did fire the effect was shattering. Mk IV Panzers whose armour had been impervious to the shot and shell of the undergunned British tanks in the tank battles of the previous winter shuddered, reared and exploded in sheets of red flame when they were hit by the 75mm armour-piercing shells of the Grants. Several Mk IVs were hit. Shocked into adopting more cautious tactics the rest of the Panzers deployed in hull-down positions and the battle for Knightsbridge degenerated into a duel – a contest of guns, gunners and armour. A battalion of the 115th Panzergrenadier Regiment motored up to the plateau and its 50mm anti-tank guns were quickly deployed to support the Panzers. When they opened fire, it was the turn of the anti-tank gunners to receive a jolt. According to Leutnant Helmut Schmidt the first shot from one of his 50mm Pak – short for *Panzerabwehrkanone* (anti-tank gun) – simply bounced harmlessly off one of the Grants. Another shot did score a hit, striking the Grant on the engine cover. The engine caught fire. But, before it exploded, the Grant had time to get off another shell, and this one was high explosive. The guns of the ordinary British 'I' tanks could not fire HE, while to the Afrika Korps infantry the HE shells of the Grants 75s were lethal.

General de Stephanie, commander of the Ariete Division

With their new leviathans, the odds seemed to be weighed in favour of the British. In fact it was not so, for the majority of the British tanks were still the old Matildas and Honeys equipped with two pounders. Furthermore the Grant's guns had practically no traverse and were mounted so low that they could not be used hull-down. The first engagement lasted about an hour and at the end of it the 15th Panzer broke off, moved northwards to lay up in a defensive position below the Rigel Ridge, and von Vaerst reported, 'Fuel exhausted. Protection requested from the 21st Panzer.' The 21st Panzer on the left, not having suffered so many casualties, was in a better state than its sister division. (On the morning of 28 May, the 15th Panzer had only 15 battleworthy tanks, but the 21st Panzer was able to deploy 80.) When the 15th Panzer appealed for protection von Bismarck's tanks were only about 12½ miles from Commonwealth Keep – an important Eighth Army supply depot. But the division halted and pulled back in response to von Vaerst's appeal, and the two divisions laagered for the night between Rigel Ridge and Bir Lefa. Not until the two divisions were actually in contact was the extent apparent of the hammering to which the 21st Panzer Panzers had been subjected. Apart from the heavy losses in tanks Oberst Roske, commanding the 115th Panzergrenadier Regiment, had been taken prisoner and a third of his regiment had been killed, or wounded, or captured. Coming on top of a report that Gause had been wounded this was more bad news for Rommel, who had spent the day, as usual, rushing around the battlefield. The 90th Light had also run into trouble with the Grants and been forced back south of El Adem where Nehring (who was with Ulrich Kleeman, the Commander of the 90th Light) and Oberst Alwin Wolz of the 135th AA Regiment had organised a belt of anti-aircraft guns in a 'Flak Front' through which even the Grants could not punch a hole. The 90th Light was out of touch with Rommel and most of the afternoon the latter had been trying to contact Kleeman and Nehring. British tanks and armoured cars had stopped him – he was almost captured; and at dusk the Afrika Korps supply column for all three divisions were held back. (During the afternoon Rommel vented his frustration on an unfortunate *feldwebel* whose Panzer was intercepted by the Commander of the Panzer Army. The tank had been slightly damaged in action, but the *feldwebel* had decided it needed workshop attention. Rommel considered it was still capable of fighting, and after dressing down the feldwebel in Swabian – the dialect into which Rommel usually lapsed when he was excited – rumour had it that he kicked the *feldwebel* in the backside and at pistol point ordered him back to his company.)

Rommel's orders for the following day, 28 May, were as follows: that Crüwell should continue his frontal attacks on the Gazala line; the Trieste Division which had gone off course during the advance the day before should persist with its attempts to force a passage through the minefields north of Bir Hacheim – and that the Afrika Korps should renew its push northwards to cut off the British in the Gazala line. For this purpose the 90th Light would forget about El Adem and move west to join the 15th and the 21st Panzer. However, with the fuel tanks of the 15th Panzer dry, and the Afrika Korps supply columns harrassed by British and South African armoured cars, the upshot was that the 21st Panzer had to move alone. Skirmishing and attacking throughout the morning, the division eventually reached the last escarpment overlooking the sea. But it was isolated and short of ammunition. Petrol and food were not such a problem because the 39th Panzerjäger Regiment had succeeded in capturing the Commonwealth Keep with its horde of Eighth Army supplies.

But the Panzers had not gone anywhere near fulfilling Rommel's hopes of penetration and destruction that day. He himself was often harried as he drove across the battlefield. Crüwell, in an attempt to find the Panzer Army commander by flying over the Gazala minefield in a Storch, was shot down and captured. Counting Gause, this meant that two senior officers in key positions had to be replaced in mid battle. The loss of Crüwell – a realist and an energetic leader – was particularly galling.

Nightfall on 27 May probably found the British more satisfied than Rommel with the day's developments, and to General Ritchie it seemed as if Eighth Army was about to enjoy a triumph. Rommel's thrust had been parried, Bir Hacheim and most of the infantry positions along the whole Gazala line had stood firm, and the sharp edge of the Afrika Korps' teeth had been blunted by the Grants and 6 pounders; indeed it was clear that while the Free French remained active and aggressive in Bir Hacheim the flow of supplies round the south of the Gazala line would be uncertain.

Major Otto, Chief Quartermaster of the Panzer Armée Afrika.

There was a full moon on the night of 28–29 May, and Rommel set off personally to find the supply columns without which his Panzers could not fight. While driving about during the day, he had spotted a gap in the ring encircling the Afrika Korps. Driving through this gap he found the petrol, ammunition, water and food his troops lacked and led them back to where the 21st Panzer, the 90th Light and Ariete had concentrated around the 15th Panzer. (Generalmajor Gustav von Vaerst, the commander of the 15th Panzer was wounded near Sidi Muftah (Gott el Ualeb) during the fighting on 28 May, when his Mk IV Panzer was hit by a shell from a Grant; his place was taken temporarily by Oberst Eduard Crasemann, the commander of the 33rd Panzer Artillery Regiment.) This replenishment ensured the Afrika Korps could fight one more day; after that it depended on whether a supply column could get through a second time, and if Ritchie had concentrated the 90 Matildas and 240 medium tanks which he had available that day and directed them first against one or other of the two Panzer divisions and then against the remainder the Afrika Korps would almost certainly have been destroyed. But Ritchie waited for Rommel to move first, and with an opponent like Erwin Rommel it was a disastrous thing to do. Things had gone badly for the Afrika Korps – Rommel found the situation 'unfavourable' – but time was to show that it was still capable of inflicting a shattering reverse on the Eighth Army.

To Rommel the best way of extricating the Afrika Korps from the unfortunate predicament they were in seemed to be by bursting through the Gazala front from the rear, and all his efforts during the next two days were devoted to this end.

The first thing to do was to try to open a gap in the minefields, and so at first light on the morning of 29 May the Sabratha Division was hurled against the northern end of the British line. The attack was a dismal failure; the Italians advanced bravely enough, but they were mown down by machine-gun fire and the assault fizzled out within an hour. Further south, however, Italian sappers had succeeded in breaching the minefields north of the Trigh Capuzzo and on the Trigh el Abd. This meant two paths had been opened between the Italians on one side of the Gazala line and the Afrika Korps behind it. Because they ran close to a strong British defensive position manned by the 150th Brigade they were exposed and hazardous routes. Nevertheless they gave Rommel an opportunity to restore his supply lines, and were to be of inestimable value when the Afrika Korps withdrew to Sidi Muftah on 30 May.

Meanwhile, back at Crüwell's old headquarters in the rear of the Italians, Major F von Mellenthin was in temporary control, when Feldmarschall Kesselring appeared – demanding to know how the battle was going. After telling Kesselring that Crüwell had been captured, von Mellenthin respectfully suggested that he, Kesselring, should assume command. Kesselring laughed and commented that as a Field Marshal he could hardly be expected to take orders from a commanding general. However, when von Mellenthin pointed out that it would not suit the Afrika Korps, or Germany for that matter, to have an Italian general take over Crüwell's responsibilities at this juncture – (the *Comando Supremo* had intended to appoint General Navarrini) Kesselring agreed to take over for a few days.

Early in the morning of 30 May the 5th Panzer Regiment tried to open up the two paths through the minefields west of Sidi Muftah. But the Panzers could not break through. The Brigade sup-

Generalleutnant Nehring.

ported by Matildas of the 44th Royal Tank Regiment were too firmly entrenched between the two lanes created by the Italians, and when eleven Panzers had been destroyed the 5th Panzer broke off the action and pulled back. For the Panzer Army the situation was now as critical as it had ever been, and Rommel knew that his force faced certain annihilation unless he could clear the two paths and open his supply lanes. Fortunately for the Afrika Korps the British had made no concerted attack so far, for the Panzers were now extremely short of ammunition and they would have been hard put to repulse it. (In fact an attack by the 2nd and 22nd Armoured Brigades was ordered during the morning, but it was called off when a number of British tanks were knocked

Above: Graves at Sidi Muftah. Below: The advance to Bir Hacheim.

out by Alwin Wolz's 88s.) During the morning Rommel, accompanied by Siegfried Westphal drove through the minefields in an armoured personnel carrier to confer with Kesselring. It was a hazardous trip during which their vehicle and the escorting armoured car which followed came under intense artillery and mortar fire. Westphal, who was travelling in the back of the personnel carrier – and who was barely on speaking terms with Rommel following a difference of opinion as to what the Afrika Korps should do next – was hit in the leg by a shell splinter and blown clean out of the vehicle. Rommel's vehicle did not stop, but Westphal was picked up by the escort travelling behind. Through the minefield as far as Kesselring's headquarters was a nightmare journey even when the shelling stopped, and when the party met Kesselring von Mellenthin proposed that Westphal should be flown back to the base hospital in Derna in a Storch. Westphal refused; the memory of what happened to Crüwell less than 48 hours before was still fresh in his mind. He was accordingly put into an ambulance to rattle back across a rough track to the Via Balbia and thence to Derna. Once he had arrived in Derna, the wretched Westphal was in such a state that the medical orderlies carrying his stretcher from the ambulance judged him to be at death's door. But Westphal had enough stamina to protest against his being placed in the ward next to the mortuary, reserved for terminal patients. Finally, therefore, he was given a bed in a room occupied by a young Afrika Korps soldier whose right arm had been amputated that morning, and who – while coming round from the anaesthetic – murmured time and time again, 'All because of Tobruk. . . .' It was a phrase which Westphal was never to forget.

Back once more with the Afrika Korps Rommel hurled the whole of his Panzer force against the 150th Brigade 'box'. The British infantry who fought gallantly put up a stubborn resistance, and no relief was forthcoming from the rest of the Eighth Army. The 4th Armoured Brigade hared off after some Panzers which someone had reported as being towed away, while a squadron of the South African armoured cars chased a

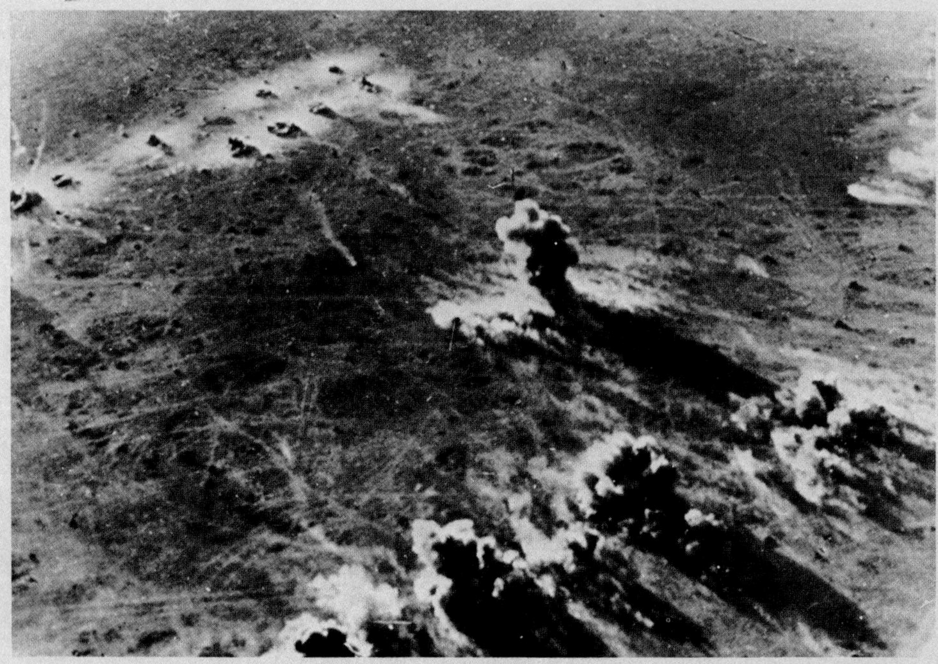

German bombers hit British tanks and motor vehicles in the vicinity of El Adem.

solitary 'tank' which turned out to be a *Sturmgeschütz* (Assault gun) in the charge of a young Afrika Korps officer, new to the desert and completely lost. Units of the 2nd and 22nd Armoured Brigades did try to break up Rommel's concentration of armour, but they never attempted to do so in concert. Among the British tank crews there were many instances of great personal gallantry, some of which were recorded, but most unseen and unsung. Clearly the British armoured force lacked leadership; it needed a Guderian or a Rommel.

By 1 June when the British 150th Brigade had expended all its ammunition, resistance collapsed and 3000 men from Britain's northern counties marched into captivity. The Afrika Korps had torn a great hole in the Gazala Line, and had earned a reprieve after tottering on the brink of disaster. That night Rommel found time to dash off a note to his wife: 'The battle is going favourably to us. . . . About 400 tanks have been shot up. Our losses are bearable. . . .'

Once again Rommel was dictating the moves, and the British response was slow, inelastic and unimaginative. Logically the next phase of the battle should have been a British counter-attack, but as, in von Mellenthin's words, 'it seemed to be very long in coming,' Rommel turned his attention to Bir Hacheim. 'What we need is a cauldron,' the Panzer Army commander declared at a conference of his senior commanders. The rest of the 'O' group looked puzzled, and Rommel explained. 'You will recall von Schwerin's attack on Mechili last year. He managed to create a whirlpool of Panzers which sucked in the enemy forces. Disorganised and disorientated they were forced to fight a battle they could not hope to win. That's what I am going to try to do here. Knightsbridge,' he said pointing to the map, 'will be our Cauldron.'

Responsibility for creating this armoured whirlpool was delegated to the two Panzer divisions, while the 90th Light-Hearted (as the Germans were now calling the 90th Light) and the Trieste Divisions moved south to reduce the now isolated French stronghold at Bir Hacheim. But the elimination of General Koenig's 3600 Free Frenchmen proved to be more difficult than expected, and the French were to earn the admiration of friend and foe alike in an epic stand. (During which they had as much help from the Eighth Army as the 150th Brigade had had in its battle.)

The situation at Bir Hacheim may be likened to a target with the French in the centre forming a bullseye, surrounded first by an inner ring of German and Italian troops, and then by an outer ring of British mobile troops harrassing Rommel's men in the rear. From the beginning it was clear that the French were determined to hold out, come what may. Pride and sheer French stubbornness were largely responsible for this determination.

An early attempt to persuade the garrison to surrender failed when General Koenig rejected an ultimatum presented by two German emissaries sent in to Bir Hacheim under a flag of truce. 'There's no question of surrender,' Koenig said. 'We shall fight on.' As the Luftwaffe had been giving Bir Hacheim an unparalleled battering since the start of the Gazala battle which apparently had not affected French morale, Rommel grudgingly accepted that Koenig meant what he said. 'I don't understand it,' Rommel growled, 'the position is lost anyway. And the British won't bail them out. . . . The British are always the same, they leave the most difficult jobs to others.'

By 8 June, however, when Rommel moved a battle group from the 15th Panzer south to join the 50th Light, it was becoming clear that the French could not hold out much longer. They were down to a 'quart' of water per man per day – and a French quart means a mere mugful. The effects of the hammering they had taken from the Luftwaffe in the air and the Afrika Korps on the ground were becoming apparent. Morally and spiritually most of the garrison may have been prepared to fight on as their commander said. Nevertheless wireless messages asking for permission to surrender were transmitted on the wavelength used by the garrison – although the French have always maintained that these were put out by the Germans. Gradually the pitch of the fighting crescendoed, and on 10 June 124 Stukas and 76 Ju 88s escorted by 170 Me 109s dropped 131 tons of bombs on French positions. That same

The despondent and anxious faces of British POWs.

evening men of Oberst Ernst-Günter Baade's 115th Panzergrenadier Regiment and some Alpine troops broke through the French perimeter and, since the British had made no significant effort to help them – as Rommel had predicted would be the case – Koenig decided his men would try to fight their way out.

Right up to the last minute they tried to maintain the impression that they would fight on to the last man and the last round. Meantime Koenig was forming up his vehicles in a huge square, with guns and prisoners in the middle. Then at 2300 hours on 10 June they marched out. Men of the 90th Light and the Trieste in the forward areas knew or guessed what was happening; in consequence the French had to run a gauntlet of shells and mortar bombs and some of their vehicles ran into a spot where they were caught in cross-fire from four directions. In spite of the losses caused by such incidents 2700 of the original 3600 defenders managed to get away. Most important of all – the fall of Bir Hacheim meant that the Gazala line was finished.

While the 90th Light and Trieste were occupied at Bir Hacheim the cauldron was beginning to bubble and seethe. By attacking the Panzer divisions and Ariete near Bir Hacheim Ritchie hoped to smash Rommel's offensive and liquidate the greater part of his forces. The first phase of this attack opened just before 0300 hours on the morning of 5 June, with an unusually heavy artillery barrage. Rommel and his staff at Panzer Army HQ watched as the sky to the east blazed with flashes. It was apparent that the British had launched an offensive, and they waited anxiously for the first reports on what was happening. But there was no need to worry. The 15th Panzer said they thought it was the 21st Panzer at the receiving end of the shells; the 21st Panzer said they thought they were falling on the 15th Panzer; and Ariete reported that if the bombardment was meant for the Italians the shells were falling well short of their target. The fact is that the barrage which was to have softened up Ariete for an attack by men of the 10th Indian Infantry Brigade was wasted on empty desert.

The Indians attacked at dawn, and in their first rush they hustled the Italians back, pushing them towards the centre of the Cauldron. Behind the Indians came the tanks of the 22nd Armoured Brigade, and these drove straight into a phalanx of anti-tank guns. After suffering considerable losses the tanks withdrew, leaving the Indians to fend for themselves. It was then the turn of the two Panzer divisions to strike which they did by first encircling the Indians and then systematically killing or capturing them. When the battle ended on 6 June the Afrika Korps alone had captured 3100 prisoners and over a hundred guns; the 10th Brigade and four regiments of field artillery were no more; the 9th Indian Brigade had suffered extremely heavy casualties – and more than a hundred British tanks had been knocked out. In sum the Eighth Army's attempt to liquidate Rommel's troops at the Cauldron had precipitated a disaster for the British.

Once Bir Hacheim had been safely disposed of, Rommel was able to turn back to the Cauldron and within hours of the fall of the French strongpoint his Panzers were on the warpath heading towards Knightsbridge. Stukas and artillery bombed and bombarded the Knightsbridge 'box' during the late afternoon of 11 June, and the 21st Panzer attacked the British positions north of the Cauldron about the same time. Meantime the 15th Panzer, with the 90th Light on the right and Trieste on the left, was driving fast through the desert, swinging in a huge arc upwards around the Cauldron. By nightfall the 15th Panzer had reached Nadunet el Ghescevasc south-west of El Adem, and the 90th Light a few miles away was positioned due south of El Adem. Rommel had returned to his original plan of a thrust against El Adem and Tobruk.

His decision to do so had no doubt been partially influenced by reports from the Afrika Korps' wireless intercept unit, whose work was eased by British commanders habitually discussing tactical moves and plans 'in clear' over the air. A well-travelled ex-representative of a Flensburg shipping company who spoke perfect English and who could talk in the clipped laconic fashion affected by British armoured corps officers was employed on occasions to chip in on conversations – or even to start them. It was reckoned that he succeeded in sending units up to divisional strength off on wild-goose chases. On 11 June however, there was no need to use the Flensburg dummy. Messages between General Messervy and his two brigadiers, disputing Messervy's orders that their brigades (2nd and 4th) should move south to Bir el Gubi from where they could operate against the flank of a German advance, were intercepted and passed to Rommel. Armed with this information Rommel ordered the 15th Panzer to stand fast on 12 June, while the 21st Panzer swung round south of Knightsbridge to take Messervy's armour in the rear.

The battle of 12 June developed slowly. In a raging sandstorm the British were trying to regroup and the whole area south and west of Tobruk was in a state of fluid ferment. A move against the El Adem box by a battle group of the 90th Light added to the confusion. The Indians defending El Adem fought stubbornly, while the Panzers and Panzergrenadiers appeared to be in real trouble when Royal Air Force and South African Air Force planes struck at them. A wirelessed SOS claiming that they were in desperate straits was sent out and the British armoured forces intercepted their appeal. To them it looked like a heaven-sent opportunity to wipe out the 90th Light. The 2nd and 4th Armoured Brigades accordingly drove south through the sandstorm, trying to get to the 90th Light before it could be extricated. On the rutted dusty track, Trigh Capuzzo, between the El Adem and Knightsbridge 'boxes', the crucial engagement took place.

The captured flag of the 259th Anti-Tank Regiment.

The British had been lured into a trap, for the bulk of the 15th and the 21st Panzer were waiting for them. The battle was fought out all along the Capuzzo track, with a little cairn-crowned hillock known as Bir Lefa as the focal point. Here the British tanks were manoeuvred into the fire of a screen of anti-tank guns. For much of the battle it was guns versus tanks, not tanks versus Panzers. Squadron after squadron of British armour roaring through the sand haze towards the scene of the action was forced on to a line of 88s and literally shot to pieces. The 22nd Armoured Brigade motoring down from the north, initially to be in at the kill of the 90th Light, and subsequently to try to rescue what was left of the 2nd and 4th Brigades, also suffered heavy losses. By the late afternoon the British had had enough. Their losses in tanks had been crippling. The Afrika Korps claimed to have knocked out 120. Churchill in the House of Commons announced that the Eighth Army's strength had been reduced from 300 to 70 on Saturday 13 June ('Black Saturday' as it came to be known in the Eighth Army). All three brigades turned about and fell back – the 2nd and 22nd withdrawing towards Knightsbridge closely pursued by the Panzers, while the remnants of the 4th Brigade fled eastwards.

The fighting simmered down during the night, but with first light the 15th and the 21st Panzer were attacking the British defensive box held by the 201 Guards Brigade below Rigel Ridge. The Guards, supported by South African field and anti-tank artillery, put up a stubborn resistance, but their positions were gradually whittled away and several half-hearted attacks by British tanks were beaten off. With the 15th Panzer forcing its way in at the eastern side of their 'box' and the 21st Panzer hammering their positions on the western side, it was obvious that Knightsbridge was rapidly becoming untenable. Rather than be annihilated like the Indians of the 10th Brigade, the Guards broke out at night and cut their way through the encircling ring of Panzers. That was the end. The Gazala battles were over; the Afrika Korps and its Axis comrades had won. The time for headlong flight had arrived and on this occasion it was the turn of the British to flee – eastwards. Their only hope of salvation now lay in holding off the Panzers until a new defensive line could be formed and a counter-attack force organised. After that both sides would have to return once more to the problems of supply, and the reinforcements marathon.

The fortified strongpoints – the 'boxes' in the Gazala area – were now redundant, for there was no mobile armoured force to operate in conjunction with them. They would have to be abandoned, and their garrison smuggled out before Rommel did to them what the British had done to Bardia and Halfaya six months before.

Rommel was about to have his revenge. 'What now?' he was asked. 'Tobruk, of course,' he replied sharply.

Two views of Tobruk on the day the South African commander of the garrison had surrendered to the Germans.

Tobruk at Last

Whether or not Generals Auchinleck and Ritchie were in favour of holding Tobruk when the Gazala Line was crumbling, Churchill unequivocally rejected the idea of giving it up. To the British Prime Minister Tobruk was a rock, like Gibraltar or Malta. On 14 June he signalled Cairo to ask, 'To what position does Ritchie want to withdraw the Gazala troops?' Then, more to the point, he went on, 'Presume there is no question in any case of giving up Tobruk. As long as Tobruk is held no serious enemy advance into Egypt is possible. We went through all this in April 1941. . . .'

But the circumstances at Tobruk on 14 June 1942 bore little resemblance to those which prevailed there in April 1941. The Panzers had already started to mop up the scattered strongpoints blocking the Afrika Korps' approach to Tobruk, and the retreat which the British Prime Minister rated as fatal was in full swing.

Formations, units and detachments of the Eighth Army were streaming back across the desert from the Gazala Line, through and past Afrika Korps units heading in the same direction. Hundreds of vehicles and thousands of men were on the move and it was often difficult to distinguish between friend and foe. Writing on the night 17–18 June, Hans-Joachim Schmidt, a wireless operator with Panzer Nachrichten Abteilung (of the 21st Panzer) recorded in his diary some of the nervous tension this provoked:

> It was already past midnight and we were still pressing on. Suddenly everything halted. We had come to the lip of a fairly steep escarpment. In front of – or rather below – us, everything was pitch dark. We could now only speak in whispers, as British troops seemed to be in the neighbourhood. It was a matter of waiting, waiting, while sappers cleared the way ahead of mines, a non-too-pleasant task in the darkness. Then the steep descent began, on no motorable track, to the plateau below. But it all proceeded without complications.
>
> After a further short, cautious advance on the level we were subjected to infantry fire, which forced us to seek cover. The shooting went on for two or three hours, and then it became light and the British ceased fire and pulled back. As we returned to our vehicles, we recognised in the light of dawn a well-constructed road running east to west. In this trackless expanse it could be only one road – the coast road, the Via Balbia. This we reached, and Tobruk was cut off.

Cutting the Via Balbia east of Tobruk meant that the Panzers could now turn back west to roll up the British forces. El Adem had fallen on 14 June and when the British lost El Adem Tobruk was virtually in Rommel's hands. As von Mellenthin was to comment later: 'the defence of Tobruk ceased to be a serious operation of war. . . .' This was a fact of which the men in Tobruk were blissfully unaware. Having assured Churchill that he had no intention of giving up Tobruk, Auchinleck had tried to make it possible for the town to withstand another siege. He knew that politically and strategically it was highly desirable to hold Tobruk, and although he did not think it was tactically feasible, the British Commander-in-Chief tried to make it so.

The two brigades constituting the 2nd South African Division, under command of Major-General H B Klopper, were already in Tobruk, and as the rest of the Eighth Army retreated through the town, bits of it were detached and ordered to stay. These included the 32nd Army Tank Brigade, with about 50 Valentines mounting the old two-pounder guns, the 201st Guards Brigade – which had shed two of its Guards battalions because they had been severely mauled a few days before (and which was therefore a Guards Brigade in name only since it had only one Guards battalion), an Indian Infantry Brigade

The final assault on the Tobruk perimeter.

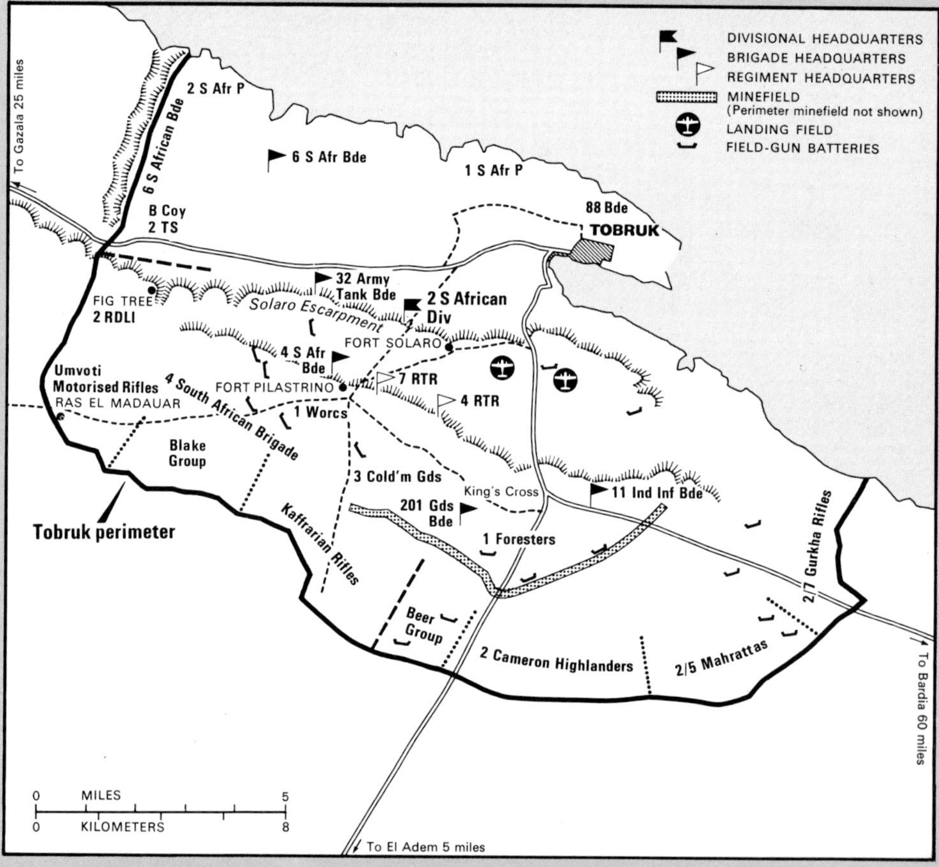

Left: A German personnel car uses the swastika on the flag as a marker for overhead aircraft.

Right: A Stuka flies over the burning Fort Pilastrino inside the Tobruk perimeter.

(the 11th), and another South African Brigade. This brought the total of men in Tobruk up to about 28,000, of whom about 15,000 were fighting troops. Klopper was appointed 'Fortress commander' and his understanding was that the tenants of Tobruk would have to hold out only while the British armoured forces were organised and refitted – ten days at the most. The Eighth Army would then launch a counter-attack in which Tobruk would once again play its vital part.

By nightfall on 18 June Rommel had effectively blocked all the overland routes to Tobruk. On the east the Trieste Division was astride the Via Balbia. Italian infantry were deployed round the perimeter north of El Adem and on the west Panzergrenadiers of the 15th Rifle Regiment and more Italian infantry were closing up to the perimeter. Afrika Korps Battle Headquarters had been set up south-east of Belhamed, and the 900th Engineer Battalion with mobile bridging equipment was on its way forward for the assault. Inside Tobruk Klopper's men were digging out loose sand that had sifted into the old gun positions, the anti-tank ditch and slit-trenches. The elaborate system of alternative communication trenches had silted up and the arrangements for reinforcements to be rushed to heavily pressed points on the perimeter had long been forgotten. The Australians, Poles and British troops who had defended Tobruk in the earlier siege were 1000 miles or more away, and the men of the new garrison manning the strongpoints on the perimeter barely knew who was on the right or who on their left, for they had had little time to familiarise themselves with the terrain, or evolve a sophisticated defensive system. All that Klopper could do was to deploy his troops around the perimeter and organise a reserve counter-attack force.

For three days, in thick brazen heat, the desert was taut with expectancy as both sides girded themselves for the coming assault, which began shortly before a cold dawn broke on Saturday 20 June. As the sun rose Rommel, standing on a hillock south of Tobruk, peered through his field-glasses, and asked, 'Where the hell is Wolf?' 'Here, Herr General,' replied the Luftwaffe Major Fuchs (Fuchs is German for Fox and Rommel pointedly always referred to Fuchs as Wolf). 'The Luftwaffe will be on time.' Sure enough at 0520 hours the combined bomber force of the German and Italian Air Forces in Africa began pounding the sector where the Panzer Army was to break through. At 0700 hours Rommel's ground troops moved in. Their attack was concentrated on a sector of a few hundred yards wide on the south-east perimeter. This was the weakest stretch of the perimeter, where Rommel had planned to attack the previous autumn; and it was defended by the 11th Indian Infantry Brigade – Mahrattas in the centre, Cameron Highlanders on one side and Gurkhas on the other.

First, two groups of Panzergrenadiers established themselves at two points opposite the Mahrattas and began to open lanes through the minefields and the wire. As they worked a box barrage laid down by the Axis artillery protected them, and as the sun rose a smoke screen was added. Simultaneously Luft-

waffe planes showered down pamphlets on the Indians. On one side there was a big circle enclosing a drawing of a spinning-wheel – the symbol of Gandhi's non-violence movement; on the back was a short message in Urdu, and at the bottom was a legend in German and Italian stating that, 'This paper is a safe-conduct pass for Indian officers and men.' Soon after this Stukas flew over to drop more lethal loads. Finally at 0800 hours, the Panzers of the 5th Panzer Regiment started to steam-roller their way through the perimeter. Mines missed by the clearance parties did not prove to be a hazard; probably many of them were faulty for they had been laid over a year before and their contents may have rusted. Led by Oberst Gerhard Müller, 40 Mk III Panzers leap-frogged forward in short bounds, alternatively advancing and halting to shoot. By 0900 hours they had reached the 'T'-shaped crossroads known to the British as King's Cross.

Right: Speed limits in North Africa.
Below: A Panzer Mk III.

Infantry of the 90th Light, and detachments of the 15th Panzer, the Trieste and Ariete Divisions followed

hard on the heels of Müller's tanks, widening the gap in the perimeter and submerging the Mahrattas. The British tanks moved forward to engage the Panzers around King's Cross and were promptly massacred by 88s which had been rushed forward to support Müller.

That was the beginning of the end. By noon Müller's Panzers were at the harbour, driving along the lines of British trucks lined up for a breakout and shooting up British demolition parties frantically trying to blow up the jetties and freshwater installations. The Panzers could not prevent some of the ships in the harbour from sailing, but one Panzer engaged and sank a small tug. Behind the Panzers the Panzergrenadiers were mopping up isolated pockets of resistance. Meantime Klopper's headquarters were being chased from one place to another as his units fell back towards the western side of the perimeter. By the middle of the afternoon there was no organised defence any more. Demolitions were taking place spasmodically, but the officer responsible for giving the order for the execution of the general demolition plan was captured before he gave it. The petrol storage tanks were set on fire and much of the petrol burned; many vehicles were smashed up. The water-towers and pumping-machines were also destroyed – to Rommel's chagrin. But huge dumps of ammunition and food – pyramids of packing cases of rations – were left. (Afrika Korps soldiers intent on 'liberating' Eighth Army rations even discovered some Münchener Löwenbräu which had come to the British quite fortuitously by way of Portugal.) Fully equipped workshops and guns and spares of every description went to swell the booty. By nightfall the battle for Tobruk was virtually over; for Rommel's men it was merely a matter of mopping up. Fighting continued through the night as the Panzergrenadiers and Italian infantrymen winkled the defenders out of their dug-outs. When the sun rose the Panzers moved in again, and shortly after 0600 hours Klopper issued an order that any man or unit of the garrison who wished to escape should try to do so. He then signalled Ritchie telling him that he wanted to avoid a bloodbath. 'I wish you and

your men God's blessing,' Ritchie's reply concluded.

Soon after that an Afrika Korps Hauptmann presented himself at Klopper's headquarters. The Panzers had halted and the fighting could stop as soon as Klopper formally agreed to surrender. However the South African commander had better hurry because the Luftwaffe were due to deliver a devastating attack at the very point on which they were now standing. Sure enough, at precisely 0700 hours, the Luftwaffe came thundering in. Klopper having agreed to surrender, the Hauptmann produced a Verey pistol and fired signal lights. Hardly had the colours faded when the formation of planes wheeled away and headed west.

Klopper was taken to Rommel's tactical headquarters which had been set up about three miles from the harbour. It was 0800 hours and the Panzer Army commander – ever intolerant and impatient – was in a nasty mood. 'Why,' he demanded of Klopper, 'didn't you stop fighting last night? You have held me up.' 'I, too, have a duty to perform,' Klopper replied.

'Why did you allow the water and and petrol to be destroyed?' Rommel shouted – gesturing angrily. 'Your men will suffer . . . they will walk . . . walk . . . walk as far as Tripoli.'

'My men are now prisoners of war and must be treated as such,' Klopper replied. 'Do as you please with me.' (In the event the 30,000 men who surrendered with Klopper did not have to march back to Tripoli. But many of them had a hard time: they were deprived of water during the first 48 hours

Rommel and Böttcher discuss the general situation.

The German 88mm anti-aircraft gun which found British tanks easy targets.

of captivity and had their rations curtailed until they reached the prisoner-of-war transit camps at Tripoli.)

After Klopper's capitulation many of the Panzergrenadiers and Italian infantrymen were occupied in the clearing and cleaning up tasks which are an inevitable consequence of battle – rounding up and coralling prisoners, collecting the wounded, burying the dead. But some of the Afrika Korps men who had seen it all before made a point of slipping off as soon as the opportunity arrived. They knew the form: if they failed to get their hands on loot within the next few hours, they would never manage to do so. They would either be pre-empted by the *Kettenhunde* (literally 'Chaindogs' – the field security police, whose badge of office was a tiny gorget hung around the neck) or Rommel would be driving them on through the same old desert towards places with different names.

Afrika Korps supply officers concerned with the official appropriation of 'loot' found it expedient to paint 'German Army Property' and *Tedesco* on packing cases and vehicles, in order to ensure it was not re-appropriated by their beloved allies. In Tobruk there was a pressing need to do this, for – as the old Afrika Korps hands predicted – Rommel was about to issue orders for a further advance, and sorting out the mess in Tobruk was to be delegated to the Italians.

That night, as Rommel was bent over a map, studying his next objective, the Nile Delta, an officer announced: 'A telegram from Berlin, General.' Rommel straightened up, turned and took the signal from the officer, Hauptmann Aldinger, his aide-de-camp. As he read it he turned a little pale, then smiled. 'The Führer has just promoted me Field Marshal,' he said.

Subsequently, after he had received his baton from Hitler in September, Rommel said to his wife, 'I would rather he had given me one more division.'

The 90th Light did not take part in the attack on Tobruk; Ulrich Kleeman and his men were driving hard towards Bardia, in the wake of Eighth Army units retreating down the Via Balbia. But, like the rest of the Afrika Korps after six days of uninterrupted fighting, the men of the 90th Light-Hearted were almost all in and many of them had difficulty staying awake even in their vehicles.

It was about this time that an incident occurred which illustrates the confusion occasioned by the use of captured vehicles – and the 90th Light was almost exclusively equipped with British trucks. Two South African armoured cars patrolling south of Sidi Barrani had

Below left: Major Barthel, one of the technical experts sent to advise the DAK. Below: Oberleutnant Behrendt, who arrived in May 1942, to look after the supply situation.

Right: Rommel in consultation with the Italian General Azzi (with moustache), outside Tobruk.

halted for the night and were preparing to move off when a turretless old armoured car was seen approaching. As the turretless vehicle was one of the type used as mobile observation posts by British gunners, none of the South Africans took any particular notice until three men leaped out brandishing rifles and hand grenades. They were Hauptmann Josef Hissmann who had narrowly escaped capture by partisans on the Russian front only three months before and who was now commanding a company of Army Flak Battalion 617, his runner Schütze Katusch, and his driver Gefreiter Hilscher, still flushed with victory after driving into Tobruk with the 21st Panzer.

'Hände hoch,' shouted Hissmann, and the Afrika Korps trio hustled the surprised South Africans on to and into their own vehicle. However in a free-for-all not long afterwards the Afrika Korps men were overpowered, thrown overboard and then captured by other South African armoured cars which had appeared. But they were left behind when Panzers came on the scene and Katusch feigned an epileptic fit.

On Monday morning, 22 June, the 361st Regiment – the 90th's vanguard – entered Bardia and found it deserted. On the horizon columns of dust created by vehicles tearing towards Halfaya suggested the Eighth Army's rearguard was at least six miles further on and that the gap between the two sides was widening every minute. However the men of the 361st Regiment could not have cared less. Bardia was no longer the smiling seaside town of a year ago – the effects of the Christmas siege were all too apparent. But the blue Mediterranean was as inviting as ever, and the ex-legionnaires of the French Foreign Legion who were the backbone of the Regiment were determined to have a bath. Oberstleutnant Albert Panzerhagen, the regimental commander – 42 years old, as tough as any of the legionnaires and probably the biggest rogue of them all – agreed.

Royal Air Force Hurricanes flew over Panzerhagen's column when it halted near the beach outside Bardia. But the 361st Regiment's vehicles were British and – apart from their Afrika Korps 'engine-driver' forage caps – the troops wore British uniforms 'liberated' from a clothing store at Commonwealth Keep.

Generalmajor Kleemann (centre), the commander of the 90th Light.

A German gun crew get their 2cm Vierling ready to fire at aircraft.

Consequently, to the pilots of the low-flying Hurricanes the 361st looked much the same as any unit in the Eighth Army. The deception was heightened by the 361st not making any hostile gesture. Satisfied that the column was not the vanguard of the Afrika Korps, the Hurricanes banked and flew off while Panzerhagen's men threw off their clothes and dashed into the sea.

The bathing interlude ended abruptly. Rommel had arrived from Tobruk – and – as the Afrika Korps' old sweats had forecast – he came with orders for a fresh offensive. The 90th Light was to press on up the Via Balbia, its next objective was Mersa Matruh, 156 miles further east.

Rommel was intent on pursuing the British into Egypt, and when Bastico arrived in Bardia on 23 June and suggested the Panzer Army had gone far enough, the new Field Marshal was livid. Seizing the Italian by the sleeve he dragged him across to a map of the world. 'There,' he said, 'is Soviet Russia. The Wehrmacht is about to sweep across the Caucasus to Baku – a distance of about 250 miles. From Baku it can carry on to Iraq, about another 600 miles further on. Haifa the terminus of the pipeline bringing oil to the Mediterranean is about 500 miles from where we are standing, and Kirkuk and Mosul in Iraq are only about another 600 miles from Haifa. So this is certainly not the time to sit on our backside here in Bardia or at Sollum waiting for the enemy to recover and hit back at us.'

Bastico argued, maintaining that the decision as to whether or not the Panzer Army advanced was his, and Kesselring, who had accompanied Bastico, sided with him. Kesselring was all for Rommel going over to the defensive – as had been previously agreed – because he wanted to see Malta eliminated. 'Rot,' said Rommel, 'I know we agreed that Operation Hercules – the Malta plan – should have priority. But with all the equipment and supplies we've picked up we can knock off Malta and knock out Egypt simultaneously.'

Neither Bastico nor Kesselring were satisfied, but Rommel had spiked their guns. He had already asked Mussolini to lift the restrictions on his freedom of movement, and he had also appealed directly to Hitler – making a very early use of his right of direct access to the Führer that went with being a Field Marshal. In the event, both Hitler and Mussolini were inclined to let Rommel have his way. 'It is only once in a lifetime that the goddess of victory smiles,' said Hitler; Mussolini concurred and

Below: Rommel and his temporary Chief of Staff, Bayerlein, review the situation following the fall of Tobruk. Right: A Focke-Wulf Fw 190 knocks out a British tank in June 1942. Inset: Rommel consults his allies.

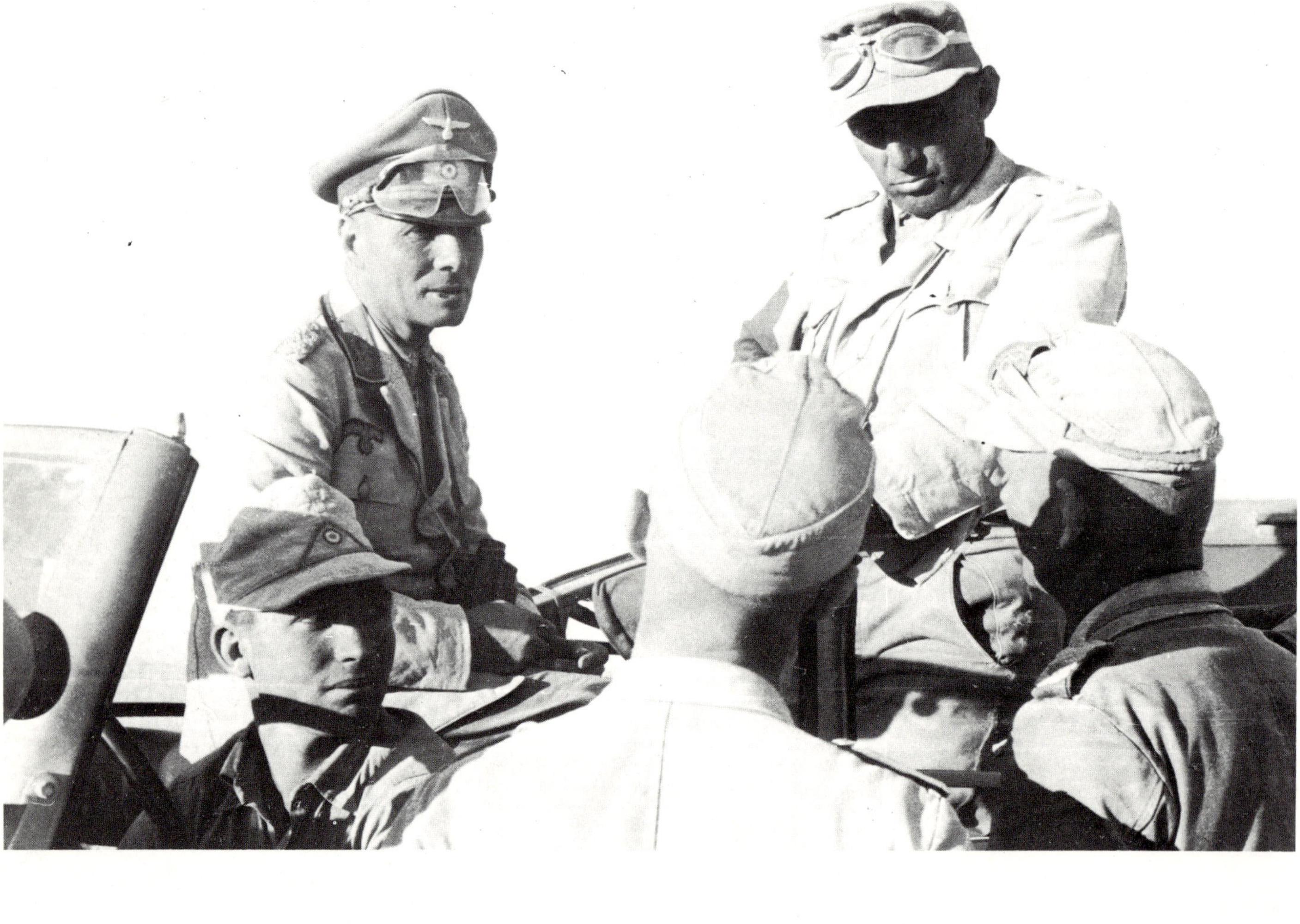

Above and Below: The British Infantry Mark III 'Valentine', which owed its nickname to the fact it was commissioned by the War Office on St Valentine's Day.

on 24 June Rommel received a signal: 'Duce approves intention of Panzer Army to pursue enemy into Egypt. . . .'

On 27 June the Duce ordered that Suez should be seized and the Canal closed. Italy would respect the rights of the Egyptian people, but Axis forces would occupy the country for the time being, with Rommel as military governor and a former Italian ambassador as governor-general. Meantime Italians writing home from North Africa declared fancifully that they could already see the tall buildings of Alexandria, while in Rome medals were being struck, occupation money was being printed, and a scheme for the civil administration of Egypt was being worked out. Finally two days after ordering Suez to be captured, Mussolini flew to Derna and uniforms, flags, bands and a white horse were got ready for his triumphant ceremonial entry into Alexandria. Rommel, confident of success, sent a message to him rashly declaring that he 'counted' on occupying Cairo and Alexandria by 30 June, i.e. in three days' time. As it turned out Mussolini's plane crashed on landing in Derna and although the Duce escaped injury a cook and a barber in his entourage were killed. Rommel did not go back to Derna and when a disappointed Mussolini returned to Rome three weeks later he was in a huff because Rommel had failed to pay his respects as well as failed to make good his rash promise.

With a little luck Rommel might perhaps have just been able to justify his forecast. But the Field Marshal's luck had run out; his men were rocking on their feet with fatigue; German tanks were being knocked out every day – not many, but enough to cause concern when no replacements were coming up; supply lines were overstretched; vehicles were showing signs of wear and tear; and – because the wells which were to provide fresh water had been salted, or oiled, or blown up by the retreating Eighth Army – every drop of water had to be brought up by truck. The Luftwaffe was also overstretched and had lagged behind in the advance. Taking advantage of this the British had put every plane they could in the air and were concentrating on the Afrika Korps' extended supply routes, and mobile columns of the British Long Range Desert Groups were hitting weak spots.

All these factors were working against Rommel; he knew that time was against him and that his only answer was to drive his men on even more relentlessly. Oberst Willy Teege, commander of the 8th Panzer Regiment, who had not slept for four days, commented on 26 June: 'My Panzers are like me – at the end of their tether.' The remark was not addressed to Rommel, but he heard it and turned on Teege. 'We're not here to give the enemy time for rest,' he snapped. Opinions and criticisms such as that of Teege were best not expressed in front of Rommel, for he never forgave and never forgot. Nor was he lavish in bestowing compliments: 'That's all in the past,' he would say icily when reminded of a recent success. 'What we are concerned with is the future.' Senior officers considered him totally unapproachable and during these days at the end of June 1942 the Panzer Army Commander was extremely short-tempered. Rommel was living on his nerves.

So too were the British in Cairo and Alexandria. Rommel had never got so close before, as people in these two cities were reminded when the German radio beamed on the Middle East predicted that ladies in Alexandria would be dating members of the Afrika Korps before the month was out. Intensive Luftwaffe activity also pointed to a crisis in the desert. Military targets along the Suez Canal were bombed and leaflets inviting the Egyptians to rise in revolt and to sabotage the British war effort were dropped over the Nile

Delta. (Fortunately for the British the Egyptians did not rise in revolt, and there was very little sabotage. Nevertheless there can be little doubt that if Mussolini had ridden in to Cairo on his white charger at the head of an Italian-Afrika Korps column, he would have been cheered all the way along the route. Many Egyptians secretly leaned towards the Germans – while feathering their nests at the British taxpayers' expense. Apart from the fact the Germans had so far been successful on nearly every front, they had never occupied any Arab country, as Britain, France and Italy had done. So far as Hitler was concerned all that was known about him was that he persecuted Jews, and with Palestine in mind the Arabs did not object to that.) Seen from Cairo it seemed more than possible that Britain might well lose Egypt. So the contingency plans drawn up at the beginning of the war when the Italians were the only menace were dusted off and revised. The Panzer Army's advance would be stopped at Mersa Matruh and if it was not stopped there another attempt would be made to stem it at El Alamein, where the British had been secretly digging and wiring a defensive line. If that failed then the South Africans would fight a rearguard action back through Alexandria. Meantime Britain's Middle East GHQ at Cairo would move to Gaza in Palestine, everything worth demolishing would be blown up and a force called 'Delta

Below: German tanks thunder down the coast to Mersa Matruh.

The flag is the battery standard of the 74th Medium Battery RA, which was awarded the battle honour 'Martinique'.

Force' would hold the line of the Nile. To top off all this planning, Auchinleck issued a 'backs to the wall' order of the day.

Auchinleck himself left Cairo on 25 June, flying up to the desert to assume personal command and to send Ritchie on leave. The Eighth Army at that moment was a tired, dispirited, formation sorely in need of a respite to rest, re-organise and re-equip, and Auchinleck, not Ritchie, was the man to be in charge. But if the Eighth Army needed a respite the British argued, it was quite certain that the Afrika Korps needed one even more. If they were weary, then Rommel's men must be well nigh exhausted, and therefore in no fit state

to launch an attack. It was a spurious conclusion. The Panzer Army was winning and that knowledge tended to keep it going. Moreover it had Rommel driving it to the limits of endurance. As he saw it only a broken army separated his men from Alexandria and a glittering conquest,

Mersa Matruh, 150 miles from Bardia, stands at the head of a defile on the road to Alexandria. At the outbreak of the war it had been transformed by concentric rings of barbed wire, minefields and trenches into a fortress base, where

Left and Below: Knocked-out Valentines, a 17-tonner with armour up to 65mm thick. The turret mounted a two-pounder gun.

Wavell's army was to stand and fight for the Middle East. Strategically Mersa Matruh was a miniature Tobruk, and for more than two years British army public relations officers had boasted that it was Egypt's 'bastion'. With good reason, therefore, Rommel expected the Eighth Army to halt there, turn and fight. So, on the evening of 26 June, orders were issued for a full scale attack. Rommel's plan followed the usual pattern; indeed those who attended his 'O' group on this occasion felt that the scenario was a repetition of others that had gone before – only the place names of the objectives had changed; everything else was the same.

'My intention is to make the enemy think we are attacking frontally,' Rommel announced. 'But, as usual, we shall use the indirect approach tactic and swing round the southern flank,' he continued. 'The 15th Panzer, under von Vaerst, will make a wide and deep right hook which will take the division around the British flank. Von Bismarck with the 21st Panzer will make a shallower hook, terminating about half-way between the sea and the southern flank of the British line. Meanwhile Kleemann and the 90th Light, advancing straight up the coast road will create the frontal diversion.'

The 361st Regiment spearheaded the frontal diversion, and at 0700 hours on the morning of 27 June the leading platoons of its 2nd Battalion were hacking their way through the barbed wire apron at the bottom of the hills west of Mersa Matruh. Beyond the wire the leading sections spread out and moved slowly up the hill, cautiously prodding the ground with their bayonets for mines. Curiously enough there was no reaction from the enemy – no shooting, no signs of life. Indeed, apart from the rumble of artillery as shells from 90th Light's guns whistled overhead and exploded somewhere in the sand beyond the hill, there was very little noise. 'They'll be waiting for us on the reverse slope,' Obergefreiter Enders of No 7 Company said, as his section marked the path they had found to be clear of mines; 'Just keep going.'

'Stupid job, this,' grumbled Oberschütze Brücker, one of those who was

supposed to just keep going. 'Mines! There aren't any mines. We're just grubbing around for nothing.' Enders suddenly realised that Brücker was probably right. Minefields were no use unless they were covered by fire, or so the text-books said. Not a single shot had been fired so far. 'All right, Brücker,' he said. 'Get on up there.'

Brücker stood up, slung his rifle and strode up the hill, stopping only when he reached a point about 10yds below the crest. This last 10yds he crawled. At the top he stood up again and shouted, 'Come and look!'

Enders' section doubled up the hill, followed by the remainder of No 7 company; behind them and to the right and left of No 7 company, trailed the rest of the 2nd Battalion with Panzerhagen, the Regimental commander, riding in a captured British carrier. Within minutes the whole battalion was standing on the ridge, gazing down in stupefaction. The scarred ruins and the mosque of Mersa Matruh were plainly visible less than one and a half miles away. Columns of smoke rising from the town hung over the buildings and one or two boats could be seen sailing east. But between the hill occupied by the 361st Regiment and the town, there was nothing. The enemy had gone.

Where had they gone, Ulrich Kleemann wondered when he was told that the 361st Regiment had advanced into a void, and that his division had failed to create a diversion. For once, he surmised, the British have anticipated Rommel's indirect approach and are facing south; if so, the 15th Panzer will run into trouble. He was right, von Vaerst's 40 remaining Panzers had blundered into the 4th Armoured Brigade and was pinned down by artillery fire and the new Grants.

Like the 90th Light, the 21st Panzer had not encountered any opposition up to the time it was supposed to terminate its encircling hook and batter a way eastwards through the British line. But at this point a signal from Nehring, the Afrika Korps commander, ordered it to make a quarter turn to the right and go to von Vaerst's aid. Meantime the 361st Regiment, followed by the rest of the 90th Light were moving down the hill towards Mersa Matruh. The town was empty and the coast road was clear, so as he had not been told what to do next, Kleeman decided to turn south where the noises of battle indicated that one or other of the Panzer divisions was in action. He advanced cautiously, expecting to run up against the British rearguard at any moment. By nightfall

Below: Damaged transports lie in the harbour of Tobruk.
Below right: Shore installations were wrecked by the intensive bombing.

when there was still no sign of organised opposition Kleemann was getting anxious and he ordered a halt. Further south the two Panzer divisions had also halted and laagered for the night.

The 27 June proved to be an eventful day. At dawn the 90th Light – moving east below the escarpment – came on a battalion of British infantry (the 9th Durham Light Infantry) 20 miles south of Mersa Matruh, cut it to pieces and took 300 prisoners. But the 90th Light was then pinned down by artillery fire and could get no further until the Panzers came up from the south to help. Meantime the 21st Panzer, continuing on its 'quarter turn right' course to join hands with von Vaerst's division, found that it was moving across the front of a ridge occupied by New Zealanders. Under cover of an artillery barrage von Bismarck's troops worked their way round the ridge to attack it from the east. Considering that the division's mainstay, the 15th Panzer Regiment, was reduced to a mere 23 tanks and about 600 very tired Panzergrenadiers, taking on a whole New Zealand division was a risky operation and the fact that they ultimately succeeded in routing it was no mean feat. But Rommel was with the 21st Panzer, and when he was around, nobody stopped to weigh the odds because they were tired.

Rommel was more concerned about the British 1st Armoured Division than the New Zealanders. With the 1st Armoured's 22nd Brigade blocking the Panzers' path forward and its 4th Armoured Brigade stopping them moving back, the 15th Panzer was marooned, short of petrol and running out of ammunition. To break out of this impasse Rommel ordered Kleeman to move north and stop the British using the coast road. He knew this would upset the British and that they would react; when they did so his opportunity would come. But the 90th Light's operation took time, and by the late afternoon both von Bismarck's division and that of von Vaerst were in dire straits. The 21st Panzer, which could make no headway against the New Zealanders, was suddenly threatened by a British tank force from the west, and the 15th Panzer was still hopelessly separated from its sister division. Although Ariete and Trieste had come up to help the combined strength of the two Italian divisions and the 15th Panzer was not enough to batter a way through to von Bismarck.

Suddenly the pressure ended and the whole situation changed. Auchinleck had decided to give up any idea of holding Mersa Matruh, but to stand at Alamein. So the Mersa Matruh positions were jettisoned and on the evening of 27 June the New Zealanders started to withdraw. As the 21st Panzer had drawn a thin ring around their positions a Maori battalion had to chop a passage with their bayonets through which the rest of the New Zealanders could follow.

In his book *Infantry Brigadier* Major-General Sir Howard Kippenberger has described how he got away:

'I was beginning to think we had found a gap when white flares went up close ahead. The column stopped, closely packed. More flares went up, no doubt a challenge, to which we had no reply to make. The Germans opened fire.

We had bumped into a laager of about a dozen tanks lying so closely together that there was no room to break through between them. Their fire simply hailed down on us. There were tank shells, 20mm shells, and automatics, all firing tracer. A petrol truck was hit at once and exploded. An ammunition truck was hit and the boxes of cartridges crackled and exploded in succession. The most dreadful sight was an ambulance a few yards away which blazed away furiously, the wounded on the stretchers writhing and struggling utterly beyond help.

Two views of Tobruk following the British capitulation on 21 June 1942; a great blow to British morale and allowed the German advance into Egypt.

My car was jammed on all sides and could not move. I told Ross and Joe to get out and for a moment we lay flat on the ground. Many others had done the same. A few seconds later I saw a truck ahead of us turning to the left, and beyond it quite clearly saw John Gray standing with his head through the roof of his car and pointing in the same direction. "We'll give it a go, Ross," I said. "Very good, Sir," he replied, as polite as ever. We scrambled back and followed the trucks ahead, all bolting like wild elephants. For a few moments we ran on amid a pandemonium, overtaking and being overtaken by other frantic vehicles, dodging slit trenches, passing or crashing into running men, amid an uproar of shouts and screams. I recognised the men as Germans, pulling out my revolver and was eagerly looking for a target when suddenly there was silence and we were out running smoothly on level desert. We were through.

I thought of Joe, who had not got out of the car with us, turned round and poked him. There was no response. I prodded him again and called anxiously and Joe woke up. He had slept through the whole affair.'

This was only one corner of the picture. The British were now pulling out all around Mersa Matruh and Rommel has recorded how his own headquarters were engulfed in the confusion when one retreating British column chose a route through Panzer Army's HQ.

'A wild *mêlée* ensued, in which my own headquarters, which lay south of the fortress, became involved . . . One can scarcely conceive the confusion which reigned that night. It was pitch-dark and impossible to see one's hand before one's eyes. The RAF bombed their own troops, and with tracer flying in all directions, German units fired on each other.'

Came the morning of 28 June the battles for Mersa Matruh were over. Mussolini was in Derna, exercising his white charger and rehearsing the details of the triumphal parade he planned to stage in Cairo, the British were back behind the Alamein line, and the Afrika Korps was burying its dead and licking its wounds. Alexandria was only two hours away.

On into Egypt

Until July 1942 El Alamein was the placeless name of a rocky rise 34 miles west of Alexandria which carried the coastal road and the railway connecting Alexandria with Mersa Matruh. But here the desert narrows down to a 53-mile bottleneck – bounded on the north by the Mediterranean and on the south by the low-lying trackless wastes of the Qattara Depression. Across this bottle-neck the Eighth Army had dug a line of trenches, with strongpoints on the coast, near the Qattara Depression, and at points between. The gaps between these defensive 'boxes' were covered with minefields and by artillery fire. Dominating the area was the bare stony Ruweisat Ridge – a narrow hill about 11 miles long but less than half-a-mile deep on which each side, in turn, was to break its teeth.

With Rommel anxious to maintain the momentum of the advance, there could be no let up for his exhausted troops. They desperately needed sleep and rest, and no doubt they would have been refreshed if the Panzer Army had stopped for a few days; it can also be argued that the Luftwaffe would have had a chance to catch up and the Panzer strength and ammunition supply of the Afrika Korps would have improved. But the bulk of the Eighth Army's in-fantry had managed to elude the Panzer Army at Mersa Matruh and to Rommel it was important to overrun Alamein before the British could reorganise and complete their defences. In any event nobody questioned the Panzer Army's *Fingerspitzengefühl* – his knack of sensing in his fingertips the occasion and the opportunity.

'We attack tomorrow,' Rommel announced to his divisional commanders at an 'O' Group conference on the afternoon of 30 June. He, von Kleist, von Bismarck, Generalmajor Graf von Sponeck (who had taken over the 90th Light from Kleemann) and the Italian commanders of the Ariete and Littorio divisions were standing on the Miteiriya Ridge looking down on the plain of Alamein. There was little to be seen: thick barbed wire entanglements marking the edge of the British perimeter, a few grey humps – fortified positions, nothing more. 'The situation is the same as it has been at all the other defensive lines,' Rommel said. 'Sea to the north, desert to the south, a line of defence works – strongpoints and minefields between the two. We will use the same tactics as we used at Gazala a month ago and at Matruh. The 90th Light will stage a frontal attack up the coast road to divert the enemy. Meanwhile the Afrika Korps will move south towards the Qattara Depression. However as we cannot get round the flank through the salt marshes, as soon as it gets dark the Panzers will swing in to penetrate the line between Alamein and the ridge called Deir el Abyad. By this time I hope the 90th Light will have worked its way round Alamein. So we should all end up behind the British and the whole line will collapse. I hope El Alamein will be in our hands by this time tomorrow.' 'Next stop Alexandria,' von Vaerst responded.

Two hours before sunrise next morning the tired men of the 90th Light clambered out of the trenches they had dug under the fire of the British artillery, and cautiously began to advance east towards the blackened entanglements of wire in front of the Alamein 'box'.

Slightly behind them and to the north, four battalions of the Italian Trento Division were moving in the same direction. Germans and Italians alike all had to cross an open strip of desert about 11 miles wide, and having arrived only the previous evening nobody had had time to see, let alone reconnoitre, the route to their objective. Nor did they know what lay on the other side of the wire. Most of the Germans were reeling with fatigue and too tired even to think. Those who did expected their opponents to be in as poor condition as they were themselves. They did not know that the veteran 1st South African Division had been in Alamein for over a week, that further south the 18th Indian Infantry Brigade and the 6th New Zealand Division had not so far seen action, and that all were fit and resolute troops whose morale was high.

The drill for the advance was routine; Panzergrenadiers stumbled forward with the wretchedly few Mk III Panzers that remained to the 190th Tank Bat-

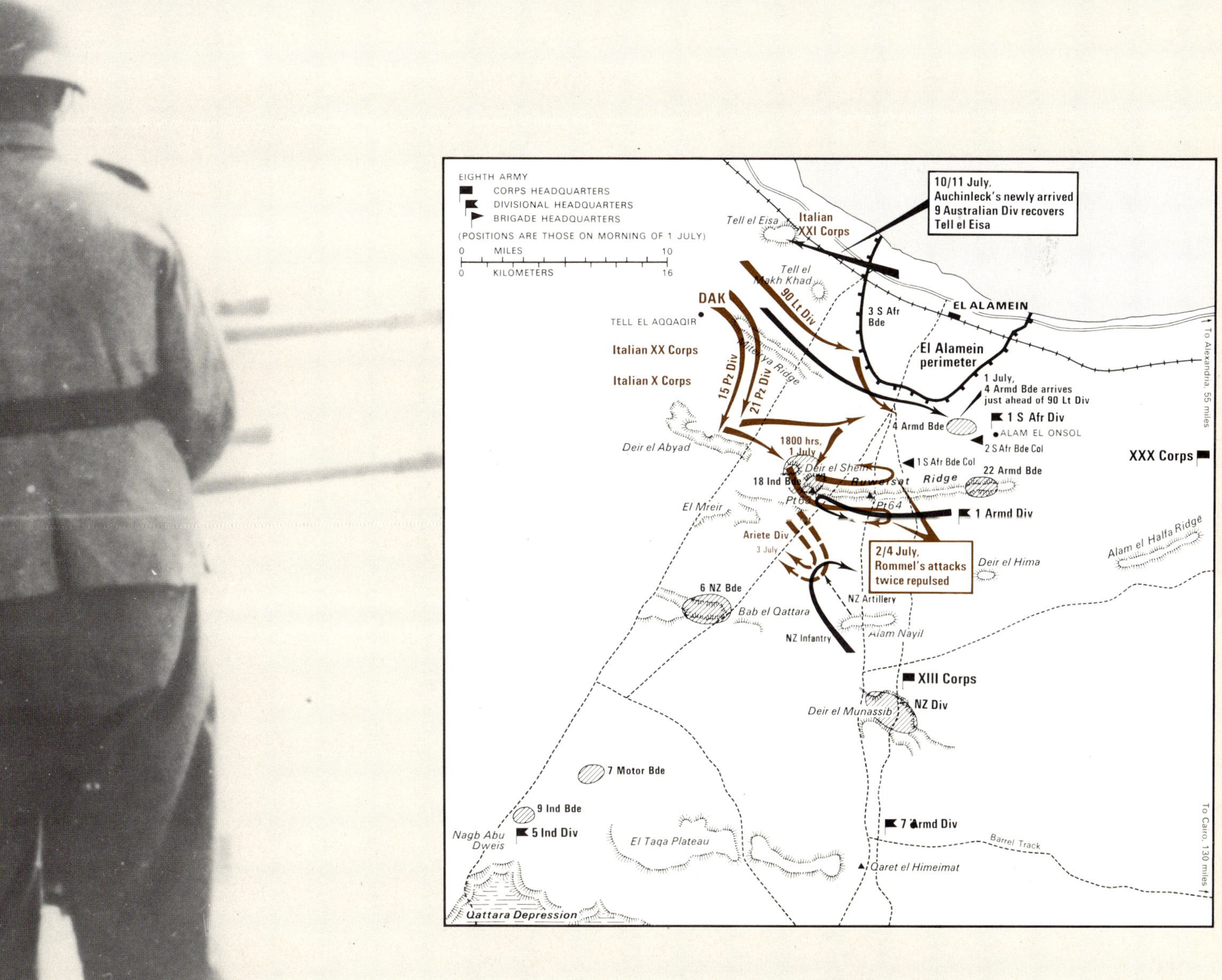

Below left: A 2cm Vierling anti-aircraft gun.
Below: The first battle of El Alamein.

talion, while the anti-tank guns bounded forward from one ridge to another. Nothing happened until after sunrise, when the forward troops had reached a point about one and a half miles from the Alamein defences. Then, as his men came under heavy machine-gun fire and his Panzers and other transport were engaged by anti-tank guns, von Sponeck realised that the 90th Light had veered too far north. But there was little he could do about it. By 0730 hours his troops were pinned down and when he tried to disengage and pull back out of range prior to seeking a way round the Alamein box von Sponeck found that it was extremely difficult to do so. Fortunately the elements came to the rescue with a sandstorm which enabled the 90th Light to slip away. But it was well after midday before the division was moving again, and by this time it had lost nearly all its artillery to bombs dropped by the South African Air Force.

By the middle of the afternoon the exhausted Panzergrenadiers were in more trouble. As they tried to turn north round the Alamein perimeter in order to get to the coast and so cut off the 3rd South African Brigade in the Alamein box they ran into fresh and unexpected resistance. An attack was mounted, but it failed to make any headway. Alamein was proving a tough nut to crack, as the entry in the war diary of the 90th Light concerning the situation about 1600 hours illustrates: '. . . a panic breaks out in the division, which is stopped just in time by the energetic action of the Divisional Commander [von Sponeck] and the Chief of Staff. Supply columns and even parts of fighting units rush back under ever-increasing enemy artillery fire. The Commanders of Battle Group, however, succeed in keeping most of their units facing the enemy and bring back the troops which have taken to flight. The Division digs itself in.'

Rommel's view was that, 'This [the Panzer Army's attack] created a deadly threat to the British. They brought into action all available artillery and blanketed the area with a hail of shells. Gradually the tempo of the assault slowed down till our units were eventually pinned down in extremely heavy artillery fire. Appeals for help from the 90th Light demanded the despatch of artillery, as the divisional artillery was no

Below: Generalmajor von Vaerst, commander of the 15th Panzer, talks to Oberstleutnant Westphal. Bottom: The advance on El Alamein.

longer fit to go into action. Immediately I sent the Kiehl Battle Group south of the 90th Light Division and drove forward myself in an armoured car so that I could gain a picture of the situation and make decisions accordingly. We soon ran into such strong British artillery fire that we had to discontinue our journey.'

Further south the Italians had also run into difficulties and retired to reorganise. Initially the two Panzer divisions had been more successful, despite their progress being hampered by bad going, a sandstorm and six air raids. By mid-morning (1 July) Panzers were rolling over Deir el Abyad and heading towards the Deir el Shein ridge held by the 18th Indian Infantry Brigade. The Indians stood their ground and fought bravely, but they were no match for the men of the Afrika Korps. Auchinleck ordered the 22nd and 4th Armoured Brigade to go and help them and when the move of 22nd Armoured uncovered the flank of the 1st South African Brigade on the north side of Ruweisat Ridge, the Afrika Korps was not slow to exploit the fact. Finding that they could look down on the South Africans from the top of the ridge the Germans poured fire and destruction on to the defences which the South Africans came to call 'The Hot Box'. Ultimately the position became untenable and the 1st South African Brigade evacuated the box and pulled back to line up with the rest of the 1st South African Division. Not that all the fire came from the Germans. When the South Africans called

An encampment before El Alamein.

for artillery support, British 25 pounders mistook their target and shelled the South Africans, and the same error was repeated by New Zealand gunners who also pounded the South African position. To make matters worse the bombs of the South African Air Force were added to the rain of German, British and New Zealand shells, for it too had been called to help and given the wrong target. Finally and unbelievably, the 1st Armoured Division also joined in. Seeing shells falling on one place the 1st Armoured's divisional artillery assumed this was where the Panzer Army was, and joined in, and over an hour elapsed before the South Africans could persuade the British gunners to stop the bombardment.

A story behind this withdrawal is worth recounting. According to Brigadier Hartshorn, who took over command of the 1st South African Brigade during the action a bitter argument developed between Major-General Dan Pienaar, the commander of the 1st SA Division and Lieutenant-General Sir Willoughby Norrie, the corps commander, when the former asked for permission to withdraw the brigade to a more secure position:

General Norrie's reaction to Dan's reasoned argument was to say, "So – the South Africans want to run away again, do they?" He went on, "Very well, I will withdraw your Brigade into reserve and replace it with a British formation." The Commander-in-Chief was evidently at Corps Headquarters, and according to reports he was drawn into the conversation. The argument went to and fro until an exasperated Dan put an end to it so effectively that, as he said to me, "You could bloody well hear their teeth rattle." The historic words with which Dan clinched the argument, and which he used more as shock tactics than anything else, were, "Look, Norrie, let me get this straight. Am I fighting you or Rommel? If it's you, say so and I will guarantee to take Alexandria in the next 24 hours and – what's more – I'll bring Rommel with me." (*Avenge Tobruk,* Purnell and Sons (SA) Ltd, Cape Town 1960. Pages 157/8.)

Meantime while all this was going on the 22nd Armoured Brigade's tanks had closed with the 15th Panzer south of the Indian defensive box and von Vaerst's division, outnumbered and outgunned was being forced slowly back towards the west. Within a few hours 15 of his Mk IIIs had been destroyed and although the division contested every yard of ground it was clear that this was a state of affairs which could not continue indefinitely. It was the anti-tank guns commanded by Leutnant Vogt of the 39th Panzerjäger which saved the division. Vogt lined up his 88s on the reverse slope of Ruweisat ridge while the 15 remaining tanks of Willy Teege's 8th Panzer Regiment were still fighting a rearguard action on the forward slope

The British left behind their tinned fruit.

of the ridge. Teege was leap-frogging his tanks back, covering the withdrawal of the hundred odd Panzergrenadiers – which was all that remained of Oberst Ernst Baade's 115th Panzergrenadier Regiment. Ammunition for the Panzer guns was already a problem and Teege had ordered his crews not to waste it on the enemy's infantry, for he knew that it was the Valentines and Matildas that he had to fear. Teege, at the back, following the enemy advance through his field-glasses, watched the British tanks moving up the slope. As they topped the Ruweisat crest there was a sharp crash as one of the 88s opened fire. A few well-aimed shots and six Matildas were out of action.

While Teege's Panzers were slowly yielding ground a few miles to the south the 21st Panzer was liquidating the 18th Indian Brigade, and by the late afternoon Nehring was able to report to Rommel the capture of 2000 Indians and 30 guns. This news – the first good news that day – prompted a change in Rommel's plan. The 90th Light, dug in and pinned down by the South African artillery was to be extricated; so too was the 21st Panzer, and the whole of the Panzer Army was to unite in a concerted effort to break through to the coast road on the east side of Alamein. Accompanied by his *Gefechtstaffel* – the vehicles and personnel of his headquarters – Rommel joined the Kiehl Battle Group for this operation.

> Again terrific British artillery fire slammed into our ranks. From north, east and south, the British shells came screaming. Tracer from British anti-aircraft guns whizzed through our forces. In such tremendously heavy fire the attack was brought to a standstill. We dispersed the vehicles hastily and sought cover. The impact of one British shell after another crashed in our vicinity. For two hours Bayerlein and I lay in the open.

Caught in this furnace of fire the Panzer Army could not move until it slackened. When it did, towards dusk, Rommel and his *Gefechtstaffel* pulled out of the battle and the 21st Panzer moved slowly back down into the plain along the route which it had used in the morning. As darkness cloaked the battlefield von Bismarck took stock of the situation. His division had started out that morning with 40 tanks, and in less than 12 hours he had lost 28 of them.

A few miles north of the 21st Panzer the 1300 men who were all that remained of the 90th Light were licking their wounds and hoping for a respite. They did not get one. At 2130 hours Rommel ordered them to fight their way to the coast by moonlight. Intelligence sources had reported that the British Mediterranean Fleet had sailed from Alexandria, that the harbour was to be blown up and that sappers were feverishly laying demolition charges under dumps and storehouses in the city. British morale was clearly flagging and the Panzer Army commander was determined to force a decision.

DAK men examine the wreck of a British transporter.

So the exhausted men of the 90th Light picked up their weapons and attempted to carry out their orders. But they were stopped by machine-gun and artillery fire, and Rommel was compelled to revise his plan. Next morning the two Panzer divisions would resume their attack advancing north-east to cut the coast road a few miles from Alamein. When they had done that they would turn back towards Alamein and wrap up the South Africans in the box there. Meantime the 90th Light would continue its efforts to advance; once the Panzers reached the road and pierced the crust of the Alamein box the pressure on the 90th should lessen. The Italians also had a part to play: Ariete and Trieste would drive south and watch the southern flank.

Below: The Germans in front of El Alamein: an observer's position, left, a protective shelter and right, building an ammunition dump.

But things did not go 'according to plan'. The battle ebbed and flowed throughout 2 July, but every effort of the Afrika Korps was thwarted by intense artillery concentrations. British tanks were now firmly ensconced on Ruweisat Ridge and the Panzers were just not strong enough to move them. The exhausted men of the 90th Light did manage to force their way forward another few yards and at one time they believed their way to the coast was clear and reported so to Rommel. But they never had any real hope of breaking through the South Africans. Moreover British aircraft were out in force; Stukas flying in to bomb the Alamein perimeter in support of the 90th Light were driven off, while huge four-engined Liberators – newly arrived in Africa – were able to bomb Afrika Korps vehicles without let or hindrance.

The struggle continued on 3 July, but the German thrust was growing perceptibly weaker. Rommel ordered the 90th Light, the whole of the Afrika Korps and the Littorio division to try once more to get round the Alamein Box. But before this operation had even started there was bad news from the south where the New Zealanders had left their 'box' at Qaret el Abd to attack the Italians. Ariete, after losing all its artillery, had been virtually wiped out.

The news did not bring any change to Rommel's plan however, and in the afternoon the Afrika Korps tried once more to advance. The Panzers gained some ground on Ruweisat, but as the two divisions now had only 26 tanks between them, they had no hope of dislodging the British and of breaking through. At nightfall when Rommel ordered his men to stand fast and dig in where they stood, everyone realised that the offensive had at last come to an end.

There was not going to be any triumphal entry into Alexandria – not yet anyway.

Rommel himself had lost his usual buoyant optimism, and on 4 July he was writing to 'Dearest Lu . . . Resistance is too great, and our strength is exhausted. However I still hope to find a way to achieve our goal. I'm rather tired and fagged out. . . .'

The Afrika Korps was worn out too, and although the offensive had ground to a halt this did not mean that the fighting stopped. While Rommel was writing home to his wife 600 men of the 90th Light, many of them literally asleep on their feet, surrendered. South of the Alamein box the remainder of the division also took a knock and pulled back; still further south the New Zealanders began to clear their area and more Italians were taken prisoners. The initiative had passed to the British and the odds were on their side. Churchill and the men in Whitehall had accorded priority to the war in North Africa and large numbers of men and great quantities of material were already on their way to Auchinleck. Within a few weeks the Eighth Army would be able to muster 200,000 men and 1000 tanks, while – with the driblets of reinforcements it was receiving – the Africa Korps and its Italian allies would be able to raise only about half its strength.

The front began to stabilise on 5 July. The Panzer Army had dug in behind a screen of anti-tank guns and settled down to await the reinforcements that were already on their way up. Behind the line the tank workshops were working feverishly to repair about 200 German and 150 Italian tanks, and every sort of supply – especially ammunition – was being rushed forward from Tripoli and Tobruk. General Alessandro Gloria's Bologna Division was trudging up the Via Balbia on foot from Gazala 406 miles away; in Tripoli the *Comando Supremo* was commandeering vehicles to send up two fresh infantry battalions and reinforcements to bring the badly mauled Brescia, Pavia and Sabratha Divisions up to strength. From Germany another 12,000 men were on their way by air. These included additional units – a mountain regiment, some artillery and some sappers. From Crete came the Ramcke Parachute Brigade which – because it was a Luftwaffe formation and thus subordinate to Herman Göring and Kesselring – Rommel regarded as a dubious acquisition: 'Göring's agents'. (This was a harsh judgement. Ramcke's paratroops, fighting as ordinary infantry, distinguished themselves and were unaffected by their Luftwaffe affiliations. They fought to the end in Africa and then 'quietly' disappeared – frittered away in operations for which they had never been intended.) To match the German paratroop contribution the Italians sent the Folgore Parachute Division; it had cost them 45 times the amount of money spent on raising a normal infantry division, and an Italian subaltern compared its employment in North Africa to washing floors with champagne. But Rommel had to have reinforcements; even the Italians recognised that. The troops had to be found somewhere and the Folgore happened to be available.

Meantime Auchinleck was intent on keeping the initiative that had passed to the Eighth Army. His technique was to concentrate on the Italian units – the weakest parts of the Panzer Army's line – so forcing Rommel to switch the exhausted Afrika Korps units backwards and forwards to meet the emergencies that the Italians precipitated.

On 10 July the Australians, the freshest and perhaps the toughest of the Brit-

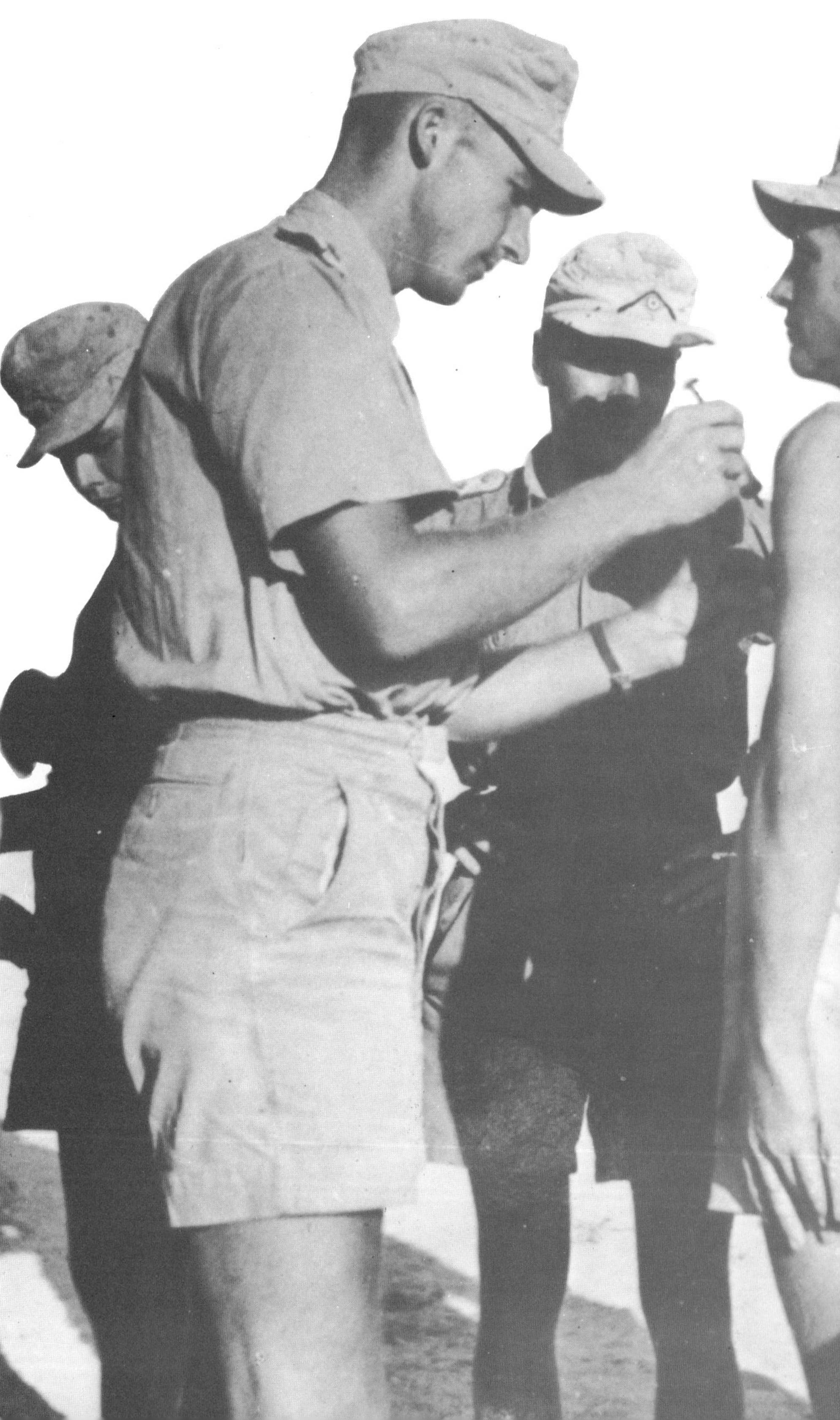

German soldiers are vaccinated prior to the battle at El Alamein.

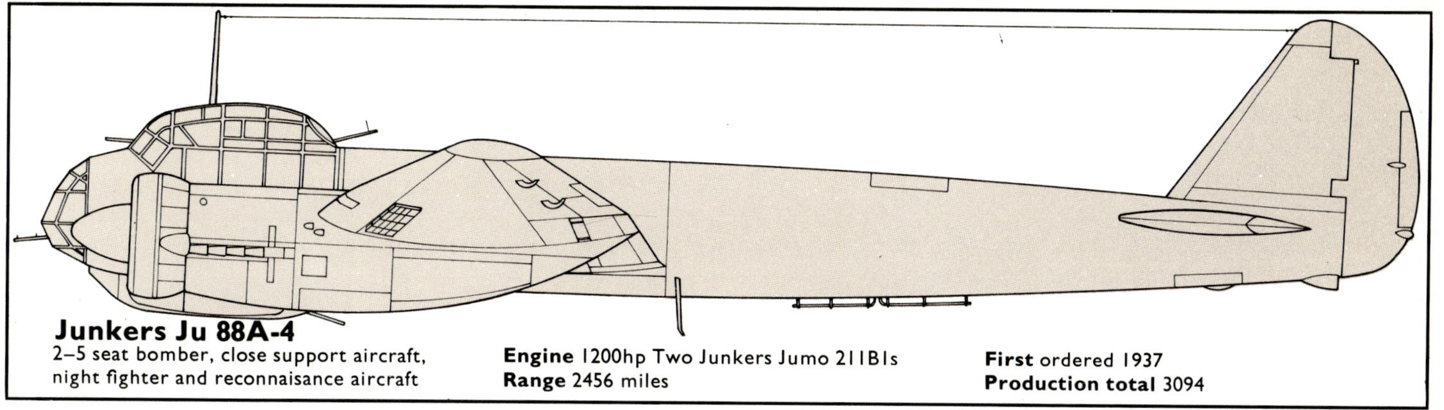

Junkers Ju 88A-4
2–5 seat bomber, close support aircraft, night fighter and reconnaisance aircraft
Engine 1200hp Two Junkers Jumo 211B1s
Range 2456 miles
First ordered 1937
Production total 3094

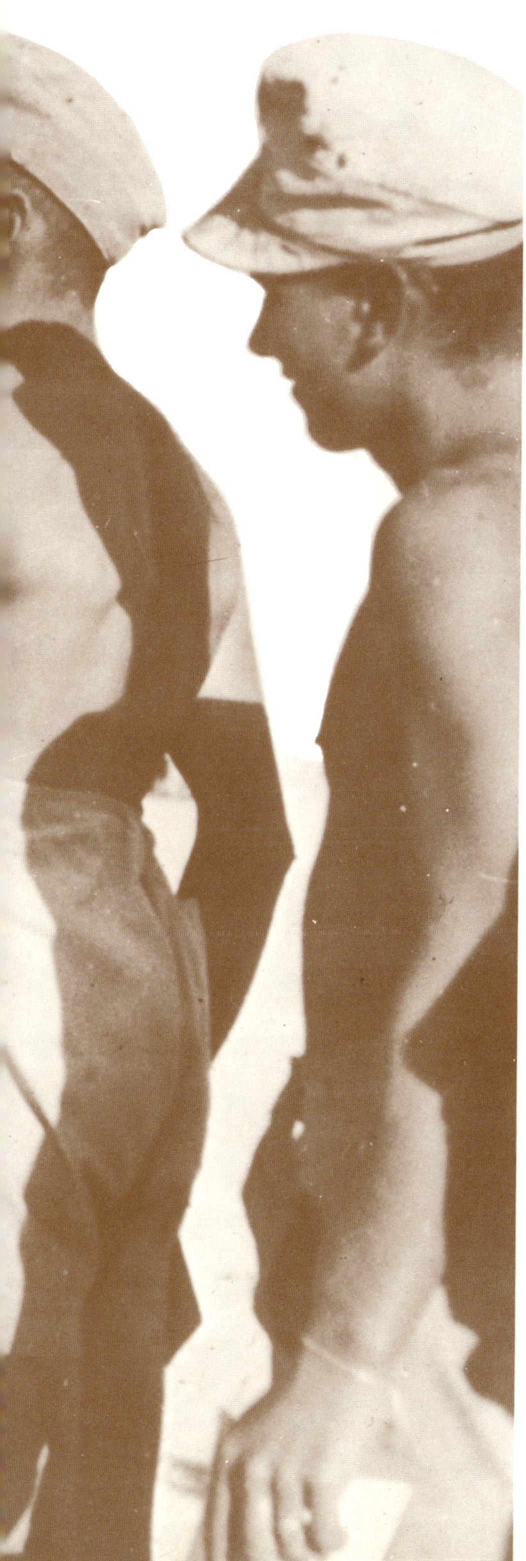

ish troops in the Middle East, launched the first attack in a series of operations that was to push the Italians back along the coast. In the first few hours they did not meet much opposition, the Tell el Eisa ridge was overrun and some 2000 Italians were taken prisoner. At one time it looked as if the Australians would overrun Rommel's headquarters on the coast a few miles further west. Rommel was away visiting, and von Mellenthin was in charge. 'Startled to see hundreds of Italians rushing past the headquarters in the final stages of panic and rout . . .' he hurriedly collected the clerks, wireless operators, cooks and miscellaneous bottlewashers who constitute a headquarters and organised a defensive position to stem the tide. The Australians were stopped but Hauptmann Seebohm, officer in charge of the Wireless Intercept Section, and most of his wireless operators were killed.

By sheer luck some of the first German reinforcements, in the shape of a Panzergrenadier battalion of the newly arrived, poorly trained and ill-equipped 164th Light 'Afrika' Division, had just arrived. With some other reinforcements going up to join the 90th Light the new arrivals were deployed across the coast road and a new front line was established. A counter-attack was then mounted and on the afternoon of 10 July Captain Vittorio Bulgarelli of the Trieste led a company of M13 and M14 tanks across the dunes in an assault on the Tell el Eisa hill – a feature known by the Australians as the Hill of Jesus. Some of the tanks bogged down en route and all but three were systematically picked off by the Australians. More were knocked out as they neared their objective and ultimately only one luckless M13 charged the hill; it suffered the same fate as the others when it reached the Australian line. When the cost was

The German column advances to the battlefield in July 1942.

counted at the end of the day it was all too clear that the Italians had suffered heavy losses, and in going to their assistance the 90th Light had also taken a heavy knock. The hole in the front had been plugged, but the enemy had not been thrown back nor the lost ground recaptured. Furthermore the events of 10 July – repeated on 11 July and again until 16 July – compelled Rommel to stiffen the Italians by dispersing units of the Afrika Korps, and this meant that his striking power was weakened.

On 12 July Rommel wrote to his wife that 'the very serious situation of the past few days is slowly being overcome. But the air is still electric with crisis. I hope to make another step forward tomorrow.' The Panzer Army Commander had decided to try another direct attack on the Alamein box. This time the 21st Panzer supported by every available gun and every aircraft that the Luftwaffe could muster was to cut off the 'fortress' from the Australians at Tell el Eisa, and then break in. The British learnt of the attack almost as soon as those who were to participate in it. British Intelligence had taken a few leaves out of the Afrika Korps book and its radio intercept service was working well. So too was the British counter-intelligence service after a couple of German agents had been caught in Cairo. Using the German code the British were transmitting spurious messages for Rommel's benefit. It was a ploy which might have been more successful if Hauptmann Seebohm and his unit had not been wiped out.

Following a raid by Stukas and Ju 88s and an intense artillery bombardment, the 21st Panzer launched the attack at noon. Once again things went wrong from the very beginning. The men of Oberst Pfeiffer's 104th Panzergrenadier Regiment shook out into their attack formation too far back and so missed the benefits of the softening up process which bombs and shells were supposed to bring. By the time they reached the enemy wire the bombardment was over and the South Africans behind the wire were recovering from its effects. An artillery concentration and a hail of machine-gun fire greeted the Panzergrenadiers and the leading sections were cut to pieces before they even got to the wire. Urgent calls for help brought the Luftwaffe back to renew its attacks on the South African artillery, and the Panzers moved forward to blaze away at the South Africans concrete strongpoints. But the South Africans resisted stubbornly and the attacks could make no progress.

Next day, writing to 'Lu', Rommel said that he was 'in an extremely bad mood' having been bitterly disappointed with the attack on 13 July. 'It achieved no success whatever,' he wrote. 'However the blow must be borne and we're

A Panzer Mk III.

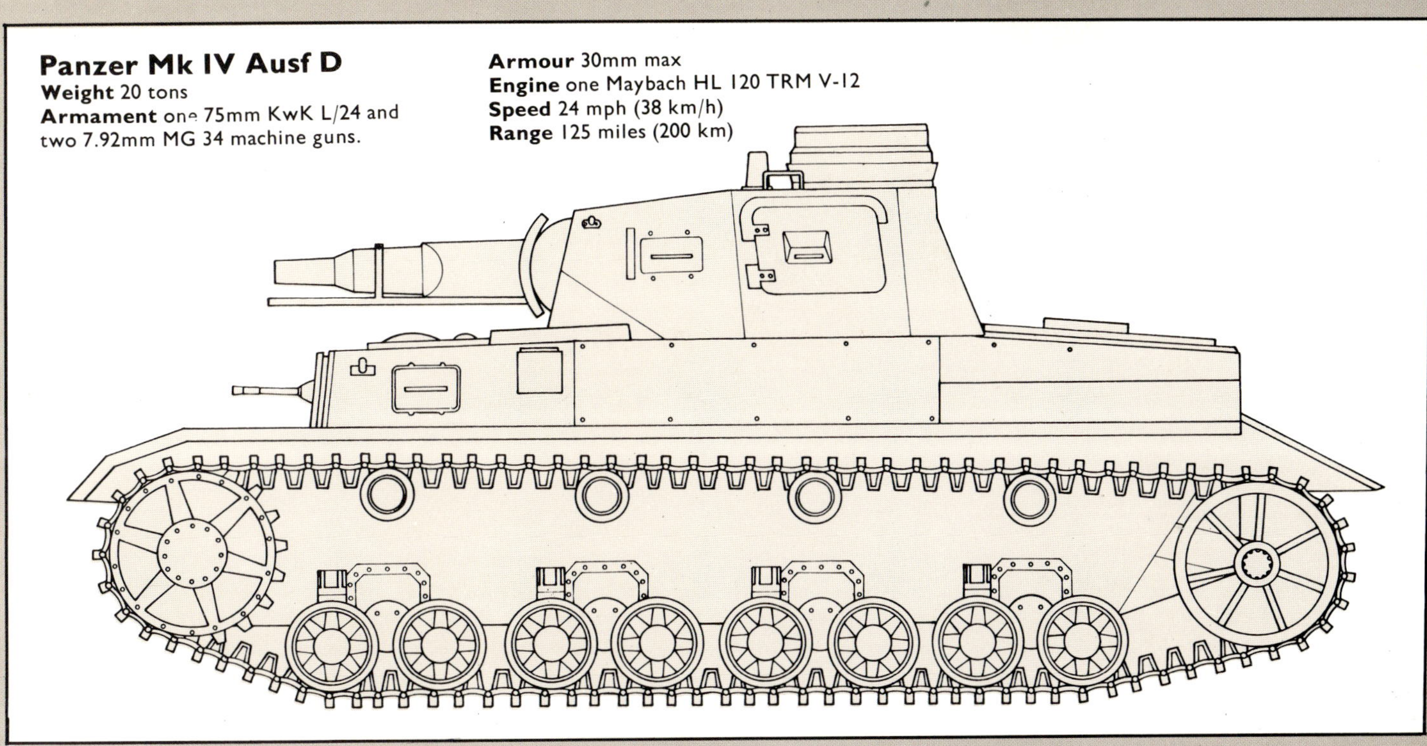
Panzer Mk IV Ausf D
Weight 20 tons
Armament one 75mm KwK L/24 and two 7.92mm MG 34 machine guns.
Armour 30mm max
Engine one Maybach HL 120 TRM V-12
Speed 24 mph (38 km/h)
Range 125 miles (200 km)

Hawker Hurricane I.

going forward with fresh courage to new operations. . . .' These 'new' operations entailed the 21st Panzer moving further west to attack the Australian positions south-east of Tell el Eisa prior to a breakthrough to the sea on the west of Alamein. The attack went in as the sun went down and under cover of an intensive air bombardment. But, as on the previous day, the Panzergrenadiers were too late and the paralysing benefit of the bombardment was lost again. Nevertheless the Panzergrenadiers did eventually manage to fight their way through to the railway and they might have got as far as the road – and perhaps even the seashore – if it had not been for murderous fire from the Alamein Box.

As this attack had been a partial success, however, Rommel resolved to renew it next day (15 July). But it was now the Eighth Army's turn to hit back. That night the New Zealanders and the 5th Indian Infantry Brigade attacked the Brescia Division on the vital Ruweisat Ridge, and smashed their way through the Italians' defences. At one stage they looked as if they might break up the whole Panzer Army front and the 15th Panzer and the 3rd Reconnaissance Abteilung were flung in to counter-attack. Eight of Willy Teege's Panzers overran the 22nd New Zealand Battalion soon after dawn and by about 1700 hours Ernst Baade's Panzergrenadiers had taken about 1200 prisoners. They had also released about 2000 Italians, many of whom were more than resigned to their forthcoming captivity and dumbfounded when they realised their change of fortunes.

The Australians renewed their attacks from their coastal salient around Tell el Eisa on 16 July, and when they overwhelmed what was left of the Sabratha Division the 382nd Panzergrenadiers were rushed up to block the gap that this had created. Attacking again just before daybreak on 17 July, the Australians now smashed through the defences held by men of the Trieste and Trento Divisions and were checked only when more Germans were brought up. Luckily when a counter-attack was launched during the afternoon, the Australians were forced back and several hundred of them were captured. But once again the Italians had borne the brunt of the fighting in which, by all accounts, they showed great courage and tenacity – a fact which Rommel made a special point of in his daily bulletin. (One battalion, the 32nd Battalion African Combat Engineers, who were holding positions between the Trieste and Trento Division had 100 men (out of a normal complement of 500) before the battle started; at the end of the day only two officers and 14 men were left.)

In the second half of July the desert war around Alamein followed the pattern set during the first half. On 21 July the Australians attacked the German front in the north and the New Zealanders attacked in the middle. Both attacks failed, as did another Australian attack on 26 July. It seemed that a position of stalemate had been reached; the Afrika Korps offensive had been brought to an ignominious halt, and the Eighth Army's counterstrokes had not resulted in Rommel's army being destroyed. The fighting did not cease completely of course, and patrols kept both sides on their toes. British patrols discovering that Afrika Korps men would leave their slit trenches and dug-outs to gather round radio trucks to listen to the special Afrika Korps programme turned this information to account in what has passed into unofficial history as the 'Lili Marlene Stonk'. Eighth Army artillery was laid on the radio trucks known locations, awaiting a prearranged signal to fire. The gunners, tuned in to the German programme waited until the final bars of 'Lili Marlene' . . . *'Mit Dir Lili Marlene.'* On the first syllable of *'Mar*lene' the guns opened fire and the effect was shattering. Not many casualties were caused, but three rounds of gunfire from between 200 and 300 25-pounders in such cir-

The 88mm anti-aircraft gun.

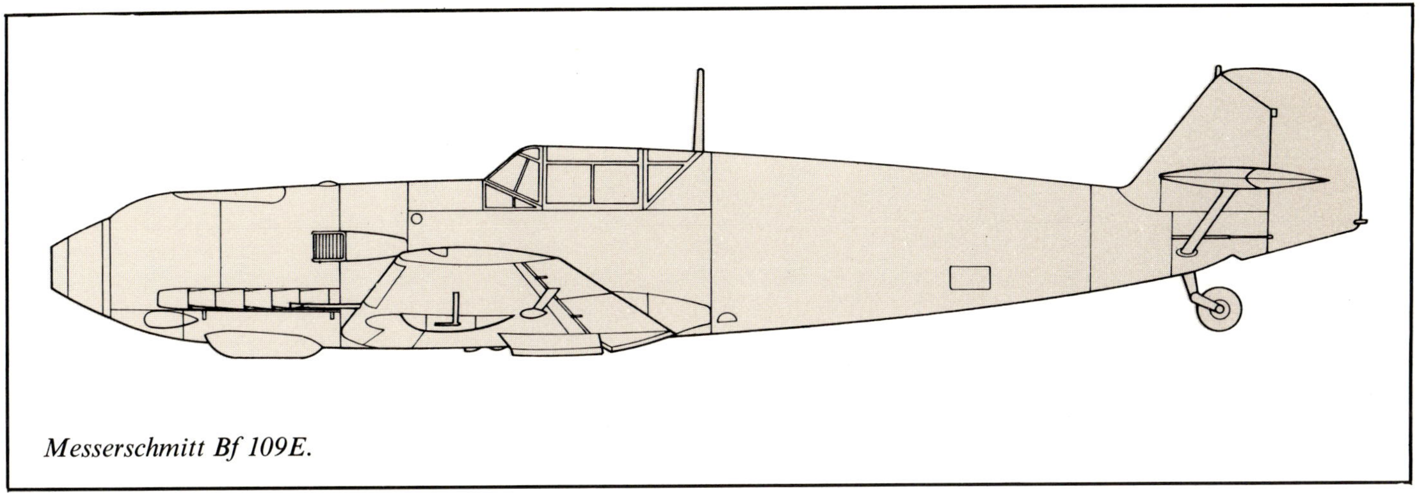

Messerschmitt Bf 109E.

cumstances was enough to teach the Afrika Korps caution.

Climatic conditions at this time were, to say the least, oppressive. It was summer again and men on both sides of the front would pray for the implacable midday sun to go down. The air was heavy, there was little natural shade and no water; compared with the arid terrain around Alamein, Cyrenaica had been a Garden of Eden. But further south at the great Qattara Depression it was even worse. 'When Allah made Hell,' runs the Arab proverb, 'He did not find it bad enough, so he created the desert and added flies.' Even the flies avoided the vast barren basin of Qattara, and there were not even any of the great sand lizards. 'Pebbles on pebbles,' wrote Auchinleck; 'A void in the void,' was Rommel's description. The Qattara was a place to avoid.

In these conditions the fighting died down while both sides waited for reinforcements. Rommel had concluded that he could not break through the Alamein line until the Panzer Army had built up its strength, and the Eighth Army's attempts to pierce the German front had convinced Auchinleck that he could not destroy the Panzer Army for the time being. Afrika Korps reinforcements were being flown across from Crete and new Panzers and guns were being shipped across to Tobruk; but men and munitions were pouring into the enemy camp at a much faster rate.

At the beginning of August Churchill and a posse of advisers on their way to Moscow to see Stalin descended on Cairo and several momentous decisions were taken. Auchinleck was not pressing forward fast enough for the British Prime Minister, and when the latter was told that the Commander-in-Chief of the Middle East considered a British offensive before September would be 'premature', Auchinleck was relieved of his command. Other major changes in the British Middle East Command followed as a matter of course. Auchinleck's place was taken by General Sir Harold Alexander and Major General 'Strafer' Gott was appointed to the command of the Eighth Army. Political considerations were largely behind the changes. Public criticism of Churchill's leadership was mounting in Britain, by-elections had gone heavily against the government, and there had been a long run of disasters: the loss of the *Prince of Wales* and *Repulse*, the fall of Singapore, the loss of Burma and of Tobruk, and the apparent success of Rommel's offensive were all contributory factors. To preserve his position Churchill wanted action there and then, and as Auchinleck was not prepared to attack before mid-September at the earliest he had to go. 'Rommel! Rommel! Rommel! What else matters but beating him!' Churchill is supposed to have snarled during a discussion on the prospects of the forthcoming British offensive.

Fate now stepped in to compel another change. 'Strafer' Gott, the Eighth Army commander designate was killed on 7 August when a couple of Luftwaffe fighters shot down the aircraft flying him back to Cairo and his new command. To take his place came Lieutenant General Bernard Law Montgomery – a new broom who was to sweep very clean indeed.

General Bernard Law Montgomery.

Rommel, who had a healthy respect for Auchinleck, knew nothing of his new adversary. Nor at this particular time did he care about the changes that were taking place in the rival camp, for the Panzer Army commander was a sick man. Like so many of his troops he was suffering from jaundice, a standard disease in the Western Desert. Apart from that the plain fact was that he was worn out. According to Professor Horster, the Panzer Army's chief medical officer, Rommel was suffering from chronic stomach trouble. 'The Field Marshal's blood pressure is too low,' Horster wrote. 'He has dizzy spells, and fainting fits. . . . His present poor state of health is due to long standing stomach and intestinal troubles which have been intensified by the physical and psychological demands of the past few weeks.' The report concluded that Rommel '. . . is not in a condition to direct the [coming] offensive. . . .'

A request by Rommel that someone else should take over command of the Panzer Army accompanied Horster's report when it was transmitted to Berlin. The man for the job he suggested, was General Heinz Guderian, the Wehrmacht's 'Father of the Panzer Corps'. A curt reply from Berlin said that Guderian was not available and so Rommel decided to soldier on – under medical supervision.

Worry over reinforcements, equipment and supplies was the root cause of the psychological 'demands' to which Rommel had been subjected. The Germans were now paying the penalty for the failure to capture Malta, and the George Cross island was fast recovering from the pounding it had taken. Attacks by long range bombers on Axis shipping in the Mediterranean were multiplying at an alarming rate, as were raids on the Cyrenaica ports through which the supplies had to be channelled – Benghazi, Tobruk, Bardia and Mersa Matruh. Because the port facilities at Benghazi and Tobruk were more sophisticated many of the ships bringing supplies had to unload there. But these places were a very long way away from the front. The desert railway was virtually useless and the long haul by road to Alamein imposed a heavy burden on the Afrika Korps' transport. The situation was further exacerbated by bickering with the Italians over equipment and reinforcement priorities. Enormous supply dumps had been captured in Cyrenaica and Egypt, but most of the captured petrol had been used and there were, of course, no stocks of ammunition for German guns. In the middle of August the Afrika Korps was down to one and a half day's petrol. Rommel reckoned that he needed six days' supply if he was to recapture the initiative, as Mussolini in Rome and Hitler in Berlin were urging him to do.

Moreover time was running out. Rommel knew that so far as equipment and reinforcements were concerned the quantities flowing to the Eighth Army exceeded those received by the Panzer Army and the relative strength of the latter compared with its adversary was deteriorating daily. There had to be an offensive soon, or it would be too late.

Over the past month the Afrika Korps had received 166 new up-gunned Mk III Panzers and 37 Mk IVs – including 27 'specials' fitted with the superb 75mm 'long' gun. Unfortunately 120 more Panzers and a mass of other vehicles together with a hundred or so guns were lying idle in Italy waiting to be shipped to North Africa. But there was a dearth of ships. For soft-skinned transport the Panzer Army was heavily dependent on captured British and American vehicles, and spares were lacking for them. The manpower situation had improved enormously, but the 15th and the 21st Panzer were still not up to strength. As for the Italians: with only half the vehicles they were supposed to have only four motorised battalions out of the ten in the XXth Corps could move by transport; if and when they had to move the rest would have to march. The Italians could contribute about 220 tanks, but as half of them were expected to break down they were a dubious asset.

Looking over the wire at the situation in the enemy camp Rommel's estimate of the Eighth Army's strength was 900 tanks and armoured cars, and about 70 battalions of infantry, supported by some 550 field guns and 850 anti-tank guns. This was a gross over-estimate.

Montgomery had deployed about 350 tanks, 40 battalions, about 400 field guns and 500 anti-tank guns. Italian Intelligence sources also reported that a British convoy carrying more than 100,000 tons of supplies and equipment was on its way round Africa and was expected to reach Suez early in September. It was now or never for the Panzer Army, and Kesselring's assurance that he could fly in 90,000 gallons of petrol a day and Marshal Cavallero's promise to use Italian submarines and warships as transports if need be, decided Rommel to gamble on another offensive.

On 28 August Rommel summoned the Panzer Army's generals – Nehring, commanding the Afrika Korps, von Vaerst of the 15th Panzer, von Bismarck of the 21st Panzer, von Sponeck of the 90th Light, three Italian corps commanders and the divisional commanders of Ariete, Littorio, Trento and Bologna to his command-post. Six miles due west of Bab el Qattara; three newcomers to the theatre – Oberst Lungershausen of the 164th Division, Ramcke, the paratroop brigade commander, and the commander of the Italian Folgore Airborne Division were also present. 'We regroup tomorrow,' Rommel announced, 'and start our attack on the 30th. The situation is broadly similar to Gazala and we shall tackle it in a similar way. As we have not been able to pierce the front here we shall have to find a way round the flank – through the minefields between where the British Line ends and the Qattara Depression. The 90th Light, Ariete and Littorio, and the Afrika Korps (the 15th and the 21st Panzer) will constitute the striking force and whilst they are going through the minefields our Italian friends – Trento and Bologna – together with the 164th Division, will attack all the way along the twelve-mile front northwards to the coast. In the far south Ramcke Force – Ramcke's brigade and two battalions from the Folgore – will advance east along the edge of the Depression from Bab el Qattara, turn north and make for the ridge called Deir el Munassib.

Once through the gap the striking force's immediate objective is the Alam el Halfa Ridge. From there we shall be able to pinch out the Alamein position and complete the destruction of the Eighth Army. After that . . . the 15th Panzer and the 90th Light will sweep on via Cairo to Suez, while the 21st Panzer occupies Alexandria.'

The 88mm anti-aircraft gun in operation against British tanks.

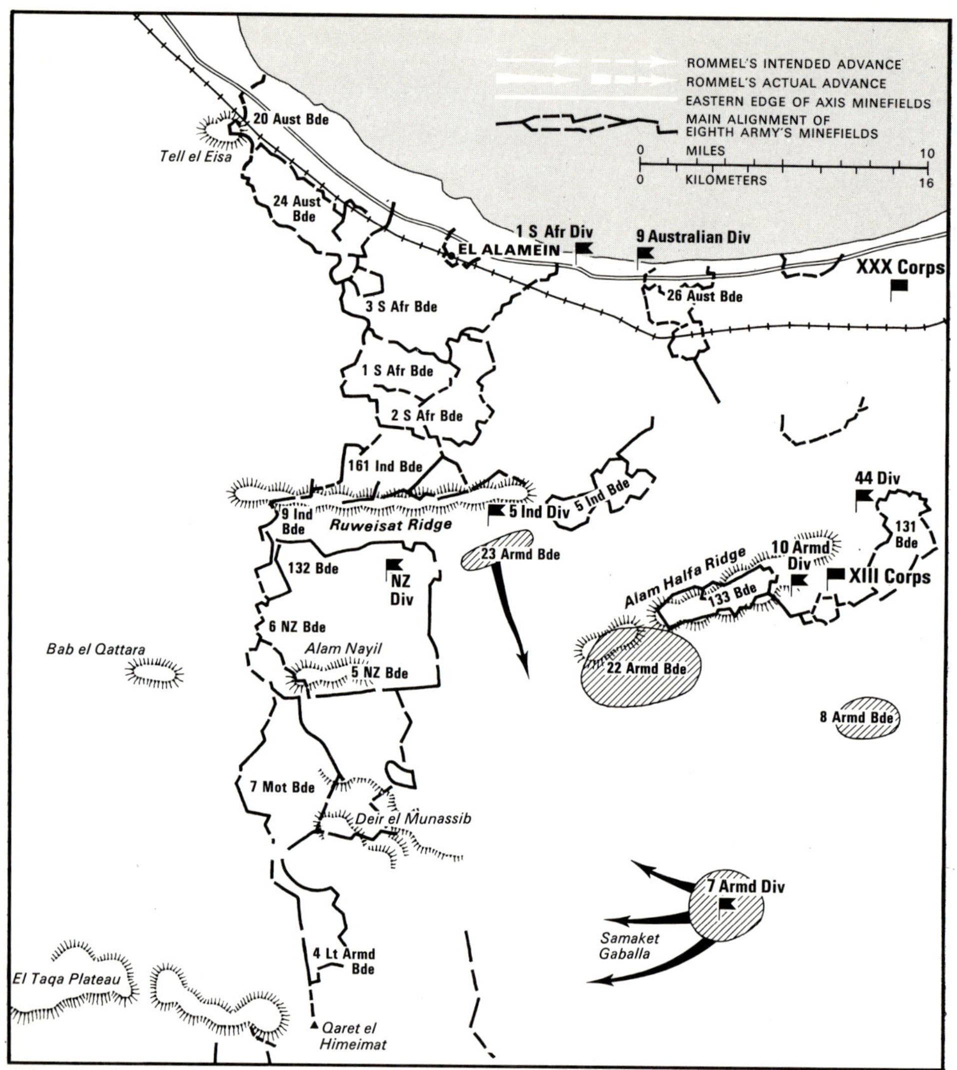

The Battle of Alam Halfa.

Rommel's plan was virtually a Chinese copy of all the other plans for his offensives – a feint attack along the front, combined with an armoured assault around the desert flank. If the plan had succeeded at Alamein, as it had elsewhere, the Eighth Army would undoubtedly have been trapped. Unfortunately for Rommel and the Afrika Korps Generals, Alexander and Montgomery had anticipated the Panzer Army commander's plan and made their arrangements accordingly. The newly arrived 44th Division had been deployed on the Alam el Halfa Ridge with artillery and tanks to support it. With his numerically inferior forces Rommel had little hope of victory and in his heart he knew it.

The Afrika Korps moved south and regrouped during the nights of 29 and 30 August, and on the morning of 30 August, Rommel issued an Order of the Day:

> Soldiers! The Army in Africa has been reinforced by fresh divisions and a new offensive will be launched today. My aim is the complete destruction of the enemy forces, and I am expecting every soldier under my command to give of his best in the decisive days which are to come.

That morning also Rommel is said to have confronted his medical adviser, Professor Horster, and told him, 'the decision to attack today is the hardest I have ever taken. Either the army in Russia succeeds in getting through to Grozny and we in Africa manage to reach the Suez Canal, or. . . .' He then made a weary gesture indicating defeat.

Ramcke's paratroops were first into action. Led by Leutnant Wagner an assault company moved off along the edge of the Depression, and the rest of the brigade followed. Shortly after 0200 hours the paratroops reached the track going north to their objective, the Deir el Munassib Ridge, and Wagner's com-

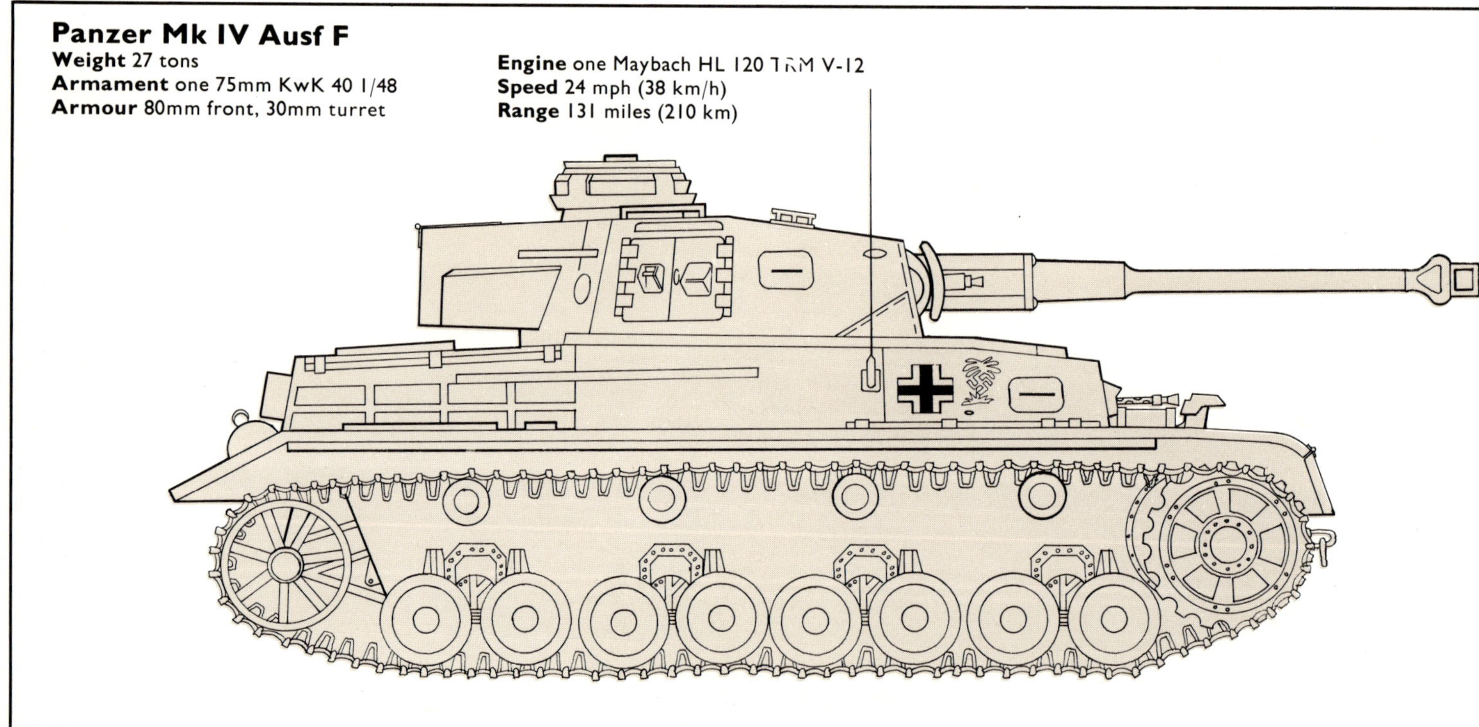

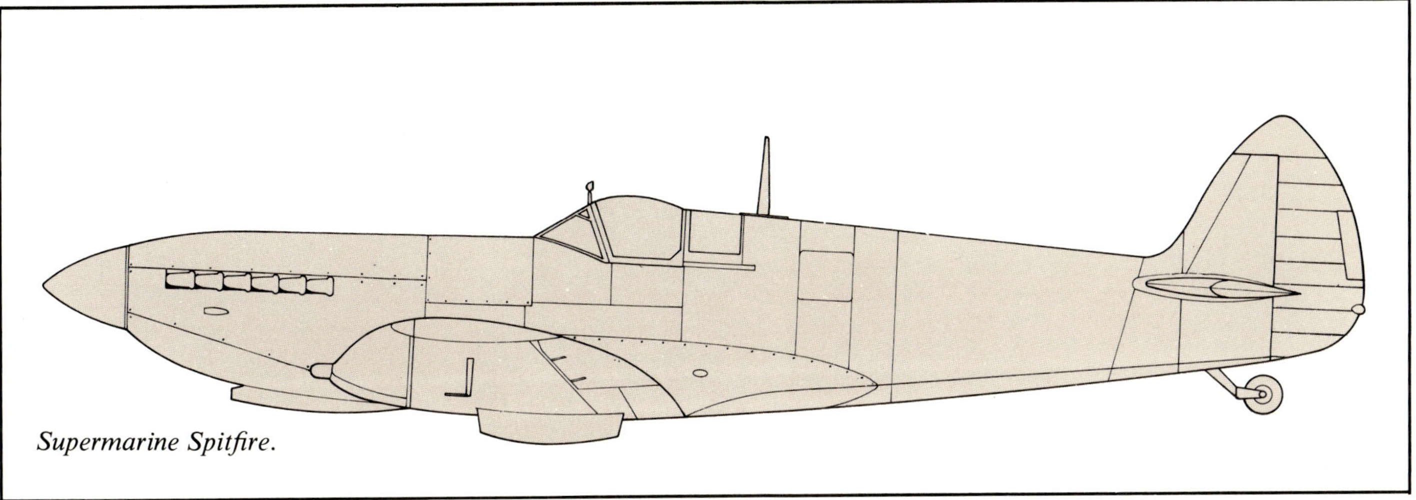

Supermarine Spitfire.

pany started to clear a corridor through the minefield protecting the British flank. No sooner had they started work when mortar bombs fell around them, exploding every now and then with a thunderous great flash as one of them hit a mine.

'Knock out the enemy mortars, the anti-tank and machine-gun positions,' Ramcke ordered his gunners, after a prolonged view of the battle front through powerful night-vision glasses. The gunners opened fire and within minutes a violent counter-bombardment duel was raging. By this time Ramcke's leading infantry was approaching the British defences and with the brigade commander leading – as was customary in the paratroop formations – the first assault wave charged into the forward positions.

By dawn Ramcke's Force had fought its way through to Wadi Deir el Ankar and were within striking distance of the objective. But the sudden detonation of mines which blew the leading scouts to pieces brought the advance to a halt; the paratroops had walked into an unknown minefield.

'Get the mine detectors up here!' ordered Ramcke. 'Kroh, get a message to the 164th Division. Tell them to send us some more engineers. If we don't look out we shall be caught here in this minefield in daylight and picked off like sitting ducks.'

With bombs from New Zealand mortars in Alam Nayil crashing around them, the paratroops hurriedly scraped holes in the stony soil of the dry wadi.

'Hübner, get your battalion ready to resume the advance,' the brigade commander ordered when the engineers reported to him. Then, as soon as a lane had been cleared through the minefield Hübner's battalion moved into the lead. But the mine-free lane was under observation from Alam Nayil and artillery and mortar barrage enveloped it as the paratroops moved in. Breaking into a run most of Hübner's men managed to get through this curtain of steel, and the minefield, to fight their way up on to Deir el Munassid Ridge. After they had attained their objective, they dug in, and there they were destined to remain for a week.

Mines had delayed the striking force also and thrown its time table out of gear. Since 0300 hours sappers had been working feverishly to clear lanes through the minefield, but when the sun rose on the morning of 31 August the two Panzer divisions were barely halfway through, for progress was difficult in the fine sand which clogged tracks and slowed movement. Within the hour Royal Air Force aircraft arrived on the scene to bomb and strafe. Casualties among the sapper mine-lifting squads began to mount when they came under fire from British covering troops.

Knowing that speed and surprise were essential to success and realising the Afrika Korps was seriously behind schedule, Nehring got out of his armoured command vehicle and was passing orders to a motorcycle despatch rider when a low flying aircraft screamed in to strafe the headquarters vehicle. Nehring fell, seriously wounded. Further forward, at almost precisely the same moment, von Bismarck was killed by a mortar bomb.

General von Bismarck.

When he heard the news about 0500 hours Rommel's *Fingerspitzengefühl* promptly came into play. Intuitively he knew that the operation had already failed. But Fritz Bayerlein, his Chief of Staff, persuaded him to let it go on, and Bayerlein took Nehring's place as a temporary measure until von Vaerst could get back from the 15th Panzer after handing over his division to Oberst Waltenberger. Meantime Oberst Karl Lungerhausen was ordered to take von Bismarck's place as commander of the 21st Panzer.

By 1000 hours the two Panzer divisions were through the minefield and moving east, aided by a raging sandstorm which screened them from the attentions of the Royal Air Force, though it also meant using more petrol. The 90th Light on the left of the Panzers was still struggling through the minefield while Trieste and Ariete had run into soft sand which slowed them down. From a vantage point on the western end of the Alam el Halfa Ridge Brigadier G B P Roberts, the commander of the British 22nd Armoured Brigade watched the Panzer divisions advancing towards the ridge and recorded:

> On they come, a most impressive array. . . . It is fascinating to watch them, as one might watch a snake curl up ready to strike. But there is something unusual too; some of the leading tanks are Mk IVs, and Mk IVs have in the past always had short-barrelled 75mm guns used for close support work and firing HE only, consequently they are not usually in front. But these Mk IVs have a very long gun on them; in fact it looks like the devil of a gun. This must be the long-barrelled, stepped-up 75mm the Intelligence people have been talking about.
>
> And now they all turn left and face us and begin to advance slowly. The greatest concentration seems to be opposite the CLY and the anti-tank

guns of the Rifle Brigade. I warn all units over the air not to fire until the enemy are within 1000yds; it can't be long now and then in a few seconds the tanks of the CLY open fire and the battle is on. Once one is in the middle of a battle time is difficult to judge, but it seems only a few minutes before nearly all the tanks of the Grant squadron of the CLY were on fire. The new German 75mm is taking heavy toll . . . the situation is serious; there is a complete hole in our defences.

Below: The Valentine was an extremely reliable tank and easy to service.
Inset: Adolf Hitler.

The Afrika Korps had made a determined attack and the 'long-barrelled stepped-up' 75mm guns which had excited Robert's attention inflicted considerable losses on the British tanks. Nevertheless the Panzers had not got a foothold on the Alam el Halfa Ridge by nightfall and petrol and ammunition was desperately low. (Reserve supplies were desperately low too, despite Cavallero's promises and Kesselring's assurances Rommel had received little petrol. Kesselring airlifted part of his quota, but most of this petrol was consumed on the long journey to the front; it was the sinking of a tanker off Tobruk which really ended any hope of success in this offensive.) Nor did they ever succeed in doing so.

The battle for the Alam el Halfa Ridge lasted for six days, although the Panzers

started to pull out on 3 September. The Afrika Korps could not fight without supplies and by the evening of 5 September the Panzers did not even have enough petrol to take them back behind the old 'front', and there was a chronic shortage of ammunition. For Rommel the gamble was over; as always the Afrika Korps had fought magnificently, but the Alam Halfa operation was a logistical disaster. Bitter and disillusioned, he flew back to Germany and was admitted to hospital at Semmering near Vienna. But before doing so he reported in person to Hitler to tell the Führer the Panzer Army was at the gates of Alexandria, but unless and until it was reinforced and the supply situation improved there was no hope of pushing these gates open. 'Don't worry,' Hitler is reputed to have said. 'We're going to give Africa priority; we'll take Alexandria all right,' and he went on, 'We are already turning out landing craft for use in the Mediterranean; we've got 200 already. They'll be better than tankers, and what is more they're going to carry a couple of 88s apiece.'

After the interview Hitler took Rommel out to show him the prototype of another 'secret' weapon which was going to bring victory in Africa – the Tiger tank. With its 88mm gun this great giant Panzer could outshoot any British, American or Russian tank in existence, the Führer boasted. 'Yes! we shall take Alexandria all right,' he said again.

Defeat and Retreat

Generalleutnant Georg Stumme took over from Rommel, inheriting the latter's plan and problems, but not his intuition. Fifty-five years old, Stumme was a little man with a big paunch and a permanent flush brought on by high blood pressure – something which Rommel considered to be a good reason why Stumme should never have been sent to Africa. But Stumme, who always wore an eyeglass and looked the part of the traditional Prussion general, was an energetic and fearless Panzer commander, idolised by his soldiers on the Russian front where his nickname was 'Fireball'. Unfortunately he had come to the desert under something of a disciplinary cloud, having lost his command because one of his staff officers carrying plans for an impending attack had been shot down in an aircraft and fallen into the hands of the Russians. Rommel, who had little time for Eastern Front generals anyway, considered that this was another good reason why Stumme should never have been sent to Africa. However Berlin thought otherwise, and as Kesselring wrote, 'Being a man of a more even and genial temperament than Rommel, he [Stumme] did much to relax the tension among officers and men, besides managing to create tolerable relations with the Italian Command.'

But not all the Afrika Korps thought so highly of the new Panzer Army commander, and his jocular familiarity with the troops and a habit of gesticulating when talking, led to him being given a new nickname, 'the Italian'.

Another Eastern Front Panzer expert, Generalleutnant Ritter von Thoma, was sent out to replace Nehring as Afrika Korps commander, and von Vaerst returned to the 15th Panzer. Oberst Bayerlein, Nehring's erstwhile Chief of Staff, and several other experienced Afrika Korps officers holding key appointments, also went on leave or were posted away during September and October. Many of those who replaced them arrived from Russia, having asked for a transfer to Africa where they imagined they would find soldiering in warm riviera-like conditions to be more amenable. Dysentery and gastric troubles brought on by lack of acclimatisation and conditions at the El Alamein front made the majority wish they had never set foot in Africa.

The conditions at the front were at this time as bad as they had ever been. Being the tail end of summer the weather was oppressively hot by day; there was little water and the ration scale had been cut in order to conserve the petrol needed to ferry food and water from Tobruk and Mersa Matruh. Men lived in holes in the ground surrounded by festoons of barbed wire, amid shell craters, burnt-out tanks and the awesome detritus of war. Empty tins littered the ground in front of the forward positions; the stench of human dung mixed with the heavy sweetish carrion smell of the dead lingered in the nostrils and penetrated the lungs. 'It puts you off *Wurst*,' one *gefreiter* complained bitterly as he watched flies paddling in the melted fat which con-

A special communications vehicle controls and oversees the German advance through Egypt.

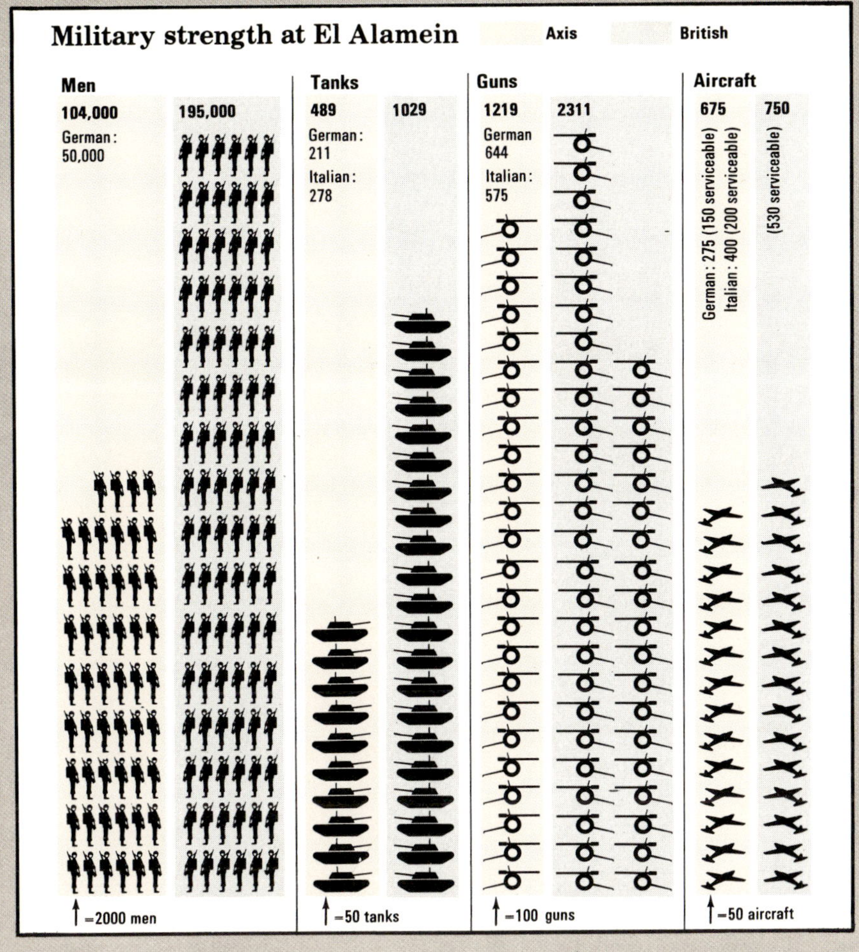

stituted his ration sausage. For the flies were at Alamein in their millions – energetic lively ones which were simply a nuisance, and sluggish bloated crawlers which were a horror.

To the men at the front each and every day in September and October 1942 was one of monotonous routine. While on the German side ammunition was short and offensive shoots were restricted. Yet it seemed there was no shortage of bombs for the Royal Air Force, since not a day passed without an air raid. In one week alone more than a thousand bombs were dropped on a single small sector of the line held by 164th Division. Bombardments alternated with the air raids and sometimes shells from British field guns sniping at Afrika Korps' positions would whistle over even during an air raid. In such circumstances it was surprising that morale was not at rock bottom, and that a grim humour flourished. 'No whistling' read a notice above one of 155 Artillery Regiment's gun pits.

At night patrols were active and there were always more mines to be laid – in two months the Afrika Korps laid over a million. But for most of the time the troops just sat and waited and the individual world of each consisted of a tiny patch of sand surrounded by barbed wire or gun pit or the turret of a Panzer. Men were filthy, unshaven and caked in layers of grey ashy dust because there was only a limited quantity of water, nearly all of which was needed for drinking and cooking. Mail arrived from time to time – letters seemingly from another world, where the writers lived among trees and green grass, deplored rain, ate real bread and butter and where water came out of a tap. But letters were few and far between; many ended up in the sea when the transport plane carrying them across the Mediterranean or in the ships sunk between Brindisi and Tripoli.

Companies and sectors were rotated and men were sent on leave of course – to rest and recuperate for a week at a

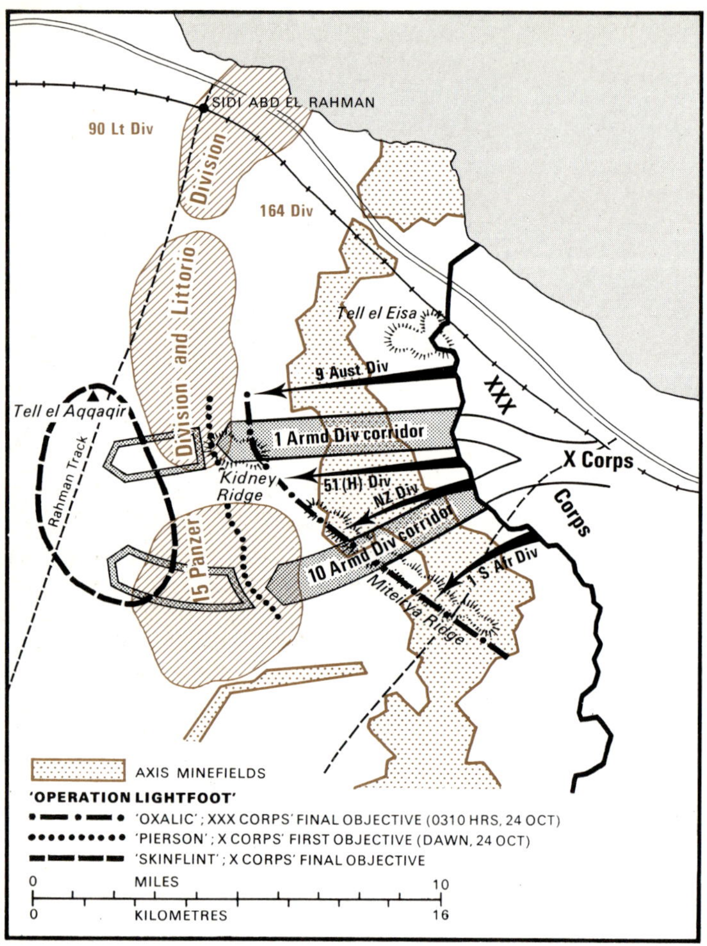

Above: Montgomery's plan to regain the offensive in North Africa.
Above right: A German tank advances along the coast to El Alamein.

time in seaside camps between Mersa Matruh and Benghazi. There it was possible to bathe and enjoy almost unlimited fresh water; even a shortage of razor-blades did not diminish the pleasure of scraping off beards. Beer was in short supply also, but every man got a couple of bottles of *Löwenbräu*. A week passed all too quickly, and when the time came to return to the front – to the air raids and the shelling – the break seemed unreal. For the battlefield had not changed, except that the filth seemed filthier and the stench to have got worse.

Meanwhile in the enemy camp General Montgomery was planning his offensive and by mid-October the preparations for it were almost complete. In an age of mechanised warfare his plan could hardly be called 'inspired' but the Eighth Army's superiority in men and machines almost guaranteed its success.

As they both fielded the same number of divisions, on paper the two sides may have looked fairly evenly matched. However the fighting strength of the British formations exceeded those of the Panzer Army in a ratio of almost two to one, and the British formations were for the most part fresh, battle-experienced and well-equipped. Moreover they had about a thousand tanks, while Stumme could muster less than half that number – and then only by including about 278 of the obsolete Italian 'coffins'. Above the battlefield also the British, with 750 aircraft, had the advantage for the Luftwaffe and the Italian Air Force together could put only 675 machines into the skies over the desert. Air superiority was a battle-winning factor, and the Afrika Korps had experienced its effects even before the British launched their offensive.

The Second Battle of Alamein – the Battle of Egypt as it is sometimes called – opened with a thunderous bombardment at 2130 hours on 23 October. Along a six-mile front in the northern sector near the Mediterranean shore the British artillery poured an unbelievable concentration of shells on the Panzer Army's positions. Stumme at his headquarters only a few miles behind the front heard the hurricane of shells sweeping over his forward troops, but there was little he could do about it. Perhaps he was all too conscious of the shortages of ammunition and petrol; and perhaps he was disconcerted by the sudden disruption of his communications system. (British bomber aircraft, specially equipped, were flying over the battlefield, jamming the German wireless nets.) No one will ever know because Stumme disappeared early on 24 October, and was not seen again until his body was picked up on 25 October by men of the 15th Panzer.

From the moment the attack started Panzer Army HQ could gain no clear picture as to what was actually happening. Montgomery had been expected to attack in the centre where the Bologna Division provocatively baited a trap in which the two Panzer divisions would close on the attackers. Although it soon became apparent that the Eighth Army had not attacked in the centre after all, reports that the British had hit hard at the strongest point of the Panzer Army's front – the south – did not reach Stumme until it was too late to hold the attack and straighten out the front. While the situation was still obscure he decided to go out and see for himself what was going on. Oberst Westphal, who was acting as Chief of Staff, begged him to take an escort and a signals truck as Rommel always did. But Stumme, veteran of the Russian front laughed at the idea; as he was going only as far as the 90th Light's tactical headquarters he would go by car and take only

Below: A British field gun in action during the second battle at El Alamein.
Left: A new German tank moves through a Libyan town in order to regain the front line.
Right: Indian troops advance to El Alamein.

Oberst Büchting with him. It was a fatal trip for Stumme, and a disaster for the Afrika Korps which found itself leaderless soon after the start of the bloodiest battle it had ever fought. (Stumme, unable to determine what was happening from the information he received at the 90th Light headquarters, decided to drive on up to the 15th Panzers' front where one battalion of Ernst Baade's 115th Panzergrenadiers had signalled it was fighting off an attack by troops of the 51st Highland Division and a second battalion had reported that it was blocking an advance by New Zealanders, who had overrun Italian-held positions in the 15th Panzer sector. Close to the front Stumme's car was shot up by enemy infantry and anti-tank guns. Büchting was killed in the first burst of fire and the driver turned the car round to get away. Stumme, apparently in the act of jumping out, had a heart attack and fell off the running board without the driver realising what had happened.)

Both the timing and the method of the British offensive undoubtedly came as a surprise to the men of the Afrika Korps. They had sensed that the initiative had passed to the enemy and they knew that the British would offer battle sooner or later. Yet only that very morning von Thoma had driven down to the Qattara Depression with Oberst Liss – a visitor from Berlin – and had concluded that a British offensive was not yet in the offing. Moreover the Eighth Army's attack when it did come was expected to come in the centre from the direction of Ruweisat Ridge. Consequently the fact that Montgomery had chosen to strike at the strongest part in the Panzer Army's line was doubly confusing – especially when the main thrust was linked with feints in the centre and south of the front.

There was a full moon that night and, as usual, when the first mighty clap of the thunderous bombardment came at 2130 hours the Afrika Korps were brewing tea and munching *Wurst*. Following a series of air raids during the day – no

heavier and no more serious than usual – the front had been quiet since nightfall. At the headquarters of the 3rd Battalion of Baade's 115th Panzergrenadiers, the battalion commander and a battery commander from Oberst Eduard Crasemann's 33rd Artillery Regiment were revising the artillery fire plan. Everything seemed to presage a normal evening. Then the bombardment started, and simultaneously messages from sentries in the forward outposts reported tanks moving up towards the eastern edge of the minefield.

The alarm was sounded and the troops ran back to their trenches and gun pits. Along the whole front the troops cowered in their trenches and waited fatalistically as the British artillery pounded their positions. Over the next 30 minutes neither the Panzergrenadiers nor the Afrika Korps' gunners dared move, as the deluge of shells from 25 pounders and the Eighth Army's new American 105mms flattened wire, demolished strongpoints and buried men in their trenches. When the bombardment did eventually ease there was a scramble to pull out the men who had been buried or half buried, and stretcher bearers were kept busy ferrying the casualties back to regimental aid posts. Meantime section commanders and artillery observation officers were now anxiously watching the front. They

Intense firing in the southern sector.

Below: A British six pounder in action. These anti-tank guns were often ineffective but they gave the troops a feeling of security.

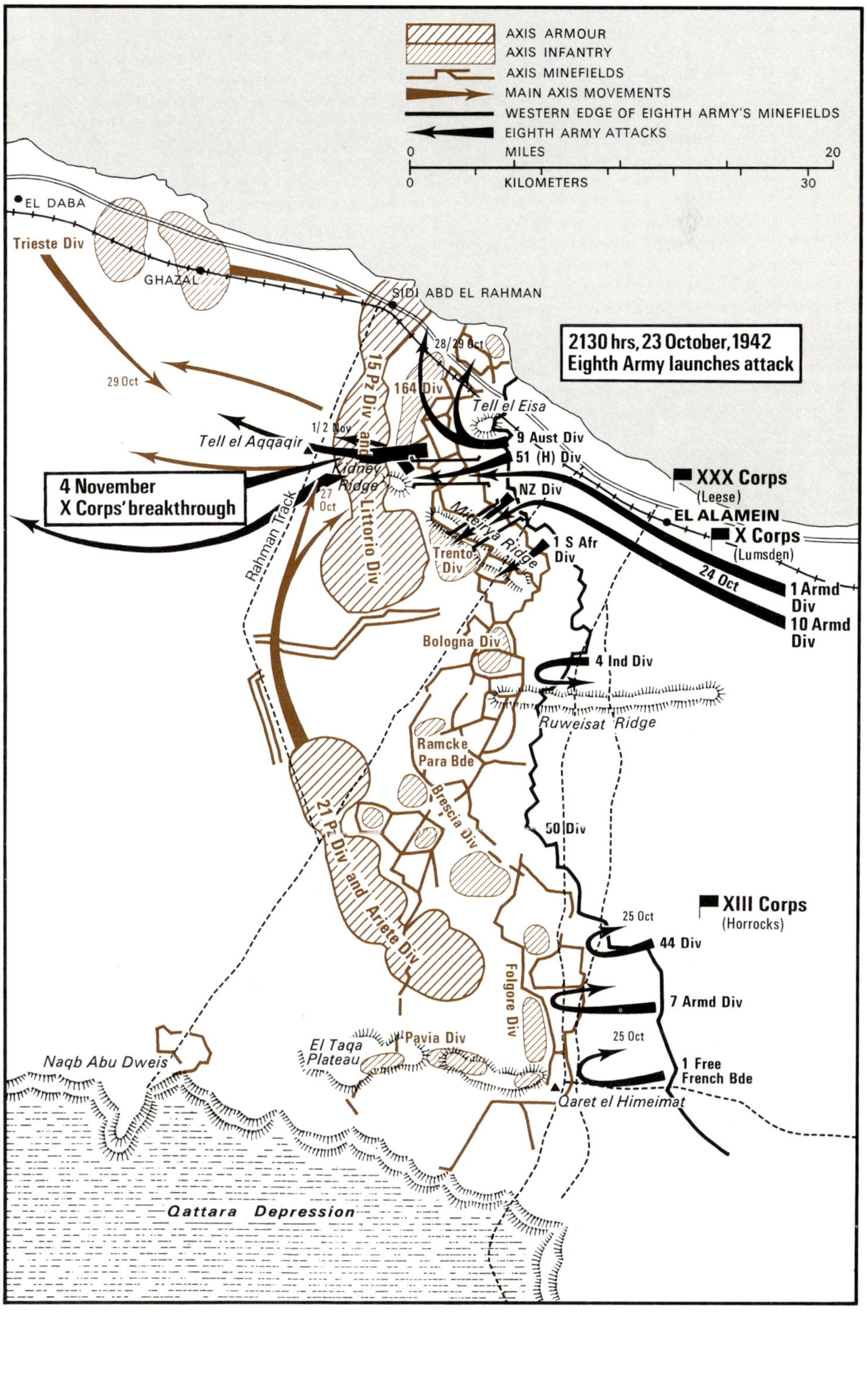

AXIS ARMOUR
AXIS INFANTRY
AXIS MINEFIELDS
MAIN AXIS MOVEMENTS
WESTERN EDGE OF EIGHTH ARMY'S MINEFIELDS
EIGHTH ARMY ATTACKS
0 MILES 20
0 KILOMETERS 30
EL DABA
Trieste Div
GHAZAL
SIDI ABD EL RAHMAN
2130 hrs, 23 October, 1942
Eighth Army launches attack
29 Oct
28/29 Oct
15 Pz Div and Littorio Div
164 Div
Tell el Eisa
1/2 Nov
Tell el Aqqaqir
9 Aust Div
51 (H) Div
Kidney Ridge
4 November
X Corps' breakthrough
27 Oct
NZ Div
XXX Corps
(Leese)
EL ALAMEIN
X Corps
(Lumsden)
Rahman Track
Miteirya Ridge
Trento Div
1 S Afr Div
24 Oct
1 Armd Div
10 Armd Div
Bologna Div
4 Ind Div
Ruweisat Ridge
Ramcke Para Bde
Brescia Div
50 Div
21 Pz Div and Ariete Div
XIII Corps
(Horrocks)
25 Oct
44 Div
Folgore Div
7 Armd Div
El Taqa Plateau
Pavia Div
Naqb Abu Dweis
1 Free French Bde
Qaret el Himeimat
Qattara Depression

knew that behind the curtain of fire enemy sappers would have been working their way through the 'Devil's Garden' of mines opening lanes for the tanks which could shortly be expected to descend on the Panzer Army's positions.

British infantry preceded the tanks and by midnight the Panzergrenadiers were engaged in bloody hand-to-hand fighting in which much use was made of machine pistols and grenades by the Germans and bayonets by the British. The tanks, Shermans, rumbled in close behind the infantry. As they emerged from the minefields and came within range, Crasemann's 88s opened fire and one or two of the leading tanks were hit. But others took their place and it was only a matter of minutes before the 88s came under intense artillery fire. One disadvantage of these guns was their size, which made them difficult to conceal. Thus when the British pinpointed their positions the enemy artillery observation officers called down a concentration of fire which lasted until the last 88 in the 115th Panzers' area was knocked out. Gunner officers reckoning the odds later estimated that at some places in this battle as many as 80 British guns concentrated on four 88s.

The Shermans seemed to be almost indestructible, and there were so many of them. Daybreak on the morning of 24 October found the two forward battalions of the 115th Panzergrenadier still clinging to some of their positions, but they had suffered heavy casualties, and some who continued to fight did so in a frenzy brought on by the shelling. On the left and the right the British had overrun flanking positions held by the Italians; while further south paratroops of the Folgore Division were fighting

hard to retain their grip on the southern extremity of the line. The British now had a bulge sticking into the Panzer Army's front, and this had created a salient along the coast, which the Australians began to nip out. Moving north from the tip of the British bulge they threatened to cut off the 164th Light Division and the Italians within the salient. On the other side of the bulge the fight revolved round a feature known as 'Kidney Ridge'. It was vital ground because it dominated the whole of the 15th Panzer's sector – something which Montgomery's men had appreciated when they seized it in the early hours of the morning.

Back at Panzer Army HQ where there was still no news of the vanished Stumme, Ritter von Thomas assumed command during the afternoon. Fifty-five years old, a Prussian aristocrat, tall with blue eyes and blond hair tinged with grey, von Thoma had a temperament similar to that of Rommel. He did not suffer fools gladly, and was given to violent and unpredictable rages. On this occasion the outburst witnessed by Stumme's staff may be considered excusable, because he had inherited a

Below: A desert armourer works on bombs in an airfield in Egypt.
Below right: A German armoured car moves towards the front line.

most difficult situation. He had taken over a static line of defences in the middle of an attack which had already breached the line at several points, and he had no mobile force available which could be rushed up to seal off the threatened areas. Stumme had not organised a counter-attack reserve because he considered that the troops in the static positions were stretched to the limit and such a force could be raised only by pulling units out of the line. Moreover Stumme had acquired his experience on the Eastern Front where the Russians generally attacked on a front extending to 60 miles. This was the traditional way of doing things. He had not imagined that Montgomery would concentrate on a narrow zone to create a breach which could then be widened when the attackers fanned out behind the front.

It was, as Rommel described it later, 'a battle without hope'. Nevertheless von Thoma decided that a counter-attack had to be attempted before the

Below: A British 2.5 pounder in August 1942.
Inset: The Sherman M4A4 Firefly.

British could extend the frontage of their break-in. So the 15th Panzer was ordered to recapture Kidney Ridge, and to ensure that the assault was a vigorous effort von Thoma himself accompanied the assault force in one of Willy Teege's Panzers. But neither this attack by the 8th Panzer Regiment nor the four others that followed could dislodge the British from the all-important ridge. Nor for that matter could the British make much progress either. Despite ceaseless shelling and round-the-clock aerial bombardment the Afrika Korps could not be budged, and their opponents began to wonder whether German reinforcements had arrived. They could not know that the Panzergrenadier and infantry companies of the 15th Panzer were down to about 20 men apiece and battalions to an average of 160 – the approximate establishment strength of a company. Panzer losses had also been heavy. By the evening of 24 October the 15th Panzer had only 36 tanks; 40 had been lost during the day.

But the British had paid dearly for the ground they had gained. The point was the Germans could not afford such losses for their reserves of men and

Rommel (seated, looking up) flew back to North Africa as soon as he was told about the situation at El Alamein.

material were almost nil, whereas the British had plenty of reinforcements waiting behind. They had won the logistical battle as Rommel appreciated when he returned to Africa on 25 October.

News that Stumme was missing had caused Hitler some rumblings of anxiety, which led to first Keitel and then the Führer himself to telephone Rommel at his Austrian retreat. 'Are you well enough to return to take command at Alamein?' Keitel asked. 'I want you to return to Africa,' said Hitler. Rommel responded immediately and flew back the following morning. Although he 'knew there were no laurels to be earned in Africa'.

Back at Alamein Rommel saw there was nothing he could do to turn the tide running against the Panzer Army. There was no petrol available for a return to mobile warfare. Moreover even if it were possible to disengage the odds against it were too high. By 1 November Afrika Korps tank strength was down to a total of 119 – of which 18 were little Mark IIs. The 15th Panzer had been reduced to a group of ten Mk IVs – the remnants of the 8th Panzer Regiment, and about 200 Panzergrenadiers – all that remained of the 115th Regiment. Both regimental commanders had gone: Teege of the 8th Panzer captured on the 30th and Baade killed on the 31 October. As a division the 15th Panzer had ceased to exist and for the rest of the campaign its decimated remnants could be used only as a battle group. (Even this tiny group ceased to exist when von Cramer, the Afrika Korps' last commander, surrendered in Tunisia. Subsequently the division was reformed in Sicily as a Panzergrenadier Division.) That night (Sunday 1 November) Rommel wrote to his wife:

> It's a week since I left home. A week of very, very hard fighting. It was often doubtful whether we'd be able to hold out. Yet we did manage it each time, although with sad losses. I'm on the move a lot in order to step in wherever we're in trouble. Things were very bad in the north yesterday morning, although it was all more or less cleared up by evening. The struggle makes very heavy demands on one's nervous energy, though physically I'm quite well. Some supplies are supposed to be on their way. But it's a tragedy that this sort of support only arrives when things are almost hopeless.

Rommel had had cause to worry about the Afrika Korps supplies – above all petrol – throughout the campaign. But never more than now. He was contemplating a withdrawal, but without petrol he had no hope of rescuing men let alone vehicles. On the morning of 26 October the Italian tanker *Proserpina* laden with 3000 tons of fuel and heading for Tobruk had been sunk.

That same evening another vessel, the *Tergestea* carrying 1000 tons of petrol and 1000 tons of ammunition for the *Deutsch-Italienische Panzer Armee* as Rommel's force was now being called, was torpedoed while she was entering Tobruk harbour. Three days later the tanker *Luisiana* with 1500 tons of petrol was sunk off Greece. Meantime the Panzer Army's vehicles were stranded with almost empty fuel tanks.

Apart from the occasional salvo of harrassing fire, Sunday 1 November was a quiet day for the Afrika Korps and in the afternoon – before he wrote to 'Lu' – Rommel had gone forward to survey the battlefield from a vantage point in the 90th Light's area. During the previous day there had been heavy fighting around here when the British tried to cut off the 125th Infantry Regiment and to push up the coast road blocked by Panzergrenadiers of the 361st Regiment (of the 90th Light). A successful counter-attack by men of the 21st Panzer and the 90th Light had restored the situation, and two battalions of the 125th Regiment had fought their way out of the trap. Montgomery had been robbed of success, but the cost to Rommel's troops in blood and bones had been heavy.

The battlefield was quiet now; the British were collecting their dead and the Afrika Korps' artillery was silent. Once again the situation had stabilised. Nevertheless Rommel had no illusion about the future. He reckoned that despite their losses the British still had some 800 battleworthy tanks and even if his mobile workshops managed to repair all the Panzers that were capable of repair he could see no more than 90 German and 140 Italian tanks taking the field. None of them could match the Shermans. British bombers and fighter bombers were also hammering the Panzer Army and exacting a grim toll well behind the front as well as in the forward areas.

'We had to evacuate Bor el Abd,' Armin Köhler recorded in his diary, '. . . the latter half of the day was made hell for us . . . . Continuous bombing attacks with 18 to 24 four-engined aircraft, with fighter bombers and low-flying aircraft rattled our nerves. The Tommies were playing cat and mouse with us. Aircraft above, aircraft in the sky – but never a German.'

On 2 November Rommel finally made up his mind. If the Panzer Army continued to fight what had degenerated into a battle of attrition it would be annihilated; a withdrawal was the only alternative. 'We must pull back to Fuka,' he said – Fuka being a defensive position based on the coastal village of that name, 62 miles west of Alamein. Italian troops had been digging defences since October, and Rommel banked on being

Above: A Bristol Beaufighter gets a thorough overhaul ready for action in the desert.
Below: The Junkers 88 was known as the 'Three-Fingered 88' because of its long engine cowlings.

able to fight a delaying action there until the Panzer Army recovered its strength. 'The dead are lucky. It's all over for them,' he wrote to 'Lu' before turning to the formidable problems presented by a retreat from Alamein.

First, however, sanction for the operation had to be obtained from Berlin. In the circumstances Rommel regarded this as a pure formality; retreat and the chance to bounce back was clearly preferable to destruction. A long signal describing the situation, outlining the problems, and requesting permission to pull back to prepared positions was duly despatched, and Rommel turned his attentions to plans for the move back. It was clearly going to be a tricky business because the troops in the forward areas had to disengage and fall back quickly, before the pursuing enemy could pin them down again. Inevitably some units fighting as rearguards would have to be sacrificed, for in any retirement operation there have to be intermediate defence lines to hold up the enemy while the forward troops get back to the new main position – in this case Fuka. In theory the men holding the intermediate lines disengage and fall back to the next line, leap-frogging back until everybody is safe behind the final defensive line. In practice, however, rearguards at intermediate positions are often isolated and overwhelmed. The Italian Bologna Division, which had no transport; the 104th Panzergrenadier Regiment of the 21st Panzer which was holding a vital sector of the

line; and the 361st Regiment whose legionnaires had done so well before Tobruk, all fell into this category.

Orders for the withdrawal were issued during the afternoon of 2 November, although some of the base installations – workshops, supply centres, medical units and the like – had moved back before then. Troops in the front line started to pull out after nightfall and by first light everything was going according to plan. When Eighth Army patrols reported that the Panzer Army seemed to be pulling out of the coastal salient, the British reacted slowly. In the event this hesitance was of little consequence, for Hitler now stepped in and prolonged their opportunity to exploit the situation.

At 1530 hours (on 3 November) Rommel was handed a telegram from the Führer. It was the latter's response

Field Marshal Erwin Rommel in his personal armoured car, which was called 'Greif'.

to his request for permission to withdraw.

It is with trusting confidence in your leadership and the German-Italian troops under your command that the German people and I are following the heroic struggle in Egypt. In the situation in which you find yourself there can be no other thought but to stand fast, yield not a centimetre of ground and throw every gun and every man into the battle. Considerable air force reinforcements are being sent to Commander-in-Chief South. The Duce and the *Comando Supremo* are also making the utmost efforts to send you the means to continue the fight. Your enemy, despite his superiority, must also be at the end of his strength. It would not be the first time in history that a strong will has triumphed over the bigger battalions. As to your troops, you can show them no other road than that to victory or death.

Adolf Hitler

Rommel was shattered; so too was everybody else in his Headquarters. Not only had Lady Luck turned against the Panzer Army, it seemed that their commander's freedom of action in the military sphere was being curtailed also. (Rommel's staff considered he should ignore the order. So too did Kesselring, who arrived at Rommel's HQ on 4 November to be promptly accused of being responsible for it. Kesselring denied this and advised the Panzer Army commander to do what he thought was right.) Always a stickler for obedience from his own juniors Rommel obeyed his Führer and a signal was sent to unit commanders:

On order from higher authority the present positions must be defended to the end. No withdrawal may therefore take place without my approval. This cancels the instruction for withdrawal in my signal timed and dated 1340 hrs 3 November.

If Hitler had not relented, his unequivocal demand for 'victory or death' would have sealed the fate of the Panzer Army six months before its ultimate demise in Tunisia. In the event, Hitler did relent, 24 hours after dictating the first signal; and in that same 24 hours Rommel had been trying to find a formula that signified obedience to the Führer's orders, but which saved his army from destruction. Without the 'victory or death' order he would have had another day for the withdrawal, and an opportunity perhaps to organise a proper defensive line at one or other of the positions his troops knew so well. As it was the day that was lost brought the sacrifice of the infantry – mainly Italian – which had no transport.

Meanwhile Rommel's standfast order had put the Afrika Korps on its mettle. Men recognised that it might be easier, as von Thoma said, 'to die in a hopeless battle, than on the evening of a victory' and von Thoma himself was prepared to show how to die. The veteran of World War I, the Spanish Civil War and the Eastern Front is reported to have said, when Oberst Bayerlein visited him late on 4 November, 'the Führer's order is madness. It is the death warrant of the Army. How can I explain it to my men?' Von Thoma was wearing his medals together with the

A German gun crew pound British positions in an attempt to hold up their advance.

shoulder straps and collar patches normally kept for the parade ground, Bayerlein noticed with some surprise.

Hitler's second signal, authorising the withdrawal had not been received when von Thoma set off to lead the survivors of the 8th Panzer Regiment on what he clearly intended to be a death and glory operation – although he described its purpose as a reconnaissance mission to ascertain whether a British force was trying to outflank the Afrika Korps. Climbing into his Panzer he gave the order, *'Vorwärts, Heia Safari!'* Some of the tank crews responded with shouts of *'Heia Safari!'* the old battle cry; others muttered *'Verdammte Scheisse!'* At this stage of the campaign most of the seasoned troops had had their fill of glory and were certainly not keen on dying.

Fifteen Panzers – all Mk IVs, moved off, crossed the semi-circle of infantry positions near Tell el Aqqaqir and clattered on towards the centre of the

A German shell burst shakes up this artillery crew.

British line. Scotsmen of the 51st Highland Division and a battalion of the 60th Rifles were deployed in this sector of the front, and behind them were Shermans of the 10th Royal Hussars. Von Thoma's charge was more of a defiant gesture than a serious attempt to gain information and it terminated in destruction. But Ritter von Thoma did not die. A scout car commanded by Captain Grant Singer of the 10th Hussars put a shot through the back of the driver's seat and the crew, including von Thoma bailed out. Singer's second car drove towards the disabled Mk IV and a tall dusty figure walking away from it. In Singer's own words, 'I thought I might as well collar him. . . .'

From El Aqqaqir von Thoma was taken to Montgomery's headquarters where that evening he was photographed and subsequently shared supper with the Eighth Army Commander.

In the far south the paratroops of the Folgore and Ramcke Brigade had to fend for themselves. The majority of the Italians – who had fought stubbornly and exceptionally well – were simply abandoned. As they had no transport they were written off. Bernhard Ramcke did not have enough transport to lift his whole brigade in one move, but he had no intention of being abandoned or of allowing the 700 men under his command to be sacrificed.

On 3 November Ramcke received a message instructing him to break contact with the enemy, pull back that night and take up new positions near Deir el Qatani. Apart from the problem of disengaging this entailed a forced march of some 16 miles – which, in desert conditions, was no mean feat; certainly nobody who took part in the march was ever likely to forget it. But the paratroopers eventually reached the predetermined area and dug in. A few men collapsed en route, but they and a few stragglers were picked up by personnel carriers operating a shuttle service along the route.

Above: General Bernard Montgomery directs operations at Alamein. On his right is Horrocks.
Left: A German motorcycle crew.

No sooner had the brigade settled in to their new positions than another message ordered another move. One battalion had to go north, and as the message had been delayed and the battalion was supposed to be already on its way, the whole of the brigade transport – amounting to 40 vehicles – was hurriedly assembled and Hauptmann Straehler-Pohl's men embussed. An hour later another message instructed the rest of the brigade to move and take up defensive positions west of Fuka. Fuka was 60 miles away, as the crow flies, so this order implied another forced march and four days trekking across open desert dominated by the enemy's air force. It looked as if the brigade was doomed, or – at least –

destined for captivity. Nor was this the end of the story. As the two remaining battalions were about to march off, the enemy attacked the positions they had just vacated. Tanks were moving ahead of enemy infantry, and the rearguard waited until they were almost on them before opening fire. These tactics succeeded; a number of enemy tanks went up in smoke and the attack fizzled out. While the enemy were still confused the paratroopers slipped away.

At midnight the brigade was still on the march, when Ramcke ordered the column to halt and rest while he, the two battalion commanders – Major Kroh and Major Fenski and Ramcke's aide Leutnant Wetter, made a brief reconnaissance forward along their route in his staff car. Topping a rise the party almost ran into a regiment of British tanks, and the car made a quick turn before it was spotted. The near presence of the enemy clearly demanded a change in direction and the brigade marched south into the desert. But the paratroops had gained only a brief respite. Next day British planes flew over the column and within an hour tanks were seen on the horizon. Ramcke's anti-tank guns put down their trails and waited while the rest of the column moved on. In the action which followed all but one of the enemy tanks were destroyed. But other tanks came to take their place and throughout the day the paratroops were under constant attack. By nightfall the anti-tank gunners had exhausted their ammunition and their guns had to be destroyed; behind them they left a trail of blackened smoking wrecks which had once been British armoured fighting vehicles.

Meantime the rest of the brigade was still marching, and during the night of 5 November the leading scouts reported that they had almost walked into a big

An Australian gun crew pound German defences in the northern sector of the front.

convoy of British vehicles; the convoy – a supply column – had stopped for the night. Ramcke, realising that this was the one – and perhaps only – chance for his brigade, said: 'They'll do for us.'

Creeping forward in small groups some of the paratroops quietly surrounded the vehicles and at a given signal sprang forward simultaneously. Seconds later the sleeping British crews woke up to find themselves looking into the muzzles of German machine pistols. Once their weapons had been seized they were ejected from their vehicles and their places taken by the Germans. Down the road the rest of the brigade waited to board the trucks as they rolled west towards safety. For the time being the paratroops had everything they wanted, since the vehicles contained food, water and weapons.

Ramcke's problem was in what direction to drive. The convoy moved by day and night without much risk, overflown on several occasions by British aircraft which undoubtedly assumed they were British. The paratroops wore their Afrika Korps uniforms with 'engine-driver' forage caps, but they were concealed by the canvas canopies of the trucks.

The convoy ploughed on for three days, 187 miles a day, on a compass course over rough terrain which brought new hazards – stoppages in patches of rough sand, breakages on rocks. Throughout all these vicissitudes Ramcke urged his men on, pitilessly – permitting little rest or sleep. He himself seemed unaffected by lack of sleep or the problems that assailed him. Driving at the head of the convoy he wore the cavalry breeches and khaki linen leggings he had taken from some *Englander* in Crete, a green pullover and a blue Luftwaffe forage cap.

On the morning of 7 November the convoy of vehicles was stopped on the coast road near Sidi Barrani by a German reconnaissance troop . . . the brigade was safe. Ramcke drove on quickly to Halfaya where he was told Rommel had set up his headquarters at Bardia. There he burst in on a conference at which the Field Marshal had just announced that he believed the paratroop brigade commander had probably been captured.

'He is alive and well . . . and still with you,' Ramcke reported. He might have added, 'And no thanks to you or the Afrika Korps,' for it was his conviction that Rommel had written off the paratroop brigade.

The Afrika Korps' move back to Fuka had been a scramble. Most of the major units were back behind the new line by 5 November and after that the retreat continued in a more orderly fashion. The summer was now over; storms raged over the Mediterranean and biting winds swept across the desert as Rommel's army prepared for the next bound to the rear. Rommel's original intention was to hold Fuka for as long as possible, giving straggling units time to rejoin the main body. In fact Fuka was abandoned on 6 November. The Panzer Army simply was not strong enough to stand up to the Eighth Army for by this time the strength of the entire Afrika Korps was down to less than 2500 men – slightly more than a tenth of its established strength – and the 15th tanks; the 90th Light with only 1100 men and no heavy weapons did not have a single tank; and the 164th, reduced to a strength of 1200 men, was in a similar state. The Italians, down to 3000 men with no tanks and no guns, were in even worse shape. Yet the Panzer Army was still capable of showing its teeth, as the Eighth Army was to learn on a number of occasions during the long trek back through Cyrenaica to Tripoli. The Panzer crews and the Panzergrenadiers were magnificently seasoned and if there had been more of them, together with more tanks and the supplies to sustain them, the Eighth Army's task would have been infinitely more difficult and the cost correspondingly higher.

After Fuka came Mersa Matruh where the remnants of the 164th Division fought a skilful action, rescuing the 90th Light's rearguard when it had run out of petrol. Petrol was tragically short – so short that when the 21st Panzer fell back from Mersa Matruh to Halfaya half its Panzers (and there were only eleven) had to be towed. Fortunately the weather came to the Afrika Korps' aid, for in the early morning of 6 November there were showers from a sky of thickening clouds. At noon the desert was deluged with water and tracks and wheels sank into the softened surface. British supply columns were delayed and the pursuit slackened.

For the men on the march the question of where they would stand and fight next was always uppermost in their thoughts. Halfaya, the scene of Padre Bach's gallant defence the year before, seemed after Mersa Matruh to be a definite possibility. But it was not to be. Rommel had just got news that American forces with British support had landed in Algeria and were advancing eastwards. It seemed that his army was not only running away from trouble, but also into it. Yet it was also clear that the sooner he got back to a line he could defend the better.

Halfaya Pass was held for two days by one Italian regiment of the Pistoria Division and a battery of artillery – 680 men in all. 'I am sacrificing you,' Rommel told the commander of this force. 'I need a day to get clear.' Doubtless the Italians, stranded with no vehicles, were happy to know that their war was nearly over. In the event 612 of them surrendered to one company of New Zealand infantry on 10 November.

Below: These Italian troops were left behind. Bottom: 8 November 1942, the first Allied landings in Morocco spelt the eventual doom of the DAK.

The next bound was El Adem, where a halt was obligatory because of the supply situation. More petrol was needed for the vehicles, and there was not enough to go round. So once again the Italians had to go short. While the Panzer Army was disentangling itself from the mass of immobilised Italian trucks another threat developed. Troops of the Eighth Army were reported to be near Derna, 60 miles to the west. This was Rommel's nightmare – an outflanking move by the British which would force him to fight facing in two directions. The answer was to do as he had done before, to bypass the place. So the Afrika Korps took to the desert again, cutting out Tobruk, Derna and Benghazi. Finally it came to Mersa Brega – the old El Agheila position – where it halted, to dig the sand out of the old fortifications and lay masses of new mines in front of them. Then winter rains came down and turned the marshes into a sticky paste; it was the end of November, and the Afrika Korps had earned a break. 'My men,' Rommel said in a letter to Berlin penned on 26 November, 'have deserved well of the Fatherland. Such an army must not be lost. Arrangements should now be made to return it to Europe. One of these days North Africa will fall to the British and Americans; to try to maintain it would be a grave error. . . .'

But the men in Berlin were not prepared to 'Dunkirk' the Afrika Korps, and another Panzer army, the Fifth, under command of Generaloberst von Arnim was on its way to Tunisia.

Death Throes

The British were not on the heels of the Afrika Korps when the latter's vehicles reached the Mersa Brega position. The plain across which von Wechmar's Fiats had charged so valiantly in the spring of 1941 had been turned into a sea of mud. Movement was further hampered by mines and booby traps laid by the Afrika Korps engineers. There was a shortage of petrol and rations were not all that plentiful, but the dumps in Tripolitania yielded a copious supply of these diabolical weapons – flat German Tellers, two-pronged French mines, thin Italian 'N' mines, 'S' mines full of ball-bearings which sprang out of the ground to burst at waist height, and a whole range of Italian booby traps. The Afrika Korps sappers made full use of the last of these. Across the wastelands on the borders of Cyrenaica and Tripolitania the road was necessarily the main axis of retreat and advance, and the German sappers lavished their most expert care on the route – laying mines with such devilish subtlety that the British dared not touch so much as a battered Italian helmet on the ground, let alone an abandoned vehicle, until their own sappers had pronounced it 'clean'. In consequence the pace of the pursuers was slowed to the pace of their mine clearance parties.

The biggest minefield of all shielded the Mersa Brega line, whose defences extended from the sea in the north to the Marada oasis about 60 miles due south of the Mersa Brega defile. Bastico, who on 22 November became Rommel's immediate superior once more, had brought up troops from Tripoli to man the defences during the retreat and when the Panzer Army's vehicles trundled across it the Spezia Division was deployed in the north and the Pistoia in the south. Bastico had been told by his masters in Rome that the Mersa Brega position must be the sticking point and held as long as possible. On the other hand, said the *Comando Supremo*, if the British attack in strength and their attack looked like succeeding then a withdrawal to Buerat might be considered. But Mussolini would have to sanction such a move and he would only do so in an extreme emergency. Hitler's instructions were that Rommel must stand at Mersa Brega, come what may.

Rommel responded by saying that if the British built up their strength in front of Mersa Brega, the chances were that his army would be thrown into the

Above and below: Successful desert tactics depended on mobility – difficult to achieve when the Axis powers were short of petrol.

sea. The Afrika Korps had been starved of reinforcements and equipment, and unless the situation improved radically and very quickly – or a miracle occurred – the best hope of saving the Panzer Army was to abandon Tripolitania and stand at the 'Gabes Gap'. There a new defensive line could be constructed to cover the narrow tongue of land separating the sea and the impassable watery expanse of the Shott el Jerid, which would serve as a Tunisian Alamein and his diminished army might then hold out until it was reinforced sufficiently to allow a return to the offensive.

But this meant abandoning Tripoli, an unthinkable prospect so far as the Italians were concerned. With *Comando Supremo* refusing to entertain the idea Rommel decided to tackle Hitler, and try to persuade him what ought to be done if this army was to remain in Africa. It was a disastrous trip. Rommel arrived at Hitler's headquarters during the afternoon of 28 November, and during the interview that followed 'there was a noticeable chill in the atmosphere'. The Führer worked himself up into a tantrum and told Rommel he was 'a defeatist . . . and you and your troops are cowards. Tripoli is to be held at all costs'.

Rommel asked, 'Is it better to lose Tripoli or the Afrika Korps . . . ? Come to Africa yourself, Führer, or send some of your personal staff to show us how to conduct a defence without reinforcements or supplies.' Hitler, close to hysteria dismissed him. 'Get out!' he shouted, 'I have other things to do. . . .' Rommel saluted and left the room, but as he was walking down the corridor, Hitler ran after him, put an arm around his shoulder and said, 'You must forgive me . . . come and see me tomorrow, and we will talk about it again, calmly. It is impossible to think of the Afrika Korps being destroyed.'

In the event neither the conversation that took place on the following day nor the discussion with Mussolini in Rome after that brought any change in direction as far as strategy in Afrika was concerned or any material improvement in the flow of supplies to the Panzer Army. Rommel, disillusioned, flew back to his troops, still sitting in the drenching rain among the salt marshes of Mersa Brega.

Not unnaturally the most frequent topic of discussion among these men was what was going to happen to them. The German armies on the Eastern Front had failed to vanquish the Red Armies and no end to the war was in sight; at the same time an end to the fighting in Africa clearly was in sight unless more German troops were sent there. Otherwise the best thing that could happen was for Rommel's army and the troops fighting in Tunisia to be returned to Europe before they were overwhelmed by the British on one side and the Americans on the other.

Of the Afrika Korps reinforcements trickling in to Tripoli – 6000 of them between the middle of November and the end of the first week in December – about half were seasoned veterans who had recovered from wounds or sickness. A shipment of Czechoslovak-manufactured high velocity 75mm anti-tank guns and some new tanks also arrived. But even when this equipment was added to that which had been recovered and repaired locally the total provided only 50 per cent of the replacements needed. The fact that there had been no sign of the famous 'Tigers' which Hitler had said would be delivered to the Afrika Korps at Alamein was galling – especially as the Fifth Panzer Army which had disembarked at Tunis had not only Tigers, but also some of the new *Nebelwerfer*, terrifying multi-barrelled mortars developed for use in Russia. Surprisingly, despite the feeling that theirs was a forgotten army – and despite the rain and cold also – the morale of the Afrika Korps' men was still high.

Meantime the Eighth Army had been assembling in front of Mersa Brega and forming up for an assault. While the 7th Armoured and the 51st Highland Divisions manoeuvred in front of the main positions a New Zealand force was quietly encircling them. On the

Scenes from Tunisia, 1943.
Above: Mud halts the advance.
Below: A Pz Mk III with a 7.5cm gun.
Inset: An 88mm anti-aircraft gun.

night of 15 December the New Zealanders moved in for the kill. Theoretically they had cut off a large slice of Rommel's army; in practice they had bitten off more than they could chew. They tried to straddle the road, but the desert was firm and level here, and when Rommel decided it was time to evacuate the Mersa Brega line his Panzers battered a passage through the road blocks, scattering the New Zealanders right and left. Rommel's men were retiring once again, and as his rearguards fell back the Afrika Korps sappers systematically went to work to scorch an earth that Nature had so ruthlessly scorched already. Telegraph poles were chopped down, buildings mined, bridges and culverts blown up, walls destroyed, air strips ploughed up – and mines were sown all the way.

Mersa Brega, Nofilia, Sirte were all familiar names which veterans of the Afrika Korps advance in the spring of 1941 remembered. Now they were stages in a relentless retreat. At Nofilia, a little town 9 miles inland from the Via Balbia, one of the 21st Panzer's battle groups ran out of petrol and a savage battle developed until it was rescued. At Sirte the 90th Light provided the rearguard giving the Eighth Army's advance guard a bloody nose when it probed too far too quickly. (The British entered Sirte on Christmas Day 1942. Except for flies it was empty and deserted. On the walls a message had been painted in German: *Englanders.* May your stay here be short and unhappy.')

The retreat was slowing down now. All those influences which had restrained Rommel in his thrust towards Alexandria the previous summer were now working in his favour. The Eighth Army's communications were stretched and its units were strung out over an immense distance. Like an advancing caterpillar it had to pause and pull in its rear portion before it could move on again.

The pause came a little west of the white-walled hamlet of Buerat, the last of three great ravines running down to the sea between Sirte and Misurata. At the coast here there is a broad strip of marshland, from which the Zemzem ravine takes off south-west while the coast – and the Via Balbia with it – turns abruptly north. Rommel had elected to make this his next bound, on a line with infantry dug in among the dunes and marshes near the coast, more infantry positions behind a great minefield extending on both sides of the road 12½ miles inland, and the Afrika Korps deployed further south. Here as the cold bright January days slid by the Panzer Army dug, wired and mined.

Buerat, like Mersa Brega, was to be defended 'to the death' – or so the authorities in Rome and Berlin declared. To Rommel instructions of this nature were worthless: Buerat had no more significance than Gazala or Mersa Brega. If Berlin was not prepared to send reinforcements and supplies he believed that the only sensible course was to ship the Panzer Army back to Europe. Failing that he was convinced he must pull back to the eastern border of Tunisia where the Panzer Army could combine with von Arnim's force facing west.

Therefore, ignoring the order to fight a death or glory battle at Buerat, Rommel began thinning out his forces, sending the 90th Light back to Misurata. This in itself probably ruled out a stand at Buerat, but an order by Mussolini on New Year's Day 1943 made it impossible. Rommel was instructed to send the 164th Division back to Sfax in Tunisia where the Americans were threatening to break through. When Rommel remonstrated, he was asked if he considered he was still fit enough to retain command of the Panzer Army. Nevertheless his arguments persuaded the Duce and *Comando Supremo* to think again. The order to move the 164th Division was cancelled; the 21st Panzer would go to Sfax instead.

Thus when the British attacked Buerat on 14 January the battle was already lost. Generalleutnant Gustav Fehn, the new commander of the Afrika Korps was wounded on the first day of the action, his place being taken by Generalmajor Freiherr Kurt von Liebenstein. All the Afrika Korps could hope to do was to block the British advance for as long as possible while the infantry got away to the west. The onus of this fell on the 8th Panzer Regiment which faced odds of 50 to one. The outcome was inevitable and late on 15 January von Liebenstein was ordered to disengage and pull the 15th Panzer back to the hills of Tarhuna.

Von Liebenstein withdrew with skill and method. Every mile or so his sappers cratered the road with explosive charges, compelling the pursuing British to leave the road and forge a new track through sticky mud. The delay was just enough to permit the 90th Light and the 15th Panzer to deploy along a new line between the ancient coastal resort of Homs and the hills of Tarhuna. The line lay 60 miles east of Tripoli, and the Italian reaction was predictable. 'Fight to the last man on the Tarhuna Line,' was the Duce's order.

For two days the Afrika Korps – or what was left of it, and two Italian in-

A German reconnaissance car and a small Italian tankette.

A general shortage of petrol created incredible logistical problems.

fantry divisions – or what was left of them – did hold the Tarhuna Line. Then *Comando Supremo* ordered the Italian infantry to pull out and fall back into Tunisia. There they would shelter behind the Mareth Line – an improvised Maginot built by the French in 1939 to keep the Italians out of French North Africa.

The Eighth Army reached the Tarhuna Line on 19 January and promptly attacked Homs, the coastal town on the left flank. In the south on the right flank, a composite Afrika Korps battle group – mainly the 15th Panzer, commanded by Rommel himself, held the pass leading into Tarhuna with 88s and heavy mortars. There was no way round the pass and Rommel's force blocked it for a good 48 hours. However, when a Luftwaffe reconnaissance pilot reported that an armoured force was making a wide detour which looked as if it would end up at Zuara west of Tripoli, Rommel decided it was time to quit. Accordingly the 90th Light retreated up the Via Balbia while the Afrika Korps drove due west for Tunisia and Mareth.

The Duce who had ordained that he should hold fast to the Homs-Tarhuna line for another three weeks at least was furious. He, Cavallero, Bastico, Kesselring and others in Rome and Berlin had been scheming for Rommel's dismissal for some time now and this latest act of 'disobedience' was the final straw. The intriguers got their way, and at noon on 26 January *Comando Supremo* signalled that on account of his bad state of health '. . . the Field Marshal may relinquish his command,' when his army reached the Mareth Line and could hand over to General Giovanni Messe (then commanding the Italian Expeditionary Force in Russia).

This was virtually an order to resign and Rommel, depressed and distressed by the tactical situation, the state to which the Afrika Korps had been reduced and all the scheming behind his back, asked Rome to send Messe to Tunisia straightway because he felt he could not carry on much longer.

The Eighth Army had entered Tripoli on 23 January, and by the beginning of February most of the Panzer Army was back in the Mareth Line; and the last of the Afrika Korps withdrew into Tunisia on 12 February – two years to the day since its advance parties landed in Africa. The desert war was over.

The Afrika Korps did not like Tunisia. Compared with Libya it was an earthly paradise of orchards, fields and flowers – too many *verdammte* flowers some of the men complained. They missed the limitless horizon, and sense of being on the ocean in the desolation of the desert.

Rommel, reluctant to take his dismissal lying down, had stayed on after all. Bastico had been relieved of his command and returned to Italy at the end of January. Messe arrived soon afterwards, but did not seem keen to take over command, and Cavallero had been sacked too. So contrary to the advice of his chief medical officer, Rommel decided to stay where he was until he was ordered to go. Possibly he felt this was not the time to abandon the Afrika Korps; the desert sand covered many graves and he had a genuine concern for his troops, despite his relentless determination and overriding ambition. Maybe he saw an opportunity to wrest back the initiative before the Allied armies closed in on him and von Arnim's army in the north.

Unfortunately there was no rapport between Rommel and von Arnim. The former had little time for veterans of the Eastern Front while Arnim – a 'traditional' Reichswehr soldier, addicted to an eyeglass and high boots – saw the highly-decorated Field Marshal as a jumped-up, publicity-seeking second-rater. Von Arnim, like Rommel, was ambitious, and the Fifth Panzer Army was his first independent command. The fact that it was independent was something he was determined to retain, with the result that although Kesselring tried to achieve some communication between von Arnim and Rommel they operated with only the minimum of co-operation. In February Rommel came forward with a plan for a counter-offensive. He had seen that the Eighth Army was so stretched that it did not pose a threat, and there was an opportunity to turn on the Anglo-American forces advancing into Tunisia from

Rommel's last plan to save Africa.

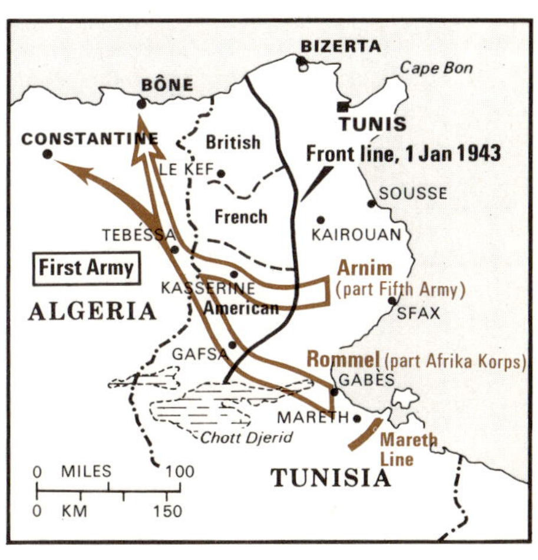

Algeria, smash them in the mountains and then return to the coastal plain to deal with Montgomery. Von Arnim did not agree with the plan and the offensive that was eventually launched took the form of two virtually independent and wholly uncoordinated operations.

In the early hours of 14 February von Arnim launched Operation *Frühlingswind* (Wind of Spring) – an attack up the Faid pass in the north and Rommel launched Operation *Morgenluft* (Morning Air) in the south the following day. *Morgenluft* opened with a battle for Kasserine Pass which was wholly successful. From there Rommel wanted to press on to capture Tebessa – a move which might well have caused the British and Americans to pull back into Algeria. But von Arnim who had different ideas held back and both operations petered out. Sick, tired and despondent Rommel ordered his troops to return first to Gafsa and then to face the Eighth Army again in the Mareth Line.

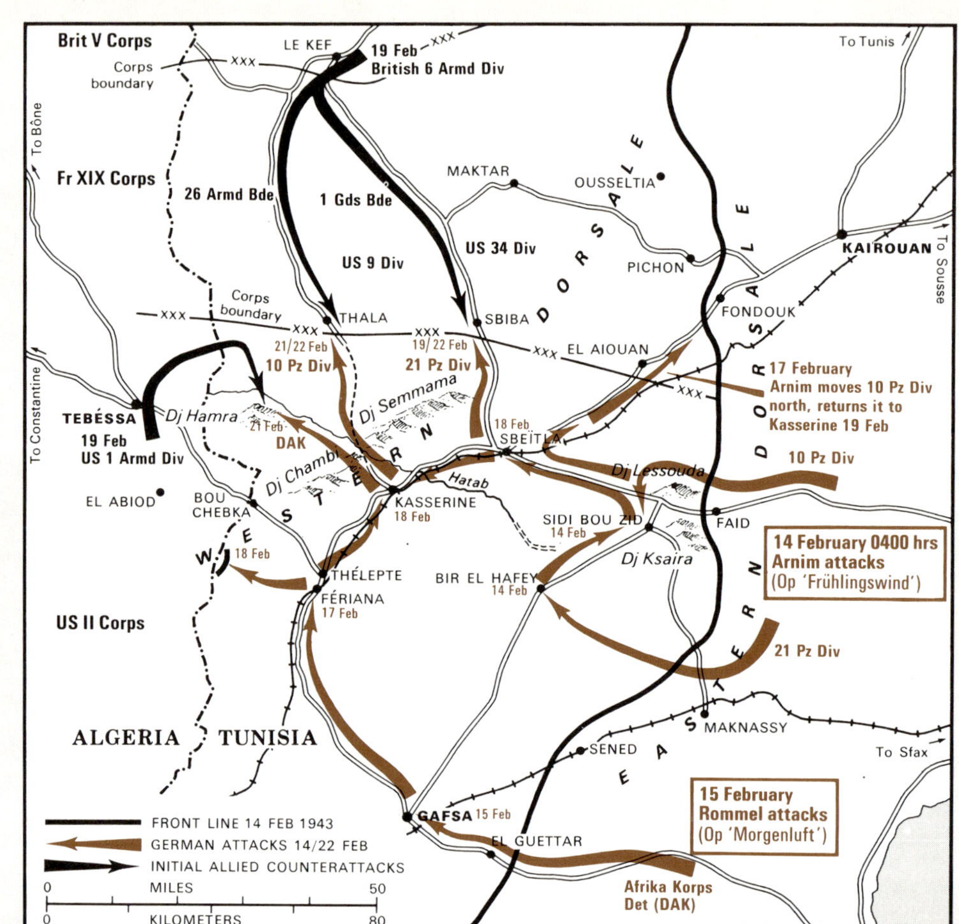

Below: A Junkers Ju 52 destroyed on the ground in Tunisia, 1943.
Right: The battle for control of the Kasserine Pass, Rommel's last victory.
Insets: Although Hitler wanted a victory in North Africa, he did not give it priority in terms of rations and equipment.

Ironically enough, while the Afrika Korps was pulling back through the Kasserine, an order from *Comando Supremo* nominated Rommel Supreme Commander of a new 'Army Group Africa' containing all the German and Italian troops in North Africa and giving him authority over von Arnim. Rommel demurred at first, but then decided he could not refuse the job. If the new group had been formed earlier he might have been able to coordinate von Arnim's Operation *Frühlingswind* which his operation *Morgenluft* and the campaign in Tunisia could have taken a very different turn. In the event the new appointment did not achieve anything because it did not resolve the differences between the 'Supreme Commander' and his deputy, von Arnim.

On 26 February von Arnim started a new *Ochsenkopf* operation (Bull's Head) with the 10th and 15th Panzer Divisions, when they advanced towards Beja. This operation, like *Frühlingswind* before it, ended in disaster and after much hard fighting and heavy casualties had to be called off. Rommel, travelling in one of the leading tanks of the 8th Panzer Regiment, watched disconsolately as units of the old Afrika Korps from the 21st Panzer and the 90th Light moved in to support the hard-pressed 10th and

Above: Two scenes of Germans marching to the Tunisian front line. Right: Breaching the Mareth Line. Below: Feldmarschall Rommel was a sick man during the Tunisian Campaign.

15th Panzer. He had no confidence in von Arnim's plan and it seemed that the omens were against it, for when the attack started at 0500 hours the sky was grey and the clouds hung low over the battlefield. By midday, when the Panzers were trying to pull out the rain was pouring down and many of the Panzers bogged down in thick mud. For the British anti-tank gunners this made them easy targets.

It was Rommel's turn now to try to pull the Axis chestnuts out of the North African fire, and on 5 March he addressed his troops in the mountains overlooking the Mareth Line. If they did not take Medenine, he said, capture the British dumps and force the Eighth Army to withdraw, their days were numbered. They attacked next day, and once again the outcome was a rous-

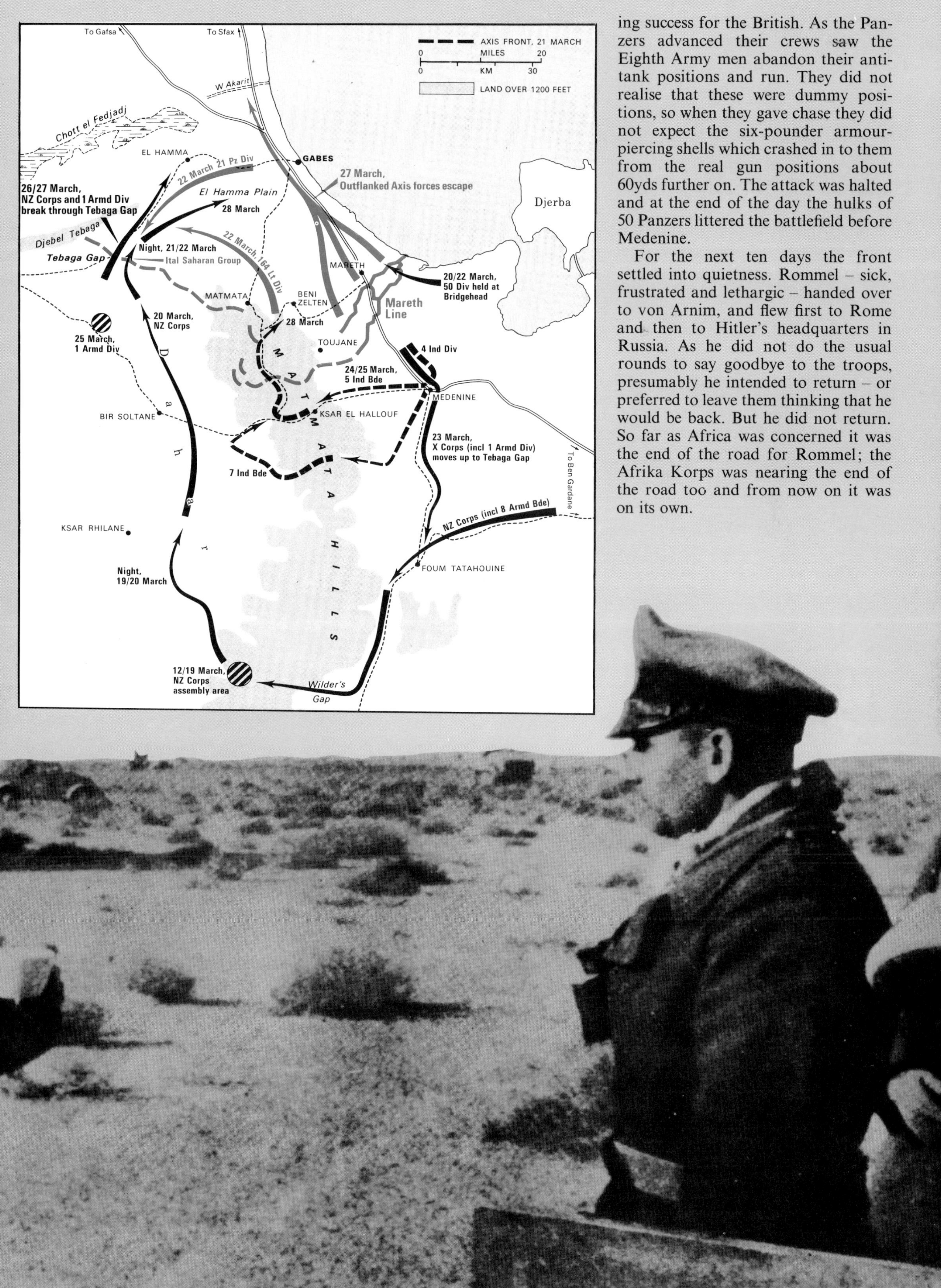

ing success for the British. As the Panzers advanced their crews saw the Eighth Army men abandon their anti-tank positions and run. They did not realise that these were dummy positions, so when they gave chase they did not expect the six-pounder armour-piercing shells which crashed in to them from the real gun positions about 60yds further on. The attack was halted and at the end of the day the hulks of 50 Panzers littered the battlefield before Medenine.

For the next ten days the front settled into quietness. Rommel – sick, frustrated and lethargic – handed over to von Arnim, and flew first to Rome and then to Hitler's headquarters in Russia. As he did not do the usual rounds to say goodbye to the troops, presumably he intended to return – or preferred to leave them thinking that he would be back. But he did not return. So far as Africa was concerned it was the end of the road for Rommel; the Afrika Korps was nearing the end of the road too and from now on it was on its own.

The Eighth Army attacked the Mareth Line on the night of 20 March. The line's main fortifications ran inland for 21 miles – following the course of a natural ravine called Wadi Zigzaou, before turning north-west for another 21 miles through the steep Matmata Hills. Across the open El Hamma valley an anti-tank ditch covered by pillboxes had been built by the French, and the rest of the way inland was blocked by a line of impassable salt lakes. All in all it was the most formidable obstacle the British had encountered since Alamein, and as it was the southern gate to Tunisia Mussolini and Hitler had issued one of their characteristic 'do or die' orders. 'You are to hold the Mareth Line to the death,' Rommel had been told. For the men of 'Army Group Afrika' who were to do the holding, what mattered was not the question of dying on the Mareth Line, but of not dying at all.

The 50th Division attacked across the Wadi Zigzaou which had been swollen by the recent rains; to get their vehicles to the far side the British troops had to heave bundles of brushwood into the flood to make a firm foundation. But by daybreak they had established a small bridgehead. The 15th Panzer was ordered to restore the situation and when a counter-attack went in the bridgehead crumbled and

Right: General 'Hap' Arnold.
Far right: A night barrage south of Medenine, 16 March 1943.
Below: Torch landings at Oran, 1942.

eventually had to be abandoned. The first phase of Montgomery's battle for Mareth had been a failure. Yet, despite the 15th Panzer's success this was a battle with no future for von Arnim's men. While the British 50th Division were fighting to establish the bridgehead and then to hold it, a force of New Zealanders were trekking round behind the Matmata Hills towards El Hamma. Montgomery outlining his strategy in boxing terms, had intended that the 50th Division should deliver a straight right into the jaws of the Mareth Line, while the New Zealanders finished it off with a 'left hook'. As the 50th Division's attack had failed, the so-called left hook became the main British thrust and no sooner had the 15th Panzer finished clearing up at Wadi Zigzaou than there was an urgent call for them to return to the mountains. The New Zealanders were through the passes and moving down into the El Hamma valley, where

A British patrol sets off in the Western Desert.

the Young Fascist Division – newly arrived from Italy – was deployed under command of General Alberto Mannerini. Mannerini complained that he could not hold the New Zealanders and appealed for help. In response the 21st Panzer moved west to El Hamma from Gabes, while the 164th Division and the Italian Spezia were brought up from the south. With the involvement of the 15th Panzer it was almost like old times; the old Afrika Korps was reassembling for action. (Von Arnim's 10th Panzer Division pinned down by General Patton's American army around Gafsa could not participate in this battle to break through the Mareth Line.)

In the event the El Hamma battle took place in a valley of grey stony hills about one and three quarter miles wide, with little side-valleys which shielded the Panzers and anti-tank guns. It started at 1500 hours on 26 March with an air strike against the German positions of such a ferocity as the Luftwaffe had never given the Afrika Korps even in its palmiest days. For three hours the British planes bombed and strafed at will, keeping anti-tank gunners away from their guns at critical moments and Panzers from the battle. If men moved or fired or did anything at all they were machine-gunned. Moreover all this time the New Zealanders had been advancing up the valley and by the evening the El Hamma Pass was in their hands. But the 21st Panzer still stood at the Gabes Gap, blocking the road to Gabes and the sea. That night the British 1st Armoured Division passed through the New Zealanders; there was no moon and the situation became very confused – so much so that some of the British tanks actually drove through the 21st Panzer's laager. Next morning the 21st Panzer woke to find itself sandwiched between the New Zealanders and the 1st Armoured Division. But the Panzers managed to extricate themselves and battle their way clear through the Gabes Gap.

The whole Mareth Line – the line which was to be 'defended to the death' – now began to crumble. Along the main part of the Line only the 90th Light, fighting the rearguard action as usual, remained on 27 March. Meanwhile the rest of the Afrika Korps was moving back northwards along the coast by a corridor which narrowed daily until it terminated at the sea.

To the desert veterans, the tactical situation in which they found themselves at this juncture was utterly bewildering and their bewilderment was exacerbated by the terrain in which they were operating. Manoeuvring in the desert, with its single coast road and nothing else had been a simple business compared with that forced on them by the maze of hills and valleys and ravines around Tunis. Not that there were many desert veterans to reminisce and compare Cyrenaica with Tunisia. By the end of April the old Afrika Korps had been reduced to a skeleton army whose total strength comprised two main composite units: the 5th Panzer Regiment – all that remained of the 21st Panzer

German Prisoners of War begin the long march to captivity.

A wounded German officer was found lying on the battlefield. A sentry was left to guard him until an ambulance arrived.

Division, and the 8th Panzer Regiment – all that remained of the 15th Panzer. There were also some infantry companies, composed of the remnants of the 90th Light and the 164th Division. Finally, over and above the Afrika Korps, there were the survivors of the 10th Panzer Division, now consolidated into the 7th Panzer Regiment.

As might be expected most of the equipment was showing signs of wear; old hits on the Panzers that had seen service at Alamein, Gazala and Mersa Brega had been covered by sections of tank tracks; the old desert camouflage paint was peeling and track pins fractured very frequently. But men and machines could still fight as the British learned to their cost at Longstop Hill in the Medjerda valley and the Americans at the 'Green' and 'Bald' hills in the Sedjenane valley. Before the battles for these places von Arnim had issued a backs-to-the-wall, fight-to-the-finish order and his troops responded magnificently. However, by the beginning of May the stage was set for the grand finale.

On 6 May the British and Americans launched the last great offensive which was to carry them to Tunis and the sea. Tunis fell on 7 May and the remnants of the Afrika Korps in the Enfidaville hills were cut off from their comrades in the Cape Bon Peninsula. The process of total collapse took six more days because inevitably there were isolated groups of brave men who fought on because they did not know that their war was over, or because they preferred to fight.

Shortly after 2000 hours on the evening of 12 May Eighth Army Headquarters announced the end of organised resistance in North Africa. Even then a large part of the Afrika Korps still had not surrendered. Rommel's old army in the Enfidaville hills was the last to surrender. In the words of one of the *landsers* – an ordinary private soldier – the men of the Afrika Korps had given in because there had been '*Ubermacht*'; they had been overwhelmed. The last commander of the Afrika Korps, von Cramer, expressed pride and defiance of the future when he sent a farewell signal to Berlin, before his headquarters were overrun:

> HQ Afrika Korps to Army Group Afrika and OKH High Command Berlin: ammunition exhausted, arms and equipment destroyed. In accordance with orders received the Deutsche Afrika Korps has fought itself to the condition where it can fight no more. The German Afrika Korps must be reborn.
>
> *Heia Safari!*

Epilogue

The focus of any story about the Afrika Korps must inevitably be on its creator, Erwin Rommel. For it was Rommel who forged it into the tough resilient fighting force that it proved to be. In the eyes of his own men, as well as those of the enemy, Rommel personified the Afrika Korps. It was Rommel who made them supremely self-confident and enterprising in battle. It was he who taught them to use their imagination and initiative, to sacrifice for the sake of speed things that other soldiers often consider essential, and to refuse to accept they were beaten. It was because they were the Afrika Korps that even as prisoners they marched into captivity with their heads high and sang: '*Wir marschieren, wir marschieren gegen England.*' More than three decades after the campaign in North Africa 'Afrika Korps' and 'Afrika' cuff-titles are prized by those who can say, 'I was in the Afrika Korps; I fought with Rommel!'

And Rommel himself? Ruthless, self-opinionated and a glory-grabber whenever the opportunity arose, he inspired his men by personal leadership, and he always seemed to be able to turn his enemies' muddled thinking to his own advantage. Yet he was capable of pig-headedness, and he persisted in sticking to the wrong course on several occasions. The rank and file respected him and – over the years and well away from the sand and the flies – their respect has developed into idolisation. Old Afrika Korps men, like all soldiers, tend to remember the more pleasant aspects of their campaign, and to forget the blood and the filth, and how Rommel drove them on when they were dead tired. He was one of the new style generals, yet one is reminded of Siegfried Sassoon's World War I character: the '. . . cheery old card (as Harry grunted to Jack; as they slogged up to Arras with rifle and pack . . .) who 'did for them both with his plan of attack'.

With the officers Rommel was often anything but popular, for he had a habit of talking down to them. 'It's a great thing to be a Field Marshal and still remember how to talk to them [officers] like a sergeant-major,' he said to his ADC on one occasion after berating one luckless senior officer whom he had caught in bed about 0700 hours one morning. But the fact that their commander had a no-nonsense approach to the officers went down well with the other ranks and helped his image. Above the company commander level, control exercised by senior officers over the men who do the actual fighting is tenuous; they exercise their authority through other officers. This makes possible a technique for cultivating popularity among the rank and file – albeit a dangerous one and often only of short term benefit. In its simplest form this technique relies on officers implementing orders issued by a commander, while the latter proffers direct sympathy to those affected by them and blaming the intermediaries for any hardships involved. Many people – British and Americans more so than Germans – have allowed themselves to be hypnotised by Rommel's legend. Without question he was courageous, a good family man, austere in his personal life and a fine professional soldier. But he had his weaknesses like anybody else, and perhaps vanity was his greatest failing. (An instance of this vanity was recounted to the author by General Bittrich, who commanded the II-SS-Panzer Corps in Normandy. Bittrich in a moment of aberration addressed Rommel as *'Herr General'* and was taken to task for not calling him *Feldmarschall.*)

Contrary to popular belief the Afrika Korps was not a *corps d'élite* of hand-picked volunteers. Whether a man was sent to Africa or Russia or to some less arduous 'front' was purely a matter of luck, so it is reasonable to suppose that the Afrika Korps represented a cross section of the Wehrmacht. Nor was there any special training for those who were posted to Africa, although young Panzer soldiers were more conditioned to war than their opponents in the desert. Most of them had been subjected to quasi-military training ever since they could remember. They had been taught camping lore and had had discipline drummed into them until implicit obedience became instinctive. As soldiers they were strong, patriotic, brave and well trained in the use of their equipment – which was of the best. Physically they did not adapt themselves to desert conditions as easily as did South Africans, Australians, New Zealanders, Indians and British. Few of them had even been outside Europe and they did not understand Africa. Nevertheless a judicious blend of propaganda, organisation, training and discipline turned them into first class desert fighters.

As part of the Afrika Korps legend it seems to have become customary for those who write about its exploits to state that Rommel's men fought 'cleanly' and 'according to the rules'. Whether this was so depends on the definition of 'cleanly' and the rules in question. In the author's experience war has never been a clean business, and it is difficult to see how it ever can be. South Africans who were refused water when they became prisoners at Tobruk did not consider the behaviour of the captors was according to the accepted rules of war. But if the definition of clean fighting means that prisoners were not beaten up and that the Afrika Korps did everything its men could do for the wounded who fell into its hands, then it rightly deserves an accolade.

Finally, when von Cramer recommended that the Afrika Korps should be 'reborn' he was probably thinking in terms of Hitler's war and a German expeditionary force to fight over the old battlegrounds. This was not to be, and the Afrika Korps renaissance has so far been limited to discussions or books about the original force. Yet the formation and employment of a second Afrika Korps is not inconceivable. Unrest in Africa is such that no great stretch of imagination is needed to envisage a scenario calling for a tough, self-contained mobile force for employment either in what the West sees as a conventional 'peace-keeping' role, or for what the East would regard as a 'peace-enforcement' task. Unless there is some dire emergency, it is unlikely that West Germany will ever consider raising a force to serve outside central Europe.

Feldmarschall Erwin Rommel, the hero of the Deutsche Afrika Korps and also of Germany in 1942.

But East Germany, the *Deutsche Demokratische Republik*, might well take a different view. Since the end of World War II the East Germans have leaned over backwards to show their Soviet masters that they are the most reliable of the latter's Warsaw Pact allies. They have pursued the strategies formulated in Moscow with true Teutonic fervour and there is good reason to suppose that East German surrogate troops might well join the Cubans in any forthcoming confrontation in central or southern Africa. In Mozambique and Angola existing stockpiles of Soviet equipment would permit East German troops – who like the rest of the Warsaw Pact armies are armed and trained with Soviet weapons – to go into action within a very short space of time. On the Angolan border the men of another Afrika Korps would operate in conditions in Ovamboland and the Kalahari Desert similar to those in which their predecessors fought in Cyrenaica. There and on the other side of the continent, on the borders of Mozambique, they would find themselves fighting the sons of the Afrika Korps' old opponents, and the latter would undoubtedly do their utmost to avenge Tobruk. Let us hope therefore that a 'reborn' Afrika Korps remains a flight of fancy, and content ourselves with the current legend.

Appendices

Appendix 1
Order of Battle

Command Organisation

COMANDO SUPREMO (ROME)

COMANDO SUPREMO IN AFRICA (TRIPOLI)

GERMAN EXPEDITIONARY FORCE/PANZERGRUPPE AFRIKA (Rommel)

ITALIAN ARMY IN NORTH AFRICA

X Italian Corps
XX Italian Corps
XXI Italian Corps

DEUTSCHE AFRIKA KORPS

The 15th Panzer Division (from March 1941)

The 21st Panzer Division (from February 1941)

The 164th Light Division (from August 1942)

The 22nd Para Brigade (from August 1942)

The 90th Light Division (from June 1941)

To put the Deutsche Afrika Korps into perspective it should be appreciated that in 1942 it was only one of the four corps in the Axis Expeditionary force in North Africa.
Deutsche Afrika Korps: the 15th Panzer; the 21st Panzer; the 90th Light Division
X Italian Corps: Bologna and Brescia Division
XX Italian Corps: Ariete (armoured) Division and Trieste (motorised) Division
XXI Italian Corps: Pavia, Trento, Sabratha Divisions

The Deutsche Afrika Korps

From 20 January until 25 July 1941 all German troops in Africa were constituted as the Deutsche Afrika Korps. On 25 July however, the Afrika Korps and two Italian corps became the *Panzergruppe Afrika* and at that time it consisted of two armoured divisions – the 15th Panzer and the 21st Panzer (formerly the 5th Light Division), and the so-called 'Afrika Division' – a motorised Infantry formation, formed especially for tropical service – subsequently being renamed the 90th Light (Afrika) Division, and sometimes known as the 'Sardinian' Division.

These units, together with several 'independent' army units – heavy AA artillery, base depots, etc – constituted the DAK element of the *Panzergruppe*.

On 22 January 1942 the DAK was further expanded when Rommel's Panzer Group became *Panzer Armee Afrika*. The only significant German reinforcements to this army were another motorised Panzergrenadier division, the 164th Light Afrika Division which arrived during July and August 1942, and Generalmajor Bernard Ramcke's 22nd Parachute Brigade which also arrived in July.

In the long retreat from Alamein in November 1942 the DAK provided the rearguard to Tripoli and Tunisia. There its units were absorbed into the *Armee Gruppe Tunisia* which ultimately surrendered at Tunis in May 1943.

Order of Battle of the original Deutsche Afrika Korps

HQ Afrika Korps: Leutnantgeneral Erwin Rommel (Chief of Staff: Oberleutnant Klaus von dem Borne)
The 5th Light Division: Generalmajor Johannes Streich
The 15th Panzer Division:Generalmajor von Prittwitz (killed 12 April 1941 and succeeded by Generalmajor Walter Neumann-Silkow

Order of the Battle of the Panzer Group Africa

HQ Panzergruppe Afrika: Feldmarschall Erwin Rommel (During October 1942 while Rommel was sick, Leutnantgeneral Georg Stumme took over, but he was killed on 23 October and Rommel returned as commander)

Formations and Units forming part of the Deutsche Africa Korps

HQ Afrika Korps: Ludwig Crüwell (July 1941–May 1942). Leutnantgeneral Walter Nehring (May 1942–August 1942). Leutnantgeneral Ritter von Thoma (August 1942–November 1943)
The 21st Panzer Division (Approximate strength 12,000) Commanders: Generalmajor Hans von Ravenstein (July 1941–January 1942). Generalmajor Georg von Bismarck (killed 23 August 1942). Generalmajor Heinz von Randow (until February 1943)
The 5th Panzer Regiment (two battalions each of 84 tanks)
The 104th Panzergrenadier Regiment (two motorised infantry battalions)
The Reconnaissance Abteilung (30 vehicles)
The 155th Artillery Regiment (three Abteilungen each of three batteries, one of which was equipped with 15cm gun-howitzers)
The 39th Anti-tank Battalion (three companies each with 14 3·7cm A tank guns)
The 220th Engineer Battalion (carried in armoured troop carriers)
The 200th Signals Detachment
The 606th Anti-aircraft Battery (two heavy batteries each of four 8·8cm dual purpose AA/A tank guns and one light battery of 2cm guns)
The 15th Panzer Division (Approximate strength 12,000) Commanders: Generalmajor Walter Neumann-Silkow (killed 6 December 1941). Generalmajor Gustav von Vaerst. Generalmajor Heinz von Randow. Generalmajor Willi Borowietz
The 8th Panzer Regiment (two battalions each of 84 tanks)
The 115th Panzergrenadier Regiment (two motorised infantry battalions)
The 115th Reconnaissance Abteilung (40 vehicles)
The 33rd Artillery Regiment
The 104th Anti-tank Battalion (transferred to the 21st Panzer Division during July 1941)

Units not counted as Deutsche Afrika Korps

The 90th Light Division (Approximate strength 8000) Commanders: Generalmajor Richard Veith. Generalmajor Ulrich Kleeman. Generalmajor Theodor von Sponeck.
After Alamein: Generalmajor Karl Lungerhausen. Generalmajor Ernst Baade. Generalmajor Siegfried Graf von Schwerin
The 115th Panzergrenadier Regiment
The 190th Tank Battalion (Transferred in February 1943 to the 8th Panzer Regiment with the 21st Panzer Division)
The 361 Infantry Regiment
The 164th Light Division
The 22nd Parachute Brigade (Fallschirm-Brigade Ramcke)

Appendix 2
Chronology

1940	AFRICA	ELSEWHERE
9 December	Opening of Wavell's offensive in Libya	
11 December	Fall of Sidi Barrani	
18 December		Directive No 21 OKW on 'Operation Barbarossa' (invasion of USSR) is issued
1941		
5 January	Fall of Bardia	
16 January		Hitler announces that 'Barbarossa' is the over-riding task for 1941
17 January		Hitler agrees to assist the Italians in North Africa
23 January	Fall of Tobruk	
1 February		Germans enter Bulgaria
6 February	Rommel summoned to Berlin	
7 February	Fall of Benghazi	
12 February	Rommel arrives in Tripolitania Luftwaffe bombs Benghazi for first time Afrika Korps starts to arrive in Libya	
2 March		British land in Greece
17 March		Hitler orders occupation of Greece
22 March	Afrika Korps reaches El Agheila	
26 March		Simovic's *coup d'état* in Yugoslavia
2 April	Capture of Agedabia	
6 April	Capture of Benghazi	Axis campaign in Greece and Yugoslavia opens
7–8 April	Battle of Mechili, Capture of Derna	
12 April	First attack on Tobruk Occupation of Bardia-Sollum-Capuzzo area	

1941	AFRICA	ELSEWHERE
End of April		British and Greeks evacuate the Peloponnese. Battle of Corinth
20 May		German airborne attack on Crete
30 May		British evacuate Crete
15 June	Wavell's 'Operation Battleaxe' against Sollum. Successful counter-attack by Afrika Korps	
18 June		German-Turkish treaty
22 June		'Operation Barbarossa' begins
6 July		Capture of Riga
10 July		Germans in front of Kiev
21 July		Siege of Leningrad begins
25 July	Formation of 'Armoured Group Afrika', and the 5th Light Division becomes the 21st Panzer Division and the 90th Light Division is allotted to the Group	
August		Battle of Smolensk
September		British enter Iran
3–10 September		Battle of Kiev
October		Germans before Moscow
18 November	Start of Auchinleck's 'Operation Crusader'	
19 November	Commando raid on Rommel's HQ at Breda Littoria	
20 November		Russian counter-offensive on Rostov. Retreat of German First Army
23 November	'*Totensonntag*' battle at Sidi Rezegh	
6 December		German defeat before Moscow Opening of Russian winter offensive
7 December	DAK withdraws to Gazala Line	Japanese attack Pearl Harbor America enters the war
8 December	End of first siege of Tobruk	
10 December	Benghazi abandoned by Axis forces	

1942	AFRICA	ELSEWHERE
3 January	Rommel's withdrawal ends at El Agheila	
17 January	Surrender of defenders of Halfaya Pass	
21 January	Rommel advances to overrun Cyrenaica	
28 January	Recapture of Benghazi	
12 February		End of withdrawal of German Army Groups Centre and North in Russia
15 February		Start of air offensive against Malta
1 March	End of first phase of attack on Gazala Line	
April		Anglo-American conference in London
26 May	Rommel's third offensive on Gazala front	
27 May	Start of battle of Bir Hacheim	
1 June	Armoured battle at 'Knightsbridge' ('The Cauldron')	
14 June	Free French troops evacuate Bir Hacheim	
20 June	Surrender of Tobruk	Churchill and Roosevelt agree on plan for invasion of North Africa
22 June	The 90th Light Division enters Egypt	Start of German summer offensive on Russian front
29 June	Capture of Mersa Matruh	
1 July	First check to Rommel before El Alamein	Capture of Sebastopol
9 July	Rommel attacks southern sector of El Alamein positions	
19 July		Dieppe raid
23 July	'Six-day battle' at El Alamein	
1 September	End of DAK offensive operations at El Alamein	
25 September		General Halder replaced by General Zeitzler as Wehrmacht Chief of Staff
23 October	Alexander's counter-offensive at El Alamein	
2 November	British breakthrough in northern sector of German position	
3–4 November	DAK starts to withdraw	
6 November	Retreating Axis forces retire across the Egyptian frontier back into Libya	
8 November	Anglo-American landing in North Africa	

1942	AFRICA	ELSEWHERE
19 November		Opening of Russian offensive Siege of Stalingrad
20 November	Rommel halts on Mersa Brega line Cyrenaica abandoned	
20 December	DAK retreats to Buerat line	
24 December	Buerat line abandoned Withdrawal to Buerat line DAK retreats towards Tunisia	
1943		
January		Heavy air raids on Germany
22 January	Tripolitania abandoned	
1 February		Surrender of Paulus' German Sixth Army at Stalingrad
12 February	Rommel pulls back to Mareth Line (second anniversary of Afrika Korps' arrival in Libya) End of 'desert war'	
14 February	Junction with von Arnim's Fifth Army	
24 February	Formation of 'Army Group Africa' with Feldmarschall Rommel as Commander-in-Chief	
31 March	Battle of El Guettar	
May		Roosevelt and Churchill agree that 'Operation Overlord' (landing in France) will take place in summer 1944
3 May	British, French and Americans break through the Enfidaville line	
7 May	Fall of Tunis	
12–13 May	German and Italian troops surrender at Cape Bon	

	FINALE
June 1943	The 5th Light Division is reformed in France and nicknamed 'The Devil's Division'
14 October 1944	Rommel's suicide, consequent on his association with others in the plot to assassinate Hitler

Bibliography

ALMAN, K
Ritterkreuzträger des Afrikakorps, Pabel Verlag, Rastatt 1968

AUCHINLECK, General Sir Claude
'Operations in the Middle East from 1 November 1941 to 15 August 1942', Supplement to *London Gazette* No 38–177 of 15 January 1948

BARCLAY, Brigadier C N
'Against Great Odds', History of World War II, The Mediterranean and Middle East, HMSO London

BARNET, Corelli
The Desert Generals, Wm Kimber, London 1960

BAUCHE, J
A Force de Vaincre, Armand Fleury, Paris 1947

BRIGHT, Joan
The 9th Queen's Royal Lancers, The Story of an Armoured Regiment in Battle, Gale & Polden, 1951

CACCIA-DOMINIONE
Alamein, an Italian Story, trans D Chamberlin, Allen & Unwin, London 1966

CARRELL, Paul
The Desert Foxes, Macdonald, London 1960

CAVALLERO, Marshal Ugo of Italy
Comando Supremo, Cappelli, Rocca Casciano, 1948

CHURCHILL, Sir Winston
The Second World War, Vol 1, Cassell & Co, London 1948

CIANO, Galeazzo
The Ciano Diaries 1939–1943, Heinemann, London 1948

CLIFFORD, A
Three against Rommel, Harrap, London 1943

CONNEL, J
Auchinleck, Cassell, London 1959

CONNEL, J
Wavell, Scholar and Soldier, Collins, London 1964

DAVIES, W J K
German Army Handbook, Ian Allan, London 1973

DOUGLAS-HOME, C
Rommel, Weidenfeld & Nicolson, London 1973

DUBREUIL, L Ardouin
La Guerre de Tunisie 1942–43, Payat, Paris 1945

ESEBECK, Hanns-Gert von
Afrikanische Schicksalajahre, Limes Verlag, Wiesbaden 1949

ESEBECK, Hanns-Gert von
Das Deutsche Afrika-Korps, Wiesbaden und München 1975

ESEBECK, Hanns-Gert von
Rommel et l'Afrikakorps, Payot, Paris 1950

ESEBECK, Hanns-Gert von
Storie Segrete dell'Ultima Guerra di Selezione dal Reader's Digest, Reader's Digest, Milan 1960

HART, Sir Basil LIDDELL
The Other Side of the Hill, Cassell, London 1948

HARTSHORN, E P
Avenge Tobruk, Purnell (SA), Cape Town 1960

HECKMANN, Wolf
Rommels Krieg in Afrika, Gustav Lübbe Verlag, Bergisch Gladbach 1976

JAN, Robert
Les Campagnes d'Afrique, Payot, Paris 1957

KESSELRING, A
Memoirs, trans Lynton Hudson, Wm Kimber, London 1953

LEWIN, Ronald
Rommel as a Military Commander, Batsford, London 1968

MACKSEY, K J
The Afrika Korps, Macdonald, London 1968

MAGDALANY, F
The Battle of El Alamein, Weidenfeld & Nicolson, London 1965

MARAVIGNA, General Pietro
Come abbiamo perduto la Guerra in Africa, Tosi, Rome 1949

MONTGOMERY, Field Marshal B L
El Alamein to the River Sangro, Hutchinson, London 1947

MORDAL, Jacques
Bir Hakeim, Presse Pockett, Paris 1970

ORPEN, N
South African Forces in World War II (Vol 3), Purnell (SA), Cape Town 1972

PHILLIPS, Lucas
Alamein, Heinemann, London 1962

PLAYFAIR *et al*
History of World War II, The Mediterranean and Middle East, Vols 1–4, HMSO, London 1954–1960

ROMMEL, Erwin
The Rommel Papers, ed B H Liddell-Hart, trans Paul Findlay, Harcourt, Brace & Co, New York 1953

ROMMEL, Feldmarschall Erwin
Krieg ohne Hass (Memoirs of Western Desert Campaign), Verlag Heidenheimer Zeitung, 1950

SCHMIDT, Oberst H W
With Rommel in the Desert, Albatross, Durban 1950

SMITH, Anthony Heckstall
The Tiger Kills (The 4th and 5th Indian Divisions in North Africa), HMSO, 1944

SMITH, Anthony Heckstall
Tobruk, Anthony Blond, London 1959

WESTPHAL, General of Cavalry Siegfried
Heer in Fesseln, Athenaum Verlag, Bonn 1950

WESTPHAL, General of Cavalry Siegfried
Macht als Vorwärts, Jungs, Pöppinghaus, Bochum-Langendreer 1960

YOUNG, Desmond
Rommel, Collins, London 1965

Index

Acknowledgements

The author would like to thank the following people for helping to prepare this book: Graham Bingham and Helen Downton for doing the line drawings, Richard Natkiel for drawing all the maps and Sue Goldblatt who did the index. The author would also like to thank the Bundesarchiv for providing the majority of the pictures and the following picture libraries for supplying the rest:

Bison Picture Library: 2–3, 13 (right), 17 (above), 64 (top), 65 (both), 69 (inset), 76–77 (all 4), 80 (below), 145 (both), 149, 150–151, 153, 160, 163 (top), 172, 179.

Robert Hunt Library: 7 (left), 11 (top), 20 (below), 58–59, 135, 146, 148, 152, 156–157, 158–159, 160–161 (both), 165 (top), 174–175 (all 3), 176 (top), 177.

Orbis: 11 (bottom), 15, 72–73, 176 (bottom).

Zwilling: 70–71, 115 (top).

Quest Library: 147 (top).

Navy Department, National Archives: 162–163.

Paul Popper Ltd: 18.